IN THE
MOON

IN THE
MOON

Dans La Lune

A Memoir of a 1930s childhood in France

ALAN HOLMES

To order additional copies of this book, contact:
Xlibris Corporation
1-888-795-4274
www.Xlibris.com
Orders@Xlibris.com
17205

ACKNOWLEDGEMENTS

I want to acknowledge those who encouraged me in the process of mining my childhood memories to create this book. My wife, Ruth-Reitinger Holmes, and my daughters, Joanna Dickson and Teresa Reitinger were especially generous with their encouragement, editing and proofreading. Jeanne Angier, the leader of my writing group, generously helped with her suggestions and proofreading, as did Miriam Silver, Adele Carney, Barbara Price and Rosalie Nelson (members of the writing group).

AUTHOR'S NOTE

The events and situations mentioned or described in this memoir are true, as best as the author is able to recollect, and the places described are real. Most of the names of people who are not part of the author's immediate family have been changed to preserve the privacy of those individuals and their relatives. I did not change the names of beloved family servants, Raimond and Françoise. (*Raimond* is usually spelled with a "y" in French, but he chose to spell his name with an "i".)

The dialogue presented is paraphrased, of course, but I made an effort to be faithful to the intent of the speakers and to capture the characteristic flavor of individual speaking styles.

The photograph on the front cover is of an oil painting done by Suzy Holmes in 1924, shortly after she and Dan moved into the house pictured. The view is the back of the house at La Closerie (in Ville-d'Avray) which, after this painting was made, underwent considerable change and improvements. The old apple tree portrayed was reputed to be as old as the house, which was built during the reign of Louis XIV (1643-1715) for one of his courtiers.

CHAPTER 1

Family Background and a Russian Nanny

> "We don't come naked into the world. We bring with us all kinds of baggage which has to do with family history and sometimes the accidents of the birth itself . . . it's why the prehistory of the characters and the manner of their arrival seems always relevant to me."
>
> **Salman Rushdie,** addressing **City Arts and Lectures,** San Francisco, May 1999

Dan, my father, had never been forthcoming about his youth, and there had always been in my mind an element of mystery about him. How had such a dyed-in-the-wool Englishman come to embrace living in France and managing a large and prosperous business in that country? For that matter, how did he happen to have a Belgian wife? I had heard that my father's frequent bouts of melancholy stemmed from the sudden death of his first wife, Suzy. That subject had always been taboo in my family. Although my mother had made veiled references to Suzy, she was hardly an impartial observer. What exactly happened? Of all those to whom I talked about my father, it was Uncle Bob who seemed to have the most valuable and plausible details of Dan's early life.

Bob was close to ninety years old when I paid him a series of visits that were especially helpful in my quest, and I was grateful and happy to find him still alert and much interested in the world around him. He was by then a widower living alone at "Broad Beech," his stately home high on a hill overlooking the town of

Dorking, in Surrey. He had owned it for over sixty years and for the previous quarter century had, since his retirement, worked almost daily in its two-acre garden. The activity had helped him retain his large, sturdy frame and had left him tanned and healthy looking. It was summer, and the garden where we usually sat having afternoon tea as we chatted, was filled with the quiet hum of bees and the English countryside's ubiquitous birdsong.

Throughout his life, Bob had never been talkative. He seemed to prefer listening attentively, looking wise as he puffed on his pipe, only occasionally making discreet utterances of doubt or concurrence, or asking a brief question. However, during these last visits, Bob displayed an unexpected loquaciousness. It seemed as if he had finally collected enough knowledge and information, and it was time to dispense some of it before it was too late. I only had to mention a time or an event, and his words flowed. He was an articulate speaker and intelligently attentive to details that matter in a narrative.

Bob's amusing description of a six-week cycling trip that he and Dan took in 1906 was probably the most revealing of Dan's character as a boy. The journey from their home in Walthamstow (thirty miles north of London) to Paris and back had been Dan's idea.

Dan had a special reason for wanting to go on the trip. After five years of patient work, he had become a serious collector of butterflies and moths. In 1905, at the age of twelve, he had added to his superb collection an extremely rare moth that he was determined to show at the next international lepidopterist's convention being held in Paris the following year. Since the family could ill afford to pay for the trip, cycling all the way seemed like the only possible means of attaining his goal.

Dan knew he had enough money saved for the steamer fare across the Channel. Then, by camping in farmers' fields and living on bread and a little cheese, he could cover the two land segments of the journey for little additional cost. However, Dan's mother strongly objected to the plan, insisting that a thirteen year old had no business setting off on such a long trip alone, most of it in a foreign country.

Dan then turned to his brother, Bob, and tried to talk him into joining him on his proposed adventure. "I was nineteen, a little wiser than Dan, and an experienced cyclist," Bob acknowledged, "so I seriously doubted that Dan had the needed stamina. He was a skinny little runt and I didn't think he could pedal a heavily loaded bike six hundred miles, which is what the round trip would be. I'd just end up having to pay our train fare home from somewhere in France, and I couldn't afford that. But Dan had a gift for persuasion, even at that age, so I reluctantly agreed. To my surprise and somewhat to my dismay, our very strict mother approved."

Bob went on to describe the trip to me in detail: "We set off on our heavy, dilapidated bikes, heading for Dover where we boarded the Channel steamer. Most touring bikes nowadays have gears to make it easier going up hills. Our old bikes had no gears and we had to walk them up any sizable hill. We could afford neither hotels nor restaurants, so we were heavily loaded down with food provisions and crude, cumbersome camping equipment. Our rain gear consisted of fishermens' oilskin capes, which we had bought in a second-hand shop near the docks in London. They were stiff and heavy, leaked at the seams, and reeked of fish.

"We now take for granted such things as good road maps and sign posts, but in 1906, they didn't exist. We relied solely on directions from local farmers along the way. They often knew less than we did and gave us incorrect information, so we frequently went astray. We probably cycled about twice as far as we should have to reach Paris.

"Dan's butterflies and moths were stored and displayed in a beautifully made cedar case with a glass lid. Before the trip, we had taken great pains to pack the case and protect it from the rain and from being bumped around on rough roads, of which we knew there would be many. The jouncing ride could damage the moths and butterflies, which were held in place in the case by a single straight pin. We'd been warned about the notoriously large cobblestones in the towns along the way, and the often unpaved roads linking the towns.

"Cars were still a rare sight in those days, and what traffic there was consisted chiefly of horse-drawn carriages, farmers' carts, and riders on horseback. The dusty road surface was littered with worn horseshoe nails, and we seldom traveled more than five miles without having to patch a tire. It rained a great deal, so the roads were often soft muddy tracks, but that didn't keep the blacksmith's nails from puncturing our tires. To patch an inner tube, its surface had to be dry, so that if the puncture happened when it was raining, we had to pitch our tent as shelter for the repair. If we were lucky, we'd find a barn nearby to use for this purpose. I counted that we made a hundred and forty patches by the time we reached Paris. Luckily, Dan had thought of bringing some spare inner tubes because we couldn't put more than two patches at the same place on an inner tube!

"It took us three weeks of dawn-to-dusk cycling and tire patching to reach Paris. When we arrived at the *Grand Rallye International des Mites et des Papillons*, we had a few anxious minutes as we unpacked the display case. We might well have come all that way for nothing. It had taken us so much time to pack that case that we were reluctant to undo it along the way to see how the moths were faring. We even worried that the case might have split or become crushed. But thank God, the case, the butterflies, and moths were intact.

"Dan, who was the only entrant under eighteen, won second prize in the 'best collection' category, as well as a three-hundred franc special prize for his rare moth, the only one of its kind found in all of Europe during the preceding three years. Thanks to the prize money, our meals improved considerably on the return trip, as Dan was especially keen on treating us to meals in good restaurants. The weather was much improved, and we continued to camp in farmers' fields every night. He was more interested in spending his hard-earned cash on good meals than on hotel rooms."

In his recounting of the trip, Bob made it sound like the greatest ordeal of his life, and commented, "I had grossly underestimated Dan's determination and hadn't expected him to last even as far as Dover. But he was always full of vigor and eager to keep pushing on. If it hadn't been for his enthusiasm, I would have packed it up a few miles from Calais where the steamer landed us in France—that's where the tire patching started in earnest." Then, after a reflective pause and another puff on his pipe, Bob added, "There's no doubt that Dan's great love affair with France was kindled on that trip."

I had once heard my father briefly mention this journey, but all I had been able to elicit from him on the subject was the comment that, for the first time in his life, he discovered that eating could be an enjoyable experience. "A slab of some local cheese on a chunk of freshly baked baguette was the most delicious thing I had ever tasted in my life."

Bob and Dan's family lived on the threshold of poverty. Their father, Peter-Christie Holmes, was a hardworking, self-effacing man. His humble position as a bank clerk meant that his four children and his wife had a roof over their heads, basic clothing, plain, monotonous meals, and very little else. All aspects of life in their household were austere.

Peter-Christie had been born nearly deaf and his speech was limited and distorted. At the time, little was being done to help the deaf. Peter-Christie's wife, Eliza, was of Scottish descent and a dour soul who viewed most conversation as superfluous. If her four offspring are to be believed, she seldom cracked a smile. However, she must have had an exceptionally charitable nature, for I have heard that before she married Peter-Christie, she had been one of the key figures in the founding of Dr. Bernado's Homes, a nation-wide charity for the housing and care of orphaned children.

Bob was also able to elaborate on the only story Father himself told me about this period of his life. Not long after their trip to France, Dan and an older friend, named A.V. Roe, worked together to build something they called "the flyer." The flyer somewhat resembled the Wright brothers' first plane which had flown a few years earlier. Dan and Roe's craft was smaller, and, unlike the Wrights' first plane, it had wheels. Three bicycle wheels allowed the craft to roll down a hill for launching. Just a glider, it had no engine. When Father was about seventy, he described to me, after a lot of coaxing, the flyer's maiden flight:

"We knew of a fairly smooth meadow with a long, gentle slope. With considerable effort, we pushed the flyer to the top of the hill. Roe climbed into the pilot's cradle and I helped push the flyer down the hill to get it started. The thing rolled easily and was soon going faster than I could run," said Father. "When it was doing about thirty miles an hour, Roe pulled back on the joy stick. The flyer leapt briefly into the air, only to lurch suddenly downward. As it hit the ground something snapped, causing it to go out of control. The beastly thing careened on, veering off to one side, and only came to a stop when it hit a hapless cow. It couldn't have been airborne more than thirty feet. I'm not even sure that it didn't just bounce upward after hitting a large tussock—if you can call that flying!" Father was never inclined to boast.

Of the three parties involved in this experiment, the cow was the least fortunate. She was impaled through an artery in her neck by one of the broken struts and died from loss of blood, despite Father's efforts to stanch the wound. "I spent the next two years paying the farmer for that wretched cow out of my own pocket money," he added ruefully. Roe's close call, the sight of the dying cow, and two years of weekly installments to repay the farmer apparently dampened Dan's enthusiasm for further aeronautical experiments. Roe emerged from the wreckage badly shaken but unscathed. He eventually went on to found Avro Aircraft, which produced a string of well-known aircraft, including the famous Lancaster bomber of World War II.

Dan attended the village school and managed to win a scholarship to London University, where he studied mechanical engineering. After getting his bachelor's degree, he went to work for the firm of Daimler, already famous for its superb motorcars. The following year, at the outbreak of World War I, Dan immediately enlisted and was assigned to an armored car battalion. Because of his training and experience at Daimler, he was soon commissioned to the rank of lieutenant and commanded a vehicle maintenance and repair depot near the front.

Bob mentioned how it was on this first assignment that Dan soon found an opportunity to show his talent. In 1915, Winston

Churchill proposed the concept of "an armored vehicle that would roll right over enemy trenches." The result of this proposal took shape a year and a half later in the form of the army tank. The first tanks clanked and rattled their way into combat at the Battle of the Somme in 1916. It was Dan's unit that secretly assembled and readied the first tanks ever to go into battle. His unit was also responsible for making repairs out on the battlefield, when feasible, or salvaging disabled tanks by towing them back to Allied lines. In 1917, Dan's outfit helped launch 400 tanks into the battle of Cambrai, which proved to be the most successful use of the tank in that war. Although Dan never fought inside a tank, his unit was never far from the front lines, and he often found himself in the thick of the fighting.

In his spare time, Dan studied and sketched design improvements for tanks, which he sent back to the War Office in London. Quite a few of his design details were incorporated into later models of the 2,300 British tanks that made it into battle during the first World War. By the end of the war, he had attained the rank of major and was awarded the Order of the British Empire.

Grim as those war years must have been, Dan's earlier love of France had been rekindled, and he resolved to remain there after the war. Instead of mustering out, he chose to stay in the army, whose chief mission in France immediately after the war was a monumental tidying up operation. All over northern France, near the Belgian border, lay the debris and devastation of four years of fierce fighting that had engaged over five million men and killed over two million in that sector alone. Dan's new army unit had to dispose of ammunition stores, weapons, vehicles, and all the other detritus of an army. During this cleanup effort, Dan was stationed at Mons, in Belgium, close to the French border.

It was in Mons that Dan first met my mother at an officers' mess dance. Jenny, the most adventurous of three sisters, had traveled alone to Mons, ostensibly to visit a former school friend who lived there. But as she later freely admitted, she knew that the British had an important army base in that town. Jenny was twenty, had spent four drab and dreadful years under the German occupation, and was looking for a little excitement.

Of my parents' first meeting, I can only conclude that it was not love at first sight. In fact, when next they met, at Jenny's home in Brussels, it became clear that Dan fancied Suzy, Jenny's older sister rather more. It was Suzy he married about two years later, in 1921. Jenny's comment about this was that marriage was not yet on her agenda; she was having the time of her life on the debutante circuit of Brussels.

Dan mustered out of the army shortly after his marriage to Suzy, and they settled in Wimereux, a small seaside village near Boulogne on the north coast of France. Dan and an old army chum and fellow officer, Captain Pickett, went into business together. They bid on the right to acquire and dispose of military matériel still stockpiled in the northern coastal sector of France.

There were few bidders. Most British soldiers were tired of the war and were anxious to return to England. During the four years of the war, Dan had spent nearly all his spare time working on special mechanical problems related to the design of tanks. He hadn't had time to spend much of his army pay and so had managed to save several thousand pounds. He and Pickett scraped up enough to submit a half plausible bid. They weren't the highest bidders, but two higher bidders never showed up with the money. Thus, for a few thousand pounds, Dan and his partner acquired well over a million pounds worth of matériel. They called their venture Franco Liquidations Ltd., and started work immediately.

Some forty years later, a few days before he died, Father talked to me about his years at Wimereux. He confided to me that it had been the happiest time of his life. He and Suzy lived in a charming, cozy, country cottage, and his job was both challenging and profitable. After the devastating years of the war, it was a time of recovery and hope. And, as Jenny intimated to me on another occasion, Dan and Suzy were deeply in love.

Jenny had always been close to Suzy and visited the newlyweds often. She described to me how Dan and Suzy explored the many small villages, seaside resorts and fishing harbors in this beautiful corner of France. They rode around on an old army motorcycle, which had a sidecar so that Suzy could take along her easel and paint box. When they stopped somewhere with a suitable view, she would set up her easel and paint while Dan read to her.

Suzy had studied to be a professional painter and had developed an impressionist brush style well suited to portraying the local landscapes and the luminous light of this area. She sold quite a few of her paintings, and it was evident that painting was the passion of her life. Of her sister, Jenny said, "She had painting in her veins and to the ends of her fingers."

As the senior partner of Franco Liquidations, Dan's job was primarily administrative. He was the one who found buyers for the salvaged materials, negotiated with customers, and took care of the bookkeeping. Pickett was out in the field supervising the actual work, which was done by a crew of local workmen. The bulk of this work involved the dismantling of artillery shells so the brass casings could be salvaged. The extracted explosives had to be detonated in large lots far from any habitation or farmland. Pickett had found an area that was especially suitable for this dangerous task. The coastal plain, some twelve miles south of Boulogne, consisted of a mile-wide strip of completely deserted sand dunes. In those days, the dunes stretched for some twenty miles down the coast. Inland, the dunes eventually gave way to a ridge of low, sandy hills covered in pine forests. A few miles farther inland, the forest ended and the landscape became the softly undulating hills of the Pas-de-Calais, some of the best and most beautiful farmland in France.

The ideal time to set off dumps of salvaged explosives piled on this wide, desolate, sandy beach was on certain days when a gentle breeze blew off the dunes and out to sea. The beach site was undeveloped public land and they had permission to set off explosions there.

By 1924, the salvaging operation was completed and their business ended. Pickett was an alcoholic whose drinking had caused major problems during their work together, and Dan was not keen on continuing their partnership. He and Pickett divided the profits and went their separate ways, both quite prosperous.

Dan and Suzy decided to move closer to Paris and soon found a house in the small village of Ville-d'Avray. They liked La Closerie (as the property was called) enough to take out a fifty-year lease on it. The main reason for their choice was the region's history as a locale favored by the impressionist painters, who liked the prevailing light and, some forty years before, had portrayed scenes of this still rural countryside northwest of Paris. For Suzy, this was an ideal place to do her landscape painting, which she always did outdoors no matter what the weather. In the meantime, Dan was casting about for a new business venture and found it convenient to be only fifteen kilometers from central Paris.

During one of their weekend motorcycle excursions along the Normandy coast, Dan discovered something that would launch him into his next business venture. At Dielette, a tiny fishing village set in a picturesque cove just south of the tip of Normandy, he came upon a masonry dome barely protruding from the rocky beach at low tide. The dome had a large manhole cover at its center. Equally mysterious was a high concrete tower set at the base of a nearby cliff, almost at beach level. Baffled as to their purpose, he set about investigating the origin of the dome and tower, and found that as early as 1855, iron ore had been mined through the manhole on the beach. The tower had been built later and was the site of another mineshaft. Both mineshafts led to seams of magnetite which angled downward towards (and under) the sea. Mining had been extremely challenging because of the high rate at which water leaked into the mine. A further problem for the mine was that magnetite was very heavy, and no easy or inexpensive overland route for its transportation was available.

Several efforts to transport the ore by ship had been made. A small pier had been built close to the mine, and shipments by small boats to nearby Cherbourg continued at a slow pace throughout the late 1800s. In 1907, a German company bought the mine and built a small steel *caisson* (artificial island) half a mile from shore. An aerial tramway was used to connect it to the mainland, and special buckets on the tramway carried ore from the mine head to larger ships moored to the *caisson*. Production started in late July 1914, but was stopped a week later when the war started, and the mine was immediately sequestered. Two years later, in what must have been a fit of patriotic (and irrational) frenzy, the *caisson* and aerial tramway were destroyed by the local authorities. They feared the Germans might somehow seize the mine and use it to their advantage in the war. It had remained inactive since then.

Dan knew that magnetite commanded high prices on world markets because of its purity and high iron content. It was much sought after for adjusting the composition of steel during its manufacture. He immediately recognized the tremendous commercial potential of a new, modern mine facility at this site.

Dan envisioned a larger concrete *caisson* that would be more efficient and set about founding a company which would purchase the rights to the mine, build the new, larger caisson, and sink new mine shafts to expand the mine's output. The new company adopted the name of the original company (Société Anomyme des Mines de Dielette), and a British holding company owned a large number of the shares, though Dan invested a large part of his own money in the venture. In organizing the financing for the new company, Dan had the help of his brother, Bob, who was by now a successful stockbroker in London.

The next four years were a period of intense activity for Dan, who personally undertook the design of the larger *caisson*, oversaw its construction, its launching and placement, as well as the acquisition of new machinery for the mine and aerial tramway. Although not schooled as a civil engineer, his *caisson* design was recognized as a significant and novel contribution to marine structural engineering, and as a result, he was awarded an honorary membership in the Institute of Civil Engineers (in Britain). The mine was operational by 1929 and the British company (Anglo-French Ltd.) now bought a controlling interest in Mines de Dielette. Dan was made a director in Anglo-French Ltd. and remained administrator and president of the mining company with offices in Paris.

In the midst of this busy period in Dan's life, Suzy, awaiting the arrival of their first child, had gone to Brussels to be with her parents where she could be under the care of her Uncle William, the much revered family doctor. Her parents had insisted; after all, her uncle had successfully delivered Suzy and her two sisters, Jenny and Mary. I met Uncle William only twice when I was child. He was a big, gruff man with an imposing black beard, not the sort of person one soon forgot. He was arrogant, full of bluster and his own self-importance.

Dan was continually traveling on mine business during this time, but knew that he could be in Brussels on a few hours notice, as soon as he received word that Suzy was in labor. The family could reach him by telegram, and he wired them promptly every time he changed his address. In those days, express train service between major European cities was already fast, frequent, and dependable. Trunk calling (as long distance phone service was called at the time) was difficult and unreliable, especially across international borders. But telegrams were fast and delivered immediately, any time of day or night.

When Suzy went into labor, the highly trusted Uncle William allowed her to remain in labor for three and a half days, right in her parents' home. During this time, he kept telling the anxious family that Suzy's condition was under control and that it was too early to wire Dan. He would advise them when they should do so.

On the third day of Suzy's labor, Jenny wired Dan without Uncle William's knowledge, and Dan arrived on the scene six hours later. As soon as he learned how long Suzy had been in labor, he immediately summoned an ambulance to take her to a hospital. It was late in the evening, and the ambulance's horses had to be hitched up, delaying its arrival by an hour. Then it was discovered that the ambulance crew had forgotten to bring their stretcher. Suzy, in extreme pain and nearly unconscious, had to be carried down three long flights of stairs. She died not long after reaching the hospital, without giving birth.

Suzy's birth canal was apparently too small for a normal delivery; the mystery remains why Uncle William did not perform a cesarean section early in the labor, as soon as the problem was evident, if indeed he was astute enough to recognize that something was wrong. The operation might well have saved Suzy's life and that of the baby.

Dan never spoke of this incident. What I know of it comes from Suzy's two sisters who were both there at the time, and their accounts do not differ. Dan never mentioned Suzy's name again. He bristled if any questions about her were addressed to him, or even if she were mentioned in passing during a family conversation.

He remained in a deep depression for over a year. He refused to have anything to do with Suzy's family. Some suspected that Dan felt the family in Brussels had abetted Uncle William in his incompetent handling of the crisis. Others thought Dan couldn't forgive himself for not being at her side during the last days of her pregnancy.

An old army friend of Dan's visited him about a year after Suzy's death and then contacted Suzy's family in Brussels. Major Hill, or just "Hill" as they called him, was by now an old friend of the family. He was one of the British officers who had accompanied Dan on his first visit to Jenny (and her sister Suzy) and had been best man at Dan's wedding. In fact, Hill had been an on-again, off-again suitor to Jenny. "He was much too shy to ever make any headway in his courting of me," was Jenny's comment on this matter.

Hill reported to the family that Dan was drowning his grief in work. He labored late into the night and through the weekend. He seldom ate a decent meal and had lost a lot of weight. His conversation was unfocused, and he couldn't be raised from his despondency by any of his friends. The live-in housekeeper and cook, Eglantine, had given up in despair and left his home in Ville-d'Avray. Auguste, the gardener, who came daily to tend the large garden, had also quit. Nothing in the house at Ville-d'Avray had been moved or touched since Suzy's death. The house was in a state of total neglect, and the garden was overgrown with weeds.

It was Jenny who "took the bull by the horns" (her own words) by writing to Dan's sister, Bessie, in England. She proposed that the two of them meet in Ville-d'Avray, ostensibly to sort out Suzy's belongings and affairs, but in fact for the purpose of helping Dan out of his depression. "I would have gone to him alone," Jenny said, "but in those days, a single woman didn't march into a widower's home without confronting raised eyebrows. I needed a chaperon, but I had a hard time convincing Bessie to join me. She said she was afraid I would fall in love with Dan, and 'that simply would not do.' Bessie insisted that if I married him, it would be an incestuous marriage."

Knowing Bessie, I'd say she was quite capable of making such an outrageous statement, but it was probably a misrepresentation of her true agenda. I have heard that Dan's family in England had originally disapproved of Dan marrying a foreigner. Bessie was probably reluctant to do anything that might lead Dan to repeat his considerable misdeed. But she eventually and reluctantly agreed to go.

The two women stayed at Ville-d'Avray for six months. They rehired Eglantine, who saw to it that Dan ate good meals. They obliged Dan to come home at a reasonable hour to be with them in the evenings, and to spend his weekends at home rather than at the office. Dan slowly came out of his depression.

After Jenny's first visit in the company of Bessie, and following Dan's recovery from his depression, Jenny revisited Dan by herself and was with him a good deal. In November 1929, three years after Suzy's death, Jenny married Dan in a quiet ceremony in Ville-d'Avray. I was born the following April.

So far, several references to my mother have been in situations where other people predominate the narrative. I now bring her into sharper focus.

My mother, Jenny, born in 1899, was christened with the ponderous name of Jeanne Adele Françoise Josephine. She was the daughter of Maurice, a successful Brussels architect who was a well known specialist in *art nouveau*, and who was also an authority on Gothic restoration. Maurice's father, Jules, was a well-known Belgian sculptor whose statues still adorned various Brussels monuments in the thirties. Maurice's grandfather, Antoine, was painter to the Royal Court of Belgium and renowned for his portraiture. Jenny's mother, Laure Loutermans, came from a prosperous Dutch family who had made their fortune in shipping.

Until she married at the age of thirty, Jenny lived almost entirely in her parents' luxurious home in Brussels, and the family spent summers at their villa in the Belgian seaside resort of Westende. Jenny and her two sisters not only led an active social life, but also traveled frequently, visiting relatives living in Belgium, England and Holland.

Like Dan, Jenny had a lot of initiative and a strong inner drive to get things done. At the age of thirteen, she took on the paid position of "companion" for the young daughters of her Aunt Marguerite, who had married a wealthy Englishman and lived in England. Marguerite wanted someone who could be with her three daughters full time and teach them French. It was here that Jenny became quite proficient in speaking English and discovered that she loved the British and their way of life. This may explain how she happened to be at a British Army officers' dance in Mons in 1919.

The first major upheaval in Jenny's well-ordered life was the German occupation of Belgium in 1914. For the next four years, Belgians were heavily restricted in all their movements, even within the city of Brussels. Commerce and most businesses were severely curtailed, or came to a complete halt, except when the nature of their activity could be diverted (under duress) to the German war effort.

The end of the war in 1918 was like warm sunshine after a bad storm. Now nineteen years old, Jenny worked for the Red Cross in rural communities of Belgium that had been devastated by the war. When not working, she enjoyed life on the debutante circuit of Brussels. And there were also those handsome British officers of the liberating army. For the next ten years, Jenny, like most well-to-do young women of the time, enjoyed a life of leisure, dabbling in painting like her sister Suzy, and taking singing lessons.

Two years after the war, Jenny's father decided he might need a car in order to visit his various construction sites. In those days, the architect working on any building was, by Belgian law, the general contractor. Because of the war, her father had numerous contracts for the rebuilding of damaged or destroyed houses and public buildings, and his work extended to several other Belgian cities such as Louvain and Liège.

Listening to Jenny tell about the proposed car, it was obvious that she was the one who put the flea in her father's ear. Jenny could see the advantage he would have in owning and driving a car, but knew her father would find excuses for not venturing into something so radically new. More importantly, she was eager to drive a car herself.

Cars were still an oddity and extremely temperamental contraptions. Just getting them started and keeping them running smoothly was quite an art, each car being a law unto itself. People who could afford the luxury of a car usually acquired a chauffeur to master the mysteries of the internal combustion engine. As an alternative to hiring a chauffeur, car buyers attended a school where they learned how cars worked, how to drive, and how to deal with the frequent tantrums of the engine.

Part of Jenny's proposal to her father was that she would attend a chauffeur school for several months. Jenny was the only woman in the class and enjoyed all the teasing that this entailed. She graduated with honors and was apparently successful in imparting her newfound knowledge to Suzy and her father, who were soon able to drive. Jenny always seemed to know what she wanted, and did whatever she felt was needed to achieve her goals.

By the time she married my father, Jenny spoke English fairly well and without hesitation. She read books in English and understood the language better than she could speak it. Her pronunciation of most familiar words was close to flawless. If anything, it was almost too good. She articulated her words so well that when she uttered the word "milk," for instance, the L and K sounds were so distinct that one could almost hear the milk sloshing in the pail.

Jenny did however, have a unique language problem. If she didn't know the English word for what she wanted to say, she forged, literally invented, a new English word on the assumption that an understandable English word could be hammered out of the French word she needed to translate. And Jenny's conviction that the rules of French grammar applied equally well to English often contributed to the capricious order of words in her sentences.

When Jenny was a teenager, her formal schooling had come to a halt during the four years of World War I. However, she was part of a well-to-do French-speaking family that thrived on sophisticated conversation and the reading of good books, so she spoke French correctly and with refinement. But when Jenny spoke English, her sense of sentence decorum often abandoned her. Impressed by her pronunciation and the verve with which she delivered her sentences, her listeners were often taken aback when she combined several barely related ideas into a single, helter-skelter, breathless sentence (something she never did when speaking French). They found it quaint, entertaining, and often very funny. And because she was good-natured and had a lively sense of humor, they found her very engaging.

By the time I reached adulthood, one of Mother's favorite pastimes during our visits together was reminiscing. This she did in both English and French, but I always enjoyed it more when she did it in English because it added a whole new dimension to any story she was telling. I will occasionally, in the coming pages, attempt to portray her comments and reminiscences in English, and to give a fair impression of the way she came across, though I make no claim to complete accuracy in this regard. I must also explain that when my mother's quoted words sound appropriate and normal in these chapters, it's because I am translating what she had said in French—correctly.

I also need to mention Mother's easily excitable nature. She had a tendency to see things at their blackest and most dramatic. Her style of storytelling lent itself well to conveying all the terror, panic, and drama she conjured up in her own mind.

One day, I happened to mention to Mother that one of my earliest memories was that of a extremely large marmalade cat, a cat so large that it must have been larger than I was at the time, and that I thought I remembered him purring and dozing beside me.

"Oh yes! I remember that great big orange cat of the neighbors!" Mother said, as she launched into one of her reminiscences. "You were a newborn of two years. I remember him because he made a big brouhaha for us. Everything was going on roller skates until this cat came. Yes! It was that awful—what did you call him—'apricot jam' cat? Anyway, that orange cat, who so much deranged our life.

"Nurse Khondakov had put you on a warm, sunny day in the garden in your pram. I was doing gardenage in a far-away corner of the garden and saw that orange cat jumping right next to your pram onto the bench. The pram was hiding nearly all the bench, so I could not see him afterward, and I thought he is just taking a walk on the bench, like cats always do. But when I looked up again, I saw the pram balancing itself backwards and forwards, all alone by itself, rather violently, and you were too small to balance yourself. I was right away suspicious and alarmed myself.

"I knew he was famous for eating rats as big as a milk bottle. The rats lived in the hen's house and were always eating the hen's food and also their eggs, and I thought he would devour you. You were not much bigger." Mother often omitted what she thought was obvious, and in this case I was left wondering whose size I slightly exceeded, the rat, the cat or possibly even the milk bottle?

"I was running to your pram with my heart in my mouth at the far end of the garden. When I arrived there, I found the cat in the pram with you, having one paw around your chest, sleeping and as if he was loving you—you did not seem to mind at all and you were wide-awaked and smiling at me. Then he waked up, seeing that I was being angry with him. He violently jumped out and I was terrified that he had scratched you leaving the pram with an awful scar on your face!

"But you were not scratched at all, thank God. While this is happening, Nurse Khondakov was smoking peacefully a cigarette nearby. I crossly called her to me by saying, 'Don't you see this cat with all his fleas in the pram with the baby?'

"And you know what that Khondakov had the nerves of saying to me?" exclaimed Mother. Not waiting for an answer, she continued: " 'This cat is always coming nearby and he loves the baby, and he never even hurts him. He is like a guard dog. When that cat is there, I take a cigarette and my eases not far away, but also not near the baby while putting smoke on him.'

Khondakov was saying this to me calmly as if it was nothing at all. Can you imagine an experted nurse doing and saying things like this?

"Then I reminded her that the cat must be having fleas—he was always killing big rats and eating them with the fleas jumping on his furs before he has them inside his mouth. And next the fleas on the cat jumps on the baby, I told her. But Nurse Khondakov was so insolent and answered me that if the baby had catched fleas she will be the first to know that. And besides, there were no fleas in the pram on the baby which I looked in, and saw she was right about that.

"Then I told her that the cat is so big he might be choking the baby like a mother pig when she is sleeping on the face of her little pigs. But even this did not make her repenting. She just said I am ridiculous being afraid of choking you under the cat who was perhaps sleeping like a mother pig on your face.

"I was so furious by this insolence that I fired her on the spot!"

At this point, I interrupted Mother's excited narrative, "But you have always said that Nurse Khondakov was such a good nurse and so devoted to me!"

"She was," Mother replied. "She was a White Russian nurse and the governess of the countess who was the cousin of the Czar in St. Petersburg. So she must be very good, living even in the Royal Palace with them, being a nurse diplomed, and also nursing the Russian soldiers who were fighting in the war against the Germans, so she must be very knowing about fleas, and had medals to prove it and many good references.

"I hired her when you were a newborn only three months and I was going with Dan for a year to Africa. I don't know what I would have done if Khondakov had not arrived [on the scene]. Granny and Grandpa in Brussels would never have been managing without Khondakov even if they did have Georgette, Philomène and Matilde. Those three were devoted domestics but they were much too old to be caring of you, still a newborn. It would have been scenes in the kitchen if Khondakov had not been there to do all the things for you that you were needing as a newborn.

"When I came after a year from Africa, you were walking around already and Granny said Nurse Khondakov had been wonderfully doing everything for you. Night and day on every day of the week and singing Russian lullaby songs that were putting you to sleep and rocking you. She was marvelous for Granny and Grandpa having the joys of you little and not having all your dirty nappies too."

"But then why did you fire her so quickly if she had been so wonderful?" I persisted.

"There was another time," she continued, "after I came back [from Africa] which also made me mad against her. One day, I came up to her when she was not realizing it, and I was hearing her talking in a baby voice so you would better understand. She was saying, 'I'm your real mother who really loves you. If Mummy was really loving you, she would not go far away and leaving you like that for so long!'

"Then I came around the door and she was turning red like a beet root, seeing me embarrassed because she knew I was hearing her. I told her she must not be saying things like that to a child, that it is not appropriated, and is being disloyal to me, and she shruggingly just said, 'Small children do not understand what you are saying to them.'

"I almost fired her on that spot, then. She was completely in the wrong and you being two years old, I know very well you were understanding, especially talking in baby voice which a baby starts to listen when he hears it. That time, she was so good when I was in Africa that I took pity on her, and I said to myself that she must badly desire a little boy like you, and that's why she is saying these terrible things—but her insolence from the affaire of the orange cat was the last straw!"

In the space of ten minutes, Mother had touched on a wide range of topics: the diet of large rodents, family life in the Czar's palace, the hazards of life on the Russian front, the migratory rationale of fleas, servant conditions in her mother's household, sudden piglet death syndrome, the speech comprehension of infants, as well as the details of how I and a large cat enjoyed our naps together. I will now return to a less strenuous form of narration.

Three months after I was born, Mother had departed on a prolonged journey to Africa with Father, and had left me with her parents in Brussels for a whole year. Father had been asked to resolve some engineering problems at one of the Kimberley diamond mines near Johannesburg. He was by then Anglo-French's mining expert. He also specialized in international law and international business negotiations, and after the Kimberley assignment, the company wanted him to travel to several other mines that Anglo-French owned in central Africa. The trip was expected to take over a year, and my parents would be doing a lot of traveling by car across the veldt or traveling through the wilderness and camping under extremely primitive conditions. It was hardly a suitable journey on which to take a three-month-old baby.

Two decades later, Mother reminisced about this journey and told me about her decision to go to Africa. She said she was torn between the duties of a mother and those of a wife, that Dan was still prone to bouts of deep depression, and that she felt it wasn't good for him to be alone. She even divulged that she felt the marriage was not on sufficiently solid ground for them to be separated so long, and that she had to prove to Dan that she could be as good a wife as Suzy had been. If this sad view of her early marriage were correct, I would say she succeeded in pulling the chestnuts out of the fire. I grew up with the unmistakable conviction that they were a contented and effective team, and that they had no major differences to resolve, except the one about my going to boarding school. Father went to great lengths to make Mother's life as pleasant and comfortable as possible, and she did the same for him.

Major Dan Holmes, 1919   Suzy (self portrait), 1918

Suzy and Dan enjoying the garden at la Closerie (Ville-d'Avray), 1925

CHAPTER 2

Wild Boars and a German Governess

My sister, Brenda, was born not long after my parents' return from Africa. Then, less than a year later, Mother fired Nurse Khondakov over the marmalade cat incident, leaving her with many chores she had previously never had to face. Father insisted that she find a replacement nurse, so Mother spent the next two years searching first for the ideal nurse, and then, as we grew older, for the ideal governess. In the meantime, Mother launched into child rearing with gusto. It was her approach to everything.

For help, Mother still had Eglantine, the cook and housekeeper who had originally worked for Dan and Suzy, and who had temporarily left Dan's empty house while he was a widower. Eglantine had a teenage daughter, Sabine, who lived with her wherever she worked. Sabine's father had been killed in the last days of World War I, before he had a chance to marry Eglantine and before Sabine was born. Sabine attended the village school, and in the evenings she helped her mother in the kitchen.

One of Mother's reminiscences about Eglantine was an event which happened before I was old enough to be aware of it. Eglantine had prepared a bouillabaisse for lunch, and among the numerous ingredients of this traditional fish stew were some mussels. Upon tasting her completed dish, Eglantine decided the bouillabaisse tasted funny; a closer examination revealed that none of the mussels had opened during cooking, a sure sign that they had not been alive and fresh when they were put to cook. Eglantine was short tempered, and, in what must have been a momentary fit of rage or disgust, she threw the whole kettle of fish stew out the kitchen door into the adjacent yard. Her intention was probably to let the chickens benefit from all the other ingredients of the stew. The yard by the kitchen, like those of many country houses in France, was populated with chickens, which spent the day scratching about for the minute morsels that chickens apparently like. Food scraps were routinely thrown out into these yards to supplement the chickens' diet, if not to constitute the mainstay thereof.

For lunch that day, Eglantine served an omelette in place of the bouillabaisse. Later that afternoon, she looked out of the kitchen window and noticed that two of the chickens were lying lifeless on the ground. She wasn't sure why the birds had died, but decided to salvage what she could of this calamity by plucking one of them and serving it for dinner. Eglantine had almost finished plucking the chicken when she thought she felt it move under her hands. Then she heard a squawk from the now featherless bird. She dropped it in horror and ran to Mother, who was in the drawing room writing a letter.

"A dead chicken has come back to haunt me!" Eglantine wailed. "Oh please Madame! Please come to the kitchen and save me from this apparition! I'm too frightened to go back in there alone!"

Under questioning, Eglantine gave Mother a confusing summary of events leading to the present crisis and explained that she thought chickens could distinguish between what was edible and what was not safe to eat. She pointed out, quite astutely, that chickens peck their way around a yard and never seem to consume anything that makes them sick, so they should have been able to avoid eating the tainted mussels. Based on Eglantine's garbled tale, Mother didn't know quite what to expect as they walked to the scene of the mystery. In a state of trepidation, the two women entered the kitchen to find the chicken strutting around naked and squawking indignantly. They continued out into the yard, and in the trash bin where Eglantine had tossed the other lifeless bird, discovered a groggy hen looking as though she were awakening from a night on the town.

The two hens recovered and returned to their assigned chores of eating scraps and converting them to eggs. Since it was late in the fall, Eglantine felt sorry for the naked chicken and kept it in the warmth of the kitchen for a few days until she had finished knitting a turtleneck sweater specially fitted to the bird. The garment was bright blue, had sleeves for the chicken's legs, but none for the wings. Eglantine had also knitted into the chicken sweater a special bulge, or bustle, for the "Pope's nose," and a vital lower opening was also included for inserting the chicken into its sweater, and through which it might lay eggs, if so inclined. This fashionably attired bird never grew its feathers back and continued to lay excellent eggs. On warm days its sweater was laundered, on which occasion the chicken was allowed to disport itself naked. She grew to a ripe old age and, like all elderly hens, was eventually relegated to the pot.

By the time I was three, Mother, still without a governess, decided I was old enough to be watched over by Sabine who was, by then, about fifteen years old. My first memories of being left in Sabine's care are of occasions when Mother dropped us off at Hardelot Beach, leaving the two of us there while she went to play a round of golf. Hardelot is a seaside resort on the north coast of France. On these occasions, Eglantine always packed a small picnic basket for our afternoon tea snack, or *gouté*, which Sabine and I enjoyed on the beach. Eglantine stayed home to look after Brenda, who was barely walking and, in Mother's eyes, too young to be left on the beach with Sabine.

In preparation for our *gouté*, Sabine would coax me into building a flat-topped sand castle to use as a table for our picnic. She then set a tea towel on the horizontal surface to serve as a tablecloth. The sand was very fine and, as it was slightly damp, I could cut vertical surfaces with my toy spade in this "castle," so that we could kneel right beside it to eat our *tartines* (bread and jam sandwiches). We had to be careful not to set anything too close to the edge of this table, which crumbled easily at the slightest provocation.

The best part of the day was riding home on a quaint, pale yellow trolley car, which saved Mother the trouble of picking us up. I was thrilled and fascinated by this little tramway, which was like a small train because the main trolley pulled two additional passenger cars. The first car, the "trolley," was fully enclosed, but its sliding windows were open to keep the tram cool. It was usually devoid of passengers because people preferred the second or third cars, which were completely open on the sides so the people could enjoy the breeze.

To my immense chagrin, and even though it was still warm and sunny during our tram rides home, Sabine always insisted we ride in the first car. I used to think this was because Sabine was afraid of falling out of the open-sided car, but of course, I was the one in danger of falling off.

Even so, I always loved the ride home. The little trolley wound its way through the gently undulating sand dunes, slowing considerably as it climbed the slight inclines, then barreling full speed down the other side of a dune. Where the open dunes ended, we plunged into the warm pine-scented Forest of Hardelot.

A mile farther on, as the trolley emerged from the pine forest, it ran past the luxurious Grand Hotel du Golf. This exotic-looking establishment had abundant flower beds brimming with color and lush green lawns on which hotel guests played croquet and enjoyed their afternoon tea or *apéritifs* under colorful beach umbrellas. The trolley didn't stop at the hotel because the tram's riders probably couldn't afford to eat or stay there. Nor, for that matter, would any of the hotel's guests have deigned to ride the trolley.

By this time, the passengers, mostly young people who had spent a day at the beach and who had consumed a fair amount of wine since departing Hardelot, started to sing. The conductor got into the spirit and clanged the trolley's bell at the appropriate moments. The trolley rattled on, its wheels grinding and screeching in the curves.

The clatter of the little trolley and the merriment of those on board created a noisy intrusion into the quiet of the late afternoon landscape we were traversing—now lush pastures and farmland. We skirted two small lakes mottled with lilies and dotted with anglers as they sat immobile on their diminutive camp stools, deep in reverie. They didn't wave or turn to look at us, fearing they might frighten away the fish. When the trolley approached an old castle in ruins, once a residence of Charlemagne, Sabine and I knew we had reached our stop in the village of Condette. We stepped off the trolley (a huge jump down for me) and waved to our fellow passengers as they continued on to Ponts-de-Briques and Boulogne.

It was a short walk to our house, "Villa La Bècque," up a street bordered by tall poplar trees and a small stream. The house was named after the stream that bordered the road we were on. Villa La Bècque was one of a series of summer houses my parents rented in this part of France every summer. The owner of our Villa, an Englishman, was doing a tour of duty in India. He had built the house in the fashion of a true Indian bungalow. I was much impressed by the novelty of a one-story house and by its rudimentary, primitive look. It was very different from our house in Ville-d'Avray, which had three stories, a mansard roof, and was very formal in appearance

Villa La Bècque was a long, narrow house laid out in a straight, unbroken line. Its nine rooms were reached by a corridor that ran the length of the house on its north side like the corridor in a railroad car. We could also move from one room to another on rainy days without getting wet by using the full-length covered terrace on the south side of the house. Each of the rooms had French doors that opened onto this wide terrace. The dining room table was moved to the terrace for meals on warm days, and a set of comfortable wicker lounge chairs on the terrace served as an outdoor drawing room.

Mother pointed out a remarkable aspect of this house, which never ceased to enchant us when it rained. From every room of the house we could look up and see the rough-hewn, sloping rafters of the peaked roof, the lath over the rafters, and the underside of the orange-brown terra cotta tiles. When we had a good steady rain, there was a pleasant and soothing sound that was not the usual pitter-patter of raindrops. Mother explained that each tile, overhanging its neighbor, acted as the site for a small waterfall, and these hundreds of tiny, trickling waterfalls created a sound resembling a stream of tiny beads rolling across the gently sloped surface of a tea tray.

Something else about this house which secured its place in my affections, was its proximity to the stream known as "la Bècque." The stream ran about twenty feet from the house, parallel to its length, and flowed just fast enough so that, standing beside it, I could hear its quiet burble. Bordered with cress and bright green water weeds that swung gently back and forth in the current, this tiny river was not much wider than ten or twelve feet. I could play in it unattended because it was about knee-deep (for me) and had a flat, sandy bottom.

I used to launch little boats, actually small sticks or little pieces of wood, from a spot near the east end of the house. I then dashed into the house through a door at that end, on down the long corridor and out the front door at the house's west end, where I made a sharp right turn onto our entrance drive. The driveway crossed over a small bridge from which I could survey the finish line of my boat race. On warm days, it was more fun to go sploshing barefoot down the stream itself in hot pursuit of the boats. Either way, there was enough fun in it to keep me happy for hours. I remember being indignantly surprised at discovering that a fancy little toy boat, intended for bath tub use, and graced with the lines of a boat meant for speed, did no better in the race than the simple little sticks.

At the end of the summer, the family left Condette in the late afternoon for the car trip back to Ville-d'Avray and stopped for an evening dinner at a small country inn on the way. This stop provided me with my first vivid recollection of nighttime. I was probably sleepy as we left the restaurant after dinner, and Father carried me to the car in his arms. He stopped outside the restaurant to point out various stars to me. It was one of those black, moonless nights in the country where the air was so clear that the larger stars sparkled jewel-like against a sky luminous with the Milky Way. For a minute or two, I was transfixed as he stood there talking softly to me, telling me the names of stars and constellations. He started walking slowly towards the car, perhaps still looking up at the stars and suddenly, we were falling!

Father had tripped over a drunk, who was lying on the ground. Fortunately, we weren't hurt. For some time thereafter, I puzzled over why anyone would go to sleep on the ground right outside a restaurant.

In the autumn of 1933, when I began to attend my first school, I was three and a half years old. I can still remember the fear and dread I experienced every day as I walked up the narrow pedestrian alley leading to the school.

Our first walk to the Ecole de la rue Pradier was on a fine autumn afternoon. In an effort to calm my fears about what she called this new adventure, Mother was putting on airs of forced cheerfulness, which only added to my nervousness. When we entered the *rue* Pradier, the street where the school was supposed to be, she started looking for the house number. Both sides of the street had high stone walls, and street numbers were clearly marked beside each entrance on blue enamel plaques set into the masonry. It was soon clear that the number she was looking for was missing. We went up and down the street, looking at the numbers over and over again.

Eventually, Mother must have noticed that an unobtrusive break in the wall occurred where the number she sought should have been. This opening vaguely suggested a pedestrian alley between two properties, but no sign or number indicated that a house might be at its far end. Nevertheless, she became convinced that this was where the school had to be. The narrow alley was bordered on both sides by those same high walls. Along one side of the alley, just over the wall, was a row of closely planted chestnut trees whose dense foliage completely obscured the sky above the alley. Nor was there light or a clearing at the end of this somber tunnel, which ended in shadows and darkness. Mother hesitated for some time and even expressed misgivings about entering so dark a passage. For my part, I was hoping it meant the school didn't exist and that she would forget the whole thing.

Just then, a gnarled old woman came tottering down the street, and Mother asked her about the school. "Ah yes, it's down that alley, about two hundred meters on your right," the old woman replied, pointing to the break in the wall we had been contemplating.

The alley was chilly and damp, and I was overpowered by the musty smell of moss and mold. There was an eerie silence, a shutting out of noise by the moss-laden walls and the canopy of foliage above. I was struck by the muffled sounds of our footsteps on the thick carpet of damp leaves on the ground, and the rapid pulse beat in my ears. I wondered who would hear us if we called for help.

We walked what seemed to me an incredible distance before we finally reached a rusty, black metal gate set in the wall on our right. Mother tugged at the bell-pull beside it, and I heard the tinkling beyond the wall. A period of eerie silence was followed by the sound of footsteps on gravel. When the gate opened, a cross-looking woman wearing a well-bleached denim apron confronted us. "*Madame Lacoste vous attends*," ("Madame Lacoste awaits you,") the woman said curtly, and led us across the small schoolyard to the entrance of a shed-like building, which turned out to be the school's only classroom.

Inside the drab, dimly lit classroom was an array of empty, dilapidated desks. Sitting at a large desk at the far end of the room was a woman who glowered at us as we approached. She was Madame Lacoste who, after some terse discussion with Mother, enrolled me. Then, she abruptly told us that the autumn semester was already in progress, that classes were held only in the morning, and that I should be brought back the following morning at nine o'clock.

The next day, as Mother and I walked down the gloomy alley to the school, I was once again filled with the dread I had experienced the afternoon before. When the black gate opened, the woman in the denim apron seemed even surlier than she had been on our first visit. This time, she greeted us by announcing angrily that we were late, and that Madame Lacoste did not like her class interrupted by late arrivals. She then told Mother that she would take over and deliver me to Madame Lacoste. Classes ran till noon, at which time I should be picked up promptly, she snapped at Mother. Without further ceremony, she seized my hand and towed me rapidly across the yard and into the classroom.

Madame Lacoste was at her desk in front of the class, and about thirty boys and girls were sitting in six rows of small desks. Each child wore a black smock that came to the knees, had full-length sleeves and, as a minor frivolity, was piped in red. The surly woman in the denim apron took one of these smocks from a row of hooks along the back wall, brusquely jammed my arms through the sleeves and buttoned up a long row of buttons at the back, tugging sharply to bring each button to its hole. I had never been treated so roughly and viewed all this with considerable dismay.

The denim woman led me to one of the empty desks, sat me down, and opened a workbook that was already at the desk. She picked up a plain nib pen lying in a special groove at the top of the desk and dipped it in an inkwell set into the desk. She then wrote on a blank line an exact copy of some cursive text printed directly above it. "Do it like that," she said, "Go on—do it—just copy the line above." She took my hand and forced my fingers to close around the pen.

Madame Lacoste was reading and seemed uninterested in what was going on in the room. The students were all busy scratching away in their notebooks with their pens and, except for a couple of them in my immediate vicinity, appeared to be unaware of my arrival. I soon learned why. If a student were caught looking around or talking, he or she was immediately slapped on the knuckles by Madame Lacoste, who descended on the student like a hawk on a field mouse. The slap was administered with the wide, flat surface of a hardwood ruler that she always seemed to have with her. She didn't hit very hard, but enough to make it sting for a while. The first time I was struck, I broke into tears, so I was immediately whacked a second time and scolded for being a crybaby. No one cried in Madame Lacoste's classroom; she didn't like crying, she explained.

I dipped my pen and struggled to copy as I had been told. The results were dismal, but my interest picked up when I discovered the pen's tendency to produce unexpected ink blobs on the paper. To my great delight, the blobs then ran or smudged.

Soon, my fingers were turning black, which, of course, was the reason we wore black smocks.

Eventually, Madame Lacoste came down the aisle looking at each workbook and praising a few that must have been far better looking than mine. The beneficiaries of this scarce praise were all girls. As for me and the other boys, she had only irate reprimands and scorn.

Mother duly picked me up at noon and was appalled by the state of my hands. When we got home, she scrubbed them long and hard, first with strong soap and when that failed, she used lemon juice and a pumice stone. Traces of ink stains would remain as badges of attendance for the duration of my stay at that school.

The following morning, Mother managed to get me to the school on time. The denim woman's tongue lashing the day before had made an impression on her. On this day, I didn't miss recess as I had the day before. When it was time for recess, we filed out of the classroom in orderly fashion into the gloomy schoolyard. I now had a chance to satisfy my curiosity about a little building which looked as if it might be a "play house" and which was set in the middle of the schoolyard. As I approached the little house, its odor quickly removed all doubt as to its intended purpose.

The line we had formed was led in a circle around the outhouse. We were told to join hands, to start singing "*Alouette, gentille alouette*," and to continue skipping sideways in a "ring-around-the-outhouse" dance.

"Who needs to go first?" Madame Lacoste cried out as we danced and sang. A small, skinny boy declared impatiently that he did and broke away from the circle to enter the outhouse. The ring re-formed, and we continued dancing around and around the outhouse as my classmates took turns dropping out of the circle to use it and rejoining us once relieved. Eventually, it was my turn.

I had already experienced the convenience of peeing behind a tree, and I had peed exultantly across and into rain puddles, but here I met defeat. Once inside this disgusting, foul-smelling place,

I found I couldn't go. The singing outside was a further cause for distraction from the chore at hand.

My long delay inside the outhouse eventually caused a halt in the singing. An ominous period of silence was broken by the sound of an adult muttering outside, followed by loud banging on the door. Then the door opened, there being no lock on it. Madame Lacoste grabbed me by the collar of my smock and pulled me out just as I was finally achieving success in my original goal. There I stood, now unable to stop what I had worked so hard to start. The short flannel pants little boys wore in those days had no fly buttons, (we just pulled up the short trouser leg), so at least I was not indecent, but the stream ran down my bare leg and into my sock and shoe.

"*Sal petit garçon—quel bébé—alors! Tu ne peux pas t'arretter?*" ("You dirty little boy—what a baby—really! Can't you control yourself?") she exclaimed, slapping me on my bare legs, taking due care to avoid the wet areas.

Embarrassed beyond words, I ran to a corner of the schoolyard where I could hide behind a large tree, and there I stayed, wiping off my wet leg and sock with fallen chestnut leaves. I had been the last to volunteer, so the dancing circle now disbanded. Before long, a boy came over to where I was still licking my wounded pride. It was Marcel, the oldest and largest boy in the school.

"*C'est une méchante—elle m'a fait ça aussi—elle est comme ça!*" ("She's a nasty one—she did that to me, too—that's the way she is!") he said, shrugging. "Come on!" He put his arm over my shoulder and gently led me back to the center of the yard where the rest of the kids were now playing. I soon recovered and joined in. Marcel's kindness made a lasting impression on me.

I was too embarrassed to tell Mother about this incident. Even so, I don't think she was ever pleased or impressed by that school. However, it was the only private school nearby, and it was convenient, being about a mile from our house and thus within walking distance. This suited Mother just fine, as she had a strong belief in the need for a daily walk. Walking was something we had to do every day, no matter what the weather was like. It rained a lot, often hard, but that didn't deter her. We had raincoats, rubber boots and sou'wester rain hats to wear on such occasions.

I was at that school for about half a year. We learned to recognize and use some of the letters of the alphabet so that we could read and write a few words in cursive. And at noon, we were sent home with about an hour of work to do with the help of our parents. We learned to count up to nine and to do sums of two numbers, as well as to multiply two numbers, but we were limited to answers that were no greater than nine. The numbers were printed large enough on the page so that we could color them with crayons. After a month of coloring numbers, we wrote them in ink. Now the numbers had to have exactly the right form and be in the right place on the sheet in a neat column when doing an addition. Gross or frivolous discrepancies from these rules would result in a knuckle rapping and a loud reprimand. In spite of the hardships involved, I enjoyed working with numbers, and I awaited with anticipation our encounter with numbers higher than nine.

The strangest thing they had us doing at that school was embroidery, and this activity became my eventual downfall. It was during an embroidering session that I somehow managed to sew my smock and embroidery material around a limb of the desk I was using. I have no idea how this came about, but the result was clear. At the end of the period, I found myself unable to stand up and leave my desk. "What have you done, you imbecile?" Madame Lacoste yelled at me, as she went for a pair of scissors to cut me free. I was trussed up like a fly in a spider web, and it took her some time to sort it out because she was determined not to cut my smock. All this time, she hurled verbal abuse at me and vigorously slapped me, either to punctuate some particularly vindictive imprecation, or to stop any part of me that I had dared to move.

When Mother arrived to pick me up, Madame Lacoste unburdened herself once more of her anger as she described my heinous crime. She declared crossly that she could not have such an unruly child in her school and that she was expelling me then and there.

Mother listened to this calmly and when Madame Lacoste finally wound down, replied that it was just as well since she didn't want me under the influence of a person with so little sense of humor. And so, not quite four years old, I found myself expelled from school. For the rest of that school year I was tutored at home by Mother whenever she felt so inclined, which wasn't very often.

For the summer vacation of 1934, we spent the month of June at my grandparents' summer house, "*Villa Fancy*" in Westende, a seaside resort in Belgium. Their four-story villa had eight bedrooms, servants' quarters, a large dining room and living room, as well as a family room, though it wasn't called that. The villa had been designed and built at the turn of the century by my grandfather, a trend-setting architect in Brussels.

A miserable event which I recall from that visit to Westende took place during a Punch and Judy show not long before our scheduled departure. The show was presented only on rainy afternoons to entertain children who would normally be playing on the beach. During the performance, a little boy sitting next to me suddenly turned towards me, let out a strange cry and threw up all over me. Mother thought he had probably been fed too many pastries and candy, and after giving the child's mother a ferocious tongue-lashing, she rushed me home and gave me a bath. I never found out what happened to Punch and Judy and was more upset about that than I was at being vomited upon.

The following morning, Mother, Brenda, and I sailed for England where we went to visit my two maiden aunts who lived in a little village called Yateley, in Surrey. Bessie and Lottie were Father's two older sisters, both in their late forties at the time. Lottie had been engaged to a young army officer who was killed in the war. She was so aggrieved by the loss that she never married nor ever went out with another man, but she wasn't visibly sad or self-pitying. Quite the contrary, she had a good sense of humor and was easily brought to a chuckle. She was a kind, easy-going person and a good listener who took a deep interest in anyone with whom she spoke. I was extremely fond of Auntie Lottie, which is my British way of saying that I loved her dearly.

Her older sister, Bessie, a small, leathery-looking and wizened woman, was completely different. She was extremely independent in the way she lived and thought. She had an abrupt way of addressing people that usually sounded taunting or challenging. She was not as easy to like, at least upon first meeting her. But I eventually became very fond of her, too. I was amused by Aunt Bessie's different slant on anything and everything, and when I grew older, I admired her considerable strength and independence.

Early in World War 1, Bessie had enlisted in a special army corps for women, which came to be known as the "The Lady Lorry Drivers." Her uniform consisted of khaki coveralls and an army officer's cap. Her job was to drive ammunition trucks right up to the front lines. On the way back, Red Cross flags were attached to both sides of her lorry, which then became an ambulance for carrying the wounded back from the front.

After the war, Bessie returned to studying fine arts at the Royal Academy of Art in London, where she distinguished herself in the painting of miniatures, tiny portraits or landscapes painted on ivory or parchment.

Father and Uncle Bob together had bought the cottage in Yateley in which their two sisters lived. The brothers had both done well in business in the early twenties and had purchased the cottage as a place for their parents to retire. Both parents were in poor health and did not use it long before they died, whereupon the house and the three acres of land around it was deeded over to Bessie and Lottie.

For all her skill in miniatures, Bessie was having trouble making a living from her art. As for Lottie, she had never left her parents' home, remaining to care for them as they grew infirm, and had never earned a penny. The two sisters had no income to speak of, so they started a small farm on their newly acquired property, which happened to have a large orchard of pippin apple trees and a small pond. As a further source of income, Bessie decided to start an apiary, on the assumption that the bees would do most of the work while she continued her painting. Yateley was an excellent spot for bee keeping because nearby Yateley Common was a heath covered with heather, and heather honey was highly prized.

Lottie later told me that she "didn't care to brave all those bees and steal their honey." So she put the pond to good use by raising ducks and geese for their eggs. She apparently chose to overlook the fact that she would be braving the ducks and geese when harvesting their eggs. For roughly ten years, the two sisters eked out a modest but adequate living in this fashion. Several times a week, a green van decorated in gold leaf lettering proclaiming it to be from Harrod's, came around and picked up several dozen goose and duck eggs, along with some neat little wooden boxes that contained unrefined combs of honey. In season, the consignment also included several crates of pippin apples. Although the weekly shipments were small, all of these foodstuffs were delicacies and commanded high prices in London's West End.

The day after we arrived in Yateley, I came down with whooping cough, obviously bequeathed to me at that Punch and Judy show in Belgium. I had a very bad case of it, and about a week later, when the worst was over for me, Brenda came down with it, also a severe case. At the time, it was one of the most serious of childhood diseases, and there was no question of going back to France while Brenda and I were still in the phase of severe whooping. For two weeks, both of us were throwing up about twice an hour all day long, and since the disease is extremely contagious, we could not be out in public.

When I was over the fever and allowed out of bed, I started exploring the farm. One morning, I managed to open the latch on the gate to the "goose meadow," which was actually the orchard. I can still picture those geese, standing as tall as I was. For some reason, upon my arrival in the orchard, the whole flock of about forty of them started to waddle slowly in my direction. They gradually gathered around me and eyed me hungrily. I faced them bravely, but slowly retreated backwards in the direction of the gate. To my horror, the flock followed me and bunched up even closer. In fact, it seemed that for every step I took, the geese only narrowed the distance between us. I panicked and started wailing for help, yelling at the top of my lungs that they were about to eat me. That only seemed to whet their appetite, for the huge birds grew even bolder and moved ever closer, completely surrounding me, until I could have reached out and touched them. Then miraculously, Auntie Lottie appeared on the scene, walking in her usual calm, deliberate pace and quietly muttering, "Now! Now! You have got yourself in a fine mess, haven't you?" She shooed the geese away gently, took my hand and led me out of the gate.

When we were safely out of the orchard, Auntie Lottie enjoined me in a solemn pact: I was never again to visit the geese without a grown-up. For her part, she promised never to tell Mother, who would be extremely upset about the incident if she knew of it. She was right about Mother, who was quite excitable and prone to over-react, at least at that time in my life. Though she didn't say so, I now believe Lottie was more worried about the hazards of the pond in the orchard than about the geese devouring me.

I also enjoyed lessons in bee keeping while watching "Auntie Bee," (the family had always called Bessie just "Bee"). Almost daily, it was time to open one of her sixty hives. She could then pull out the racks to which the honeycombs were attached. A rack for honeycombs was a wooden rectangle supporting four smaller, wooden "picture frames," each about a ten-inch square and, when ready for harvesting, neatly and completely filled with a honeycomb and its honey.

Once Bessie had lifted a rack out of the hive, she carried it to a garden shed where, working at a special table, she gently pushed each comb out of its frame directly into a light wooden box. The elegant boxes were made of clean, seasoned wood and were slightly larger than the honeycomb so that the latter could fit without breakage. Auntie Bee then carried the rack and its now-empty picture frames back to the hive, where the bees dutifully started rebuilding new combs and filling them with honey all over again. In a couple of months, the full rack would be ready for another harvesting. In exchange for all this work, the bees received a pile of plain granulated sugar to see them through the winter. I wasn't there to witness this generous reimbursement, so I don't know how it was executed. It seemed to me that the taste of honey was infinitely nicer than that of plain sugar, and I asked Auntie Bee if the bees didn't mind this exchange. She insisted the bees were quite happy with the arrangement, but I had my doubts.

As Auntie Bee went through this procedure, always moving slowly so as not to attract the attention of the bees or excite them, she wore a beekeeper's bonnet with an extremely wide brim, which supported protective netting. She shrouded herself in a cloud of blue smoke, some of which came from her ever-present cigarette that she held between her lips and somehow managed to smoke beneath the netting without setting it on fire. To maintain a generous cloud of smoke close to her at all times, she also carried a special tinder burner that had a handle like a watering can. The bees buzzed around her constantly as she worked, but would not enter the little cloud that seemed to hover in her vicinity. The few bees that might enter the cloud would become dizzy and rendered harmless because, as she put it, "Once in the smoke, they're drugged into a stupor and no longer know who or what to sting."

I watched all this with great interest, but not having a little cloud of my own, I did so from twelve feet away. I not only had to avoid the indignant bees, but I was still contagious and had to stay well clear of the honey. The honey gathered and sold this way, still in the comb, was eaten wax and all. People who could afford the premium price that this "honey-in-the-comb" commanded, insisted that the texture of the wax comb added to the eating pleasure. Some also believed that this form of honey possessed special curative powers, though I forget for what ailments. The honey did little to help my whooping cough, but I enjoyed it on my toast every morning for breakfast, as I did a daily soft-boiled egg—a soft-boiled duck egg, of course.

Though by no means cured—we now only whooped about once every two hours—we were eventually deemed well enough to travel, and Father came to get us with the car so we would not be traveling on crowded public conveyances. On the ferryboat leg of the journey, we stayed out on deck, well away from other passengers, or sat in the car to be out of the wind. We could not have come near any of the other passengers even if we had wanted to. The boat authorities made Brenda and me wear black arm bands on which the word CONTAGIOUS was embroidered in large yellow letters.

We spent the remaining three weeks of the summer at "Les Buissons," in Condette, a summer house not far from Villa La Bècque. All I remember of that sojourn is how bitter I was that we couldn't ride the pale yellow trolley to Hardelot because we were still considered contagious.

Not long after our return to Ville-d'Avray in September, Sabine was caught stealing some bauble from Mother's jewel box. She was reprimanded and given a second chance. A month later, a valuable ring of Mother's disappeared. Under questioning, Sabine denied that she had stolen it. Mother promptly visited the closest pawn shop, which was in the nearby town of Sèvres, barely within walking distance of Ville-d'Avray, and sure enough, there was her ring. The pawnbroker said a middle-aged woman, who was with her teenage daughter, had brought it in. Other details in his description confirmed Mother's suspicions as to the thieves. Eglantine and Sabine were packing their bags the same day.

That autumn, Mother enrolled me in my second school, which went by the strange name of Le Cours Boutet de Monvel. Technically, it wasn't even called a school, since *cours* has roughly the meaning of "course." Mother, it seems, had a knack for finding odd schools in strange places. The classes were held in a spacious attic studio, up five long flights of stairs in a building directly behind the American Embassy in Paris. The school's single room had large, south-facing windows, which extended from floor to ceiling, and an oversized potbellied stove in one corner of the room to keep us warm on winter days. The walls and ceiling had once been white but were now an uneven gray. A mass of sooty cobwebs floated slowly up and down in the air currents above the potbellied stove and were so thick and numerous that they appeared to attach the ceiling to the walls.

While sitting in the classroom, I could look out across the flat roof of the embassy and beyond to the Place de la Concorde, where communist rallies frequently took place. Cars would be stopped by unruly crowds and sometimes get turned on their side and set ablaze. If it wasn't the riots distracting me, it was the pigeons on the roof of the embassy doing strange little dances, something that I found quite puzzling. Why did those fatter pigeons, with their feathers all puffed up, insist on climbing on top of much smaller pigeons, who didn't seem to mind at all?

We did most of the schoolwork at home. It was a strange arrangement by which the class met only once a week for two hours. The parent who brought the child was expected to attend the class for the full two hours, and sit at the back of the room taking notes that would help in tutoring the student during the week that followed. Before returning home, each pupil received a mimeographed sheet listing, in neat, purple, cursive handwriting, the work we had to do at home before the next class. Mother had her hands full on the days I didn't attend the school, for she literally stood over me two or three hours a day, coaxing me to do my homework assignments. Since we were tested on what we did at home each time we went to the school, her reputation as a dedicated mother was as much on the line as mine was as a hardworking student.

Shortly after Eglantine and Sabine's sudden departure from our household, my parents hired Raimond and Françoise. This couple stayed with us for six years, until the onset of the German invasion in 1940, but they will remain in my heart forever. They were from Perpignan, a town in the south of France, near the Pyrenees. They had a son, André (two years older than I), who lived with Raimond's parents in Perpignan. Raimond and Françoise visited him for three weeks every February.

They were the ideal servant couple: hard-working, devoted, honest, caring, and both extremely likable. Françoise was given to fiery temper tantrums, but this happened rarely.

Françoise did the cooking, housecleaning, and bed making. She also did the mending, and almost every day she walked a mile to the village to shop for all our daily provisions. Raimond served the meals wearing a yellow and black striped waistcoat and white apron. They both worked at keeping our five-bedroom house spotless. Raimond polished the silver, the furniture, the wood floors and even our two cars. He was Father's valet, seeing to it that Father's suits were brushed and pressed, for there was no dry cleaning to be had in Ville-d'Avray. Along with this, Raimond somehow managed to be a first-rate gardener in a huge garden that was a mass of flowers and provided us with a cornucopia of fruit and vegetables almost the year round. Raimond also worked in the kitchen, doing such chores as peeling vegetables, plucking all manner of fowl, eviscerating fish and poultry, and doing heavier jobs, such as keeping the coal-fired cookstove burning, and hauling the stove's ashes. I marvel at how they managed to do it all, and always in good cheer.

They were on duty long before breakfast, with Raimond waking Father by presenting him with a cup of tea; for Mother, it was a cup of coffee. Meanwhile, Françoise was serving freshly pressed grape juice to Brenda and me and coaxing us to get dressed. They did not retire at night until well after dinner, when all the washing up was done. The meal was usually at eight in the evening and was served even later whenever guests were invited.

Raimond and Françoise were given Sunday and Thursday afternoons off. But often there wasn't much left of their Sunday afternoon. When this happened, they had Monday afternoon off instead. Occasionally, if they wanted to see a show in Paris, they also took Thursday evening off. On those occasions, Mother stepped in and prepared dinner, a thing she always did very well and with enthusiasm. Mother had learned to cook while still a child, which she did surreptitiously in her parents' kitchen, a place she was not supposed to go.

Raimond and Françoise were not experienced servants when they first arrived. But after interviewing them, Mother liked them so much that she agreed to hire them if they would be receptive to instruction in the refinements of an elegant home. They gladly accepted the offer and made rapid progress under her tutelage.

Father told me years later that Raimond and Françoise were frequently offered positions in other households. Obviously, they never accepted these offers. "Once it was clear to me how good they were, I paid them a salary which no one else was willing to match," he explained. After World War II, my parents no longer lived in France, so Raimond and Françoise found a similar position in Triel, a village near Ville-d'Avray. When I visited them in Triel, Raimond mentioned to me that Father had paid them at least twice what they would have earned anywhere else, plus a generous bonus when they went off to visit their son. Then Raimond added, "Those were the happiest years of our lives. We had nothing to worry about. We were respected and treated kindly. We loved our work and our surroundings. Most of all, we loved you two kids as if you were our own."

Raimond had one unfortunate trait that drove Father crazy. He was always bursting to talk as he served the meal and would find the slightest pretext to do so. If addressed, he was unable to keep his reply brief and to the point, and once he started talking there was no stopping him. He had an opinion or information about any subject under the sun. An avid reader who daily managed to read almost every page of *Le Paris Soir*, Raimond was a walking encyclopedia for the sort of information one finds in newspapers. Of course, I found this trait very entertaining, not to mention informative, but Father thought it was inappropriate to have the butler telling him all the latest Paris gossip during meals. Fortunately, Raimond had the good sense not to do this when we had company. The whole problem was easily avoided by not talking to him in the first place. Raimond knew full well that he must not speak if he had not first been addressed.

At meal times when Father was not there, Mother generally enjoyed Raimond's chitchat. She was a lot more down-to-earth than Father was—a bit surprising considering their respective backgrounds. Still, she was careful not to trigger Raimond's avalanche of words too early in the meal and she cautioned Brenda and me to follow her example, explaining that she didn't want to abet what could become a bad habit. There were meals during which she did not address Raimond at all, and I'd see him fidgeting, rocking back and forth from one leg to another, biting his lip, dying to say something based on our conversation at table. When not serving, Raimond usually stood behind and to one side of Mother, so she couldn't see his torment. I would give Raimond a little smile to let him know I understood his problem. He usually acknowledged me with a wink and, when the meal was over and as soon as he found me alone, he would tell me all about what he had wanted to say in the dining room.

It was Raimond who launched me on my career as a gondolier. My parents had started a subscription to *National Geographic* magazine which I devoured visually until I was old enough to read it as well. In one issue, I saw an article on Venice and was entranced by the thought of a city where the streets were canals and the vehicles were boats. It seemed so utterly perfect, that I asked Raimond why they had not transformed Paris into a city of canals like Venice. After all, didn't he always maintain that Paris was the most beautiful city in the world? Surely, there was no arguing that canals were more beautiful than streets and boats and barges more beautiful than cars and trucks.

Raimond pointed out that many of the streets and boulevards in Paris were not horizontal, and that locks (like the ones I saw along the Seine) would be needed wherever there was the slightest hill. That would make movement around the city too slow for Parisians, who generally liked to go fast, he explained in all earnestness. He had obviously given the matter some thought himself.

The article on Venice stirred my interest in gondolas and started me thinking about ways I could have a gondola of my very own. We had an old perambulator Mother had used when Brenda and I were toddlers. The pram resided, discarded, in the back of our spacious chicken coop where its well-upholstered interior served as a comfortable (if unofficial) place to lay eggs. The sight of this pram relegated to such an ignominious fate had always struck me as lamentable. I had already eyed it as a candidate for conversion to something of a more worthy nature. Now, at last, I had found just the thing. With Mother's permission, I talked Raimond into sawing off the top half of the wooden body of this large pram and removing its push handle. Raimond thoroughly scrubbed and restored the interior upholstery to near-pristine condition. *Et voilà!* I had my Venetian gondola, complete with a rounded undersurface at each end.

I poled (or "punted") my wheeled gondola happily along various garden paths with a broken rake handle, pretending I was a gondolier on the Venetian canals. I didn't know that gondoliers don't pole their craft, but poling is a reasonably close visual approximation of what gondoliers do. When Raimond saw how seriously I was taking my gondoliering, he nailed onto my gondola a carefully scroll-cut board to represent a classical gondola prow. Then he painted the whole thing with shiny black enamel and embellished it with other painted decorations like the ones in the *National Geographic's* pictures. The gondola was big enough so that Brenda and her dolls enjoyed being my passengers in upholstered comfort, though I never serenaded her as gondoliers serenade their female passengers. The magazine mentioned the serenading but did not mention the song "*O sole mio!*" It was just as well—I have never been able to carry a tune.

Raimond's artwork didn't alter the fact that Father disapproved of my graceful craft, which he described as "tawdry, at best," and which he didn't want to see in the front garden when he was home. He promulgated his edict to me through Mother, who took the double precaution of having Raimond scan the front garden before Father's return from work. On weekends, when Father was home, I couldn't punt my gondola because most of the paths in the back garden sloped enough to make punting of a wheeled craft impractical—it rolled back every time the punting pole was moved forward for the next stroke.

A playful camaraderie quickly developed between Raimond and me, and I soon came to regard him as my closest friend and someone I could trust. In the meantime, since Brenda and I were still very young, Mother continued her search for a nanny or, more correctly, for a governess because we were no longer babies.

The first one she hired was a German girl. Despite the fact that Pia was barely eighteen, she was authoritarian and devoid of any warmth or humor. Pia had a stern look about her and was severe in nearly all her dealings with us. Brenda and I were terrified of her from the start.

Pia's relations with Raimond and Françoise were scarcely better. One day, Pia was receiving some tutoring in French from Raimond as the two of them sat at the kitchen table shelling peas in the presence of Françoise. Something Raimond said caused Pia to laugh—a rare enough event in itself. Françoise immediately assumed that Raimond was flirting and flew into one of her famous rages. Later, Raimond staunchly maintained before Mother that he had not been flirting and that he had been explaining to Pia some word usage that sounded funny to her. At the time, it seemed unlikely to me that someone of Raimond's stature would find it easy to be friendly with a sourpuss like Pia.

The incident was our first encounter with Françoise's hot temper. Raimond and Pia came running from the kitchen to Mother, begging her in a state of alarm to intervene on their behalf. Raimond and Pia had both tried to assuage Françoise's anger and had failed. She was hurling epithets and kitchen utensils at anyone who so much as poked a nose through the doorway to the kitchen.

Mother wanted no part of it, so she hastily rounded up Brenda and me, as well as Pia, and took us for a drive in the country that lasted until sundown, leaving Raimond to his own devices. When we returned we found him waiting at the front gate, profuse with apologies, and explaining that Françoise always recovered quickly from these fits of anger. Mother asked him if it happened often, and he replied that it was seldom, and it was always directed at him—him only, he added emphatically.

We later discovered that the mere presence of Brenda and me could cool the fiery Françoise temper. One day, unaware that anything was amiss, I entered the kitchen through its garden door and started a conversation with Françoise, who was kneading some dough and had a rolling pin on her worktable. When she was through kneading, she proposed that we go out to the orchard and pick some gooseberries for the pie she was making.

As Raimond recounted the story to us later while serving us lunch, he had overstayed a visit with Auguste, our neighbor's gardener. When he returned, one of Françoise's temper tantrums had come upon her, and he had been forced to make a hasty exit into the dining room. Fearful for the safety of anyone who might want to enter the kitchen, he valiantly stood guard in the dining room. Then, remembering there was another door into the kitchen, he set about stealthily moving a large buffet against the door he was guarding and transferred his furtive surveillance to the kitchen's outer approaches. It was there, spying from behind a large gooseberry bush, that he saw Françoise and me happily picking gooseberries. It was quite obvious that the *crise de colère* had subsided.

"I knew all she had to throw was a basket of gooseberries," he told us. So he approached Françoise cautiously, but the gooseberries never flew. She had calmed down and was acting as though nothing had happened; Raimond silently joined Françoise and me in the berry picking. Thereafter, Brenda and I were the ones called upon to be the oil on stormy seas. Mother enjoyed no such immunity, and more than once had to duck flying utensils. However, during Françoise's six years of service, these blowups only happened a few more times, and we soon learned how to deal with them. Most of the time, Françoise was pleasant and amicable, a devoted servant, always ready to do her absolute best on any occasion, and patient to a fault with Brenda and me.

That spring, we went to Condette (on the north coast of France) for the Easter holiday. There, one afternoon, Mother left Brenda and me with Pia to play in the sand dunes near Hardelot while she went off for a round of golf. A very dark and threatening sky gradually materialized, and by the time we began our picnic tea, the sound of distant thunder was growing louder and louder. Brenda and I were terror-stricken.

On a previous occasion, Mother, Brenda and I had set out on an afternoon's long walk in the forest of St. Germain near Ville-d'Avray. The sky had grown steadily darker, and thunder had begun rumbling almost from the start of our walk. Despite constant pleas from me, Mother insisted on continuing in a direction away from the car. Finally, the downpour started, thunder was all around us and, in pelting rain and hail, we had to run for cover into a woodsman's hut. Each time a thunderclap had sounded, I had been paralyzed with fear. I never understood why Mother hadn't turned back at the first sound of the approaching thunderstorm.

And now, here we were, once more in the path of an ominous storm, without a car or hut to which we could run. It started to rain, and Pia walked us to a nearby pine tree under which she hoped to find shelter. The tree stood alone not far from the main forest of Hardelot and was roughly a hundred yards from the road. We had a car blanket we had used as a mat for our picnic and, when it started to rain hard, Pia tried to cover us with it as we stood under the tree. In a state of panic, I wriggled myself free of the blanket and told Brenda to come with me to the edge of the road where I was sure we would soon be picked up. I shouted to Pia, the way people do in heavy wind and rain, that Raimond had once told me never to stand under a tree in a thunderstorm if the tree stood alone or without other taller trees nearby. I begged Pia to take us to the edge of the road, telling her that I expected Mother to appear with the car at any moment.

Angrily, Pia ordered me to get back under the blanket and to stay put. I was having none of it. I grabbed Brenda's hand and, dragging her behind me, started to run towards the road. About a hundred feet out, I stopped, turned and saw Pia running after us with the blanket draped over her head. I could just barely hear her shouting at us through the din of the storm. I resumed running, with Brenda still in tow, and reached the edge of the road. There I stopped, not knowing what to do. Pia was almost upon us, and I couldn't see Mother's car coming from the direction of the golf course.

As I watched Pia approaching, there was a blinding flash and a deafening crash. The tree we had been standing under was filigreed in light and was instantly engulfed in a fountain of sparks, like fireworks. I must have seen this out of the corner of my eye, for I had been watching Pia when it happened. My eyes had probably shifted their attention to the tree instantly after the flash, for I can still see clearly the entire tree glowing momentarily like a light bulb filament. I also remember the multicolored tree outlines and the ensuing shower of sparks that darted across my vision for some time after. Lightning had struck the tree under which Pia had wanted us to take shelter.

Pia hadn't seen the lightning strike as she rushed headlong after us, shrouded in the blanket, but when she reached us, she shouted, "That was very close! I hope it doesn't get any closer!" I told her what I had seen, and she replied, "I don't believe it! Now we go back to the tree, so the rain won't hit us so hard!" Then she took us both by the hand and tried to lead us away. At that moment, I looked up the road and saw our car coming towards us. .

By the time we were in the shelter of the car, Brenda was crying hysterically and, through faltering sobs and the chattering of my teeth, I was angrily chastising Mother for not having come sooner. I was sure she had dilly-dallied this time as she had in the forest of St. Germain; that was her way of acting before an approaching storm. She had heard the rumble of thunder early in the afternoon, as we had, and she had chosen to keep on playing golf until the downpour had forced her to stop, I remonstrated. I was livid, in a hysterical state, and continued to heap protestations and condemnations upon her. All this caterwauling did not improve my credibility when I told her about the lightning strike I had witnessed. Neither Brenda nor Pia had been facing the right way to see it and so could not substantiate my story. Pia conceded that there had been no time interval between the flash and the thunderclap, that it had been the brightest flash and loudest noise she had ever known, and that she had felt as if a wave of pressure from the crash had almost knocked her over. Mother still refused to believe me.

That entire Easter vacation at Condette was a disaster for Brenda and me. Mother had taken us there so she could shop around for a beach-front villa that she and Father wanted to rent the following summer. Hardelot, so cheery and colorful in summer, looked more like a ghost town, its villas still boarded up for the winter and not a soul around. The beach, a half-mile wide at low tide, was completely desolate. Under a dense, gray April sky it looked like the loneliest place on earth. But there was worse.

Hardelot had no hotel, and the beautiful Grand Hotel du Golf on the way to Condette was still closed for the winter. Mother was forced to settle for the next nearest hotel, which was in the tiny farming village of Condette, about six kilometers inland from Hardelot. The shabby-looking "Hotel Metropole" fell far short of its grandiose name. It was a dingy, low-priced hotel used by traveling salesmen and by hunters during the hunting season.

South of Condette was a forest that was still well populated by pheasant, rabbit, deer, and wild boar. Hunters gathered at the Hotel Metropole all through the hunting season. Its drab, dreary dining room possessed just one decorative feature, if you can call it that. It was the head of an immense wild boar, stuffed and mounted high up on the wall, with its sinister glass eyes angrily surveying the entire room.

I remember the boar's head as being a yard in height and protruding out from the wall about as far. The head of a mature rhinoceros could not have been any larger. The hotel proprietor, whose pride and joy the boar's head apparently was, could not resist the temptation to regale the hotel guests with its story. He boasted that it was the head of the biggest boar ever killed in the Pas-de-Calais, a region that stretched roughly fifty miles east, north and south of Condette.

Three bullets fired from a distance of a hundred meters had hit the animal, but had not mortally wounded it. Streaming blood, it had started a charge towards the hunting party that continued to reload and fire at the enraged boar. It plunged into a pack of hunting dogs and managed to kill three of them, then turned its fury towards one of the men who had approached the mêlée in an attempt to save the dogs. The man was severely gored as the other hunters struggled to find a place to aim their rifles at the debacle before them. It was the hotel owner's grandfather who had led the hunting party and who had succeeded in delivering the *coup de grâce* to the beast. To substantiate this tale of gore and horror, the stuffed head had two huge tusks the size of goat horns protruding from its lower jaw. Its mouth, which dangled half open, revealed a further array of fearsome teeth and was festooned with "drips" of red sealing wax intended to suggest blood. The taxidermist had doubtless been carried away in his zeal to portray the animal's ferocity and viciousness. The gleam in the wild boar's eyes was one of pure hatred and fury.

This superb piece of taxidermy was hardly conducive to sustaining a healthy appetite in two young children. The sight of the boar's head completely overwhelmed Brenda and me. In fact, it was quite impossible for us to sit in that dining room and eat anything at all. We tried sitting with our backs to it, but that was no help because I kept visualizing the creature creeping up behind me, and I constantly looked over my shoulder to make sure it wasn't there, which in fact it was. We tried sitting under it, where we could not see it, but that placed us even closer to it. I kept looking up, afraid that blood would drip down on us. We ended up having to eat in the hotel's kitchen, which proved to be only a minor improvement, as the cook eviscerated a steady procession of chickens, rabbits and fish on a worktable in full view of where we sat trying to eat our meal.

The pernicious influence of the boar's head extended to all other aspects of our stay there. Nightly, Brenda and I had nightmares in which the beast chased us. In the daytime, when we were left in the sand dunes to play in the company of Pia, we feared the creature would stumble upon us as it foraged for food. The hotel proprietor had cheerfully assured us that there were still plenty of boars about and that they roamed the region freely, though perhaps they might not be quite as big as this one! We couldn't wait to get back to the tranquility of Ville-d'Avray. However, when we returned to Ville-d'Avray, more excitement awaited us there.

Shortly after our return from Condette, Pia disappeared. Mother, who had spent the day shopping in Paris, returned in the late afternoon to find Brenda and me alone in our playroom. She asked where Pia was and I told her I didn't know. She went off to interrogate Raimond and Françoise, and when she returned a few minutes later, Mother wanted to know how long we had been alone. I replied that I was sure Pia had not been with us since lunchtime.

In the guest room where Pia slept, Mother found some of her things, but her suitcase was gone, as were her more important belongings. It had the look of a hasty departure. Raimond and Françoise had not seen her leave and had assumed that she was upstairs with us. Pia did not return that day, nor ever after. Raimond and Françoise said that Pia acted normally enough at lunch and insisted there had been no altercation between them.

Mother went to the village *gendarmerie* (police station) where she was told that National Police Headquarters would be notified. (In France, all local police are under the jurisdiction of a national organization.)

Several days later, two very sinister-looking men came to the house to ask Mother a lot of questions. They were wearing trench coats, black, broad-rimmed fedoras, and to Mother's great disgust, they had cigarettes dangling from their mouths the whole time they were there. She hated the smell of Gauloises Bleues cigarettes. Afterwards, as the two men walked away from the house, I heard her mutter under her breath, "*Crottes de chameau!*" ("Camel dung!")

Raimond also smoked Gauloises Bleues cigarettes, though never around Mother or in the house. Once, in the garage, where Raimond had been smoking as he worked, Mother and I had come upon the detested smoke. As we left the garage, she had used the same words. That time, though, there had been no anger or contempt in her voice, and I took her words literally, assuming, with some amazement, that she was describing the nature of the tobacco in the cigarettes.

On the occasion involving the police detectives, however, her tone was quite different; it was contemptuous and angry. Having never heard her use such a tone, I was baffled and curious, so I asked her if she were describing the tobacco or perhaps, referring to the policemen. "Both!" she exclaimed scornfully, "Just because they are the police doesn't give them the right to come into my house and keep smoking their foul cigarettes as if they were in a third-rate café!" Mother's intense aversion and contempt for people in a position of authority stemmed from her years under the German occupation in World War I.

Our two unwelcome visitors had questioned her about Father's business and his frequent movements across the French border, and they seemed to have almost no interest in the matter of Pia. They returned to our house two more times, both times on a Saturday when Father was home. Once more, lighted cigarettes dangled from their mouths the whole time they were there.

Father told me years later that they were from the French equivalent of the FBI, and that they had grilled him at length about the purpose of his frequent travel outside of France. Eventually, the agents were convinced that Father wasn't some sort of an accomplice of Pia's and that his international travel was of a legitimate nature.

The agents then explained to Father that Pia had been under police surveillance for over a year, and was suspected of being a German spy. They had, it seems, lost track of her about a month before she arrived in our household. The police report that Mother had submitted and the accompanying description of Pia had been the first clues they had of her whereabouts in over three months.

Father surmised (after World War II) that Pia may have stumbled onto key information concerning the strategic materials (iron, copper, mercury) being mined by the various companies with which he was associated.

I asked Father how he had found Pia. "I saw an ad in *Le Figaro*," he said. Then he added, "She had good references from a family in Paris. I gave this family's name to the two agents the first time they came by to interrogate me. We never heard anything more about the matter, or about Pia."

The dislike Brenda and I had for Pia had grown from the moment of her arrival. Neither of us shed any tears over her disappearance.

Jenny, Brussels, 1925

Jenny and Alain at Les Buissons, Condette, 1934

Alain's first car, Jock in center background, 1934

Raimond and Françoise (date unknown)

CHAPTER 3

Sand Yachts and Fine Tailoring

Mother had savored freedom, and after the disappearance of Pia the search for a governess resumed in earnest. Quite soon, one appeared from an unexpected quarter. "Tweet" was a young, cosmopolitan woman who was fluent in both English and French. In fact, she spoke both languages flawlessly and elegantly, having gone to finishing schools in both England and Switzerland. She was the daughter of Leonard Aldridge (or just "Aldridge," as everyone called him), the president of Anglo-French Ltd., Father's boss and one if his close friends.

Father had once lent Aldridge a considerable amount of money and, in so doing, had bailed him out of a very sticky situation. The loan was made at the time of the great stock market crash of 1929, which had left Aldridge penniless and in considerable debt. By 1935, Aldridge, with the help of Father, had recovered his financial aplomb but was drifting into a messy divorce. Both Aldridge and his wife, a good friend of Mother's, wanted their daughter, Tweet, out of London and far from the fray. Our house in Ville d'Avray seemed like the ideal refuge.

Tweet was a sweet, refined, and charming young woman of about eighteen, whose natural enthusiasm around Brenda and me clearly showed the pleasure she derived from our company. She was well informed about fashion, the arts, contemporary events, and, as a good conversationalist, she was also a good companion for Mother. She was a great help to me with my homework for the Cours Boutet de Monvel and was able to substitute for Mother as the "parent-in-attendance" at the weekly sessions held at the school. Tweet also contributed substantially to the progress of my spoken English. Most importantly, she never went near the kitchen and, at Mother's suggestion, gave Raimond a wide berth, thereby avoiding the arousal of Françoise's uncontrollable jealousy.

Tweet arrived in late April, and after a few remaining weeks of school, we left on our annual summer migration to the north coast of France. That dreadful Easter sojourn in Condette had brought about one excellent result: my parents had rented a villa at the seaside resort of Hardelot for the summer.

The villa was called "Le Green Cottage," but by no stretch of the imagination could Le Green Cottage be viewed as a cottage. Like all villas in Hardelot, it was a spacious, three-story house with numerous bedrooms, a huge dining room suitable for expansive entertaining, a superbly equipped kitchen, and comfortable servants' quarters. Rather amazingly, this house, which had beds for twelve people (including two servants), had only one cramped and barely adequate bathroom. No one dawdled there.

Hardelot, an amorphous community of summer villas dispersed throughout roughly a square mile of sand dunes, had streets without names and villas without house numbers. Instead, each villa was clearly labeled with its name, and it was reputed that only the postman could tell you where each of the three hundred or so villas in the community was to be found. The flimsiest of pretexts served as a basis for naming a villa, and Le Green Cottage derived its name from the fact that it did indeed have green trim. Another villa also had green trim, but had presumably been built before Le Green Cottage for it bore the imaginative and preemptive name of "La Villa Verte."

This was Raimond and Françoise's first summer at the seaside. They both loved the change of scene and the change of pace. Since the house was rented completely furnished, one of Raimond's first tasks upon arrival was a complete inventory of the *mobilier* (movables). Mother assisted him in this major undertaking because it was his first inventory, and he wasn't familiar with the values assigned to the items listed. All the items on the inventory (crockery, silverware, furniture, carpeting, wall paintings, bedding, towels, and such) were of the highest quality and would have to be paid for at the end of the season if anything were missing or damaged. The glassware was crystal and the silverware was sterling. There were silver serving platters and such exotic items as a soup tureen and ladle created by the same silversmith. Every movable article in the house appeared on the inventory list, which was organized by room. Mother and Raimond worked on this project for two days.

Of all the houses in which we summered, Le Green Cottage was my favorite. Not only was it a pleasant house, but it was marvelously situated within Hardelot. The better houses of the resort were clustered around a vast rectangle of brick-red tennis courts, ingeniously sunken below street level and the surrounding terrain. The purpose of this design, according to Mother, was to shelter the courts from the wind, but the result was an unintentional "amphitheater." With its sloping sides covered in colorful flower beds, shrubs, and well-kept lawns, it made a handsome focal point for the community. Le Green Cottage was located at midfield, and its veranda had a commanding view of the amphitheater. The house's center-stage location especially suited me because it was the place where small boys my age congregated to decide on the day's activities. We played all kinds of games together, and it was here that I first honed my skills in the engineering of game plans and rules. The villas were not cheek-by-jowl, but had stretches of sand dunes between them, forming wonderful venues for all sorts of games. The vastness of the play area made it imperative that rules and boundaries be established. Further constraints were placed on us by parents, governesses, or nannies who kept an eye on us from various nearby verandas. There was very little traffic in Hardelot, and it was an ideal place for us to play.

Tweet had to accompany me when I and one of my little friends headed for the nearby beach, which was only a hundred yards from the house and off limits to me unless I was with a grownup. Like so many French coastal resorts, the beach at

Hardelot was planned and organized for maximum convenience and pleasure. A gently sloping granite seawall had been built to protect the houses from the ravages of the occasional storm. This dominant feature obliterated the natural aspect of the beach. Where the mile-long seawall ended, the original sand dunes and the beach's natural character resumed. Father had little use for the "urban" aspect of Hardelot, and on the rare occasions when he joined us on the beach, we all had to traipse with him to a spot well beyond the end of the seawall. In the dunes out there, far from anything man-made, and away from the crowds that populated the beach in front of the seawall, Father would set up his beach chair and read until he felt ready for a swim. While he read, Brenda and I resumed our usual sand castle building. I'm not sure whether it was the man-made aspect of the surroundings or the crowds that he disliked more. I suspect it was both—equally.

The slope of the seawall was quite shallow and this made it possible for beach cabins on wheels to be rolled down its smooth stone face onto the sand at the start of each summer season. These tiny wooden houses rolled on crude, concrete wheels and were neatly parked in a straight line on the beach, with four-foot spaces between them. All beach cabins were identical in construction and size, but painted in colors that matched the color scheme of the villas to which they belonged. Beach cabins were parked near their owner's villa, which placed us centrally, since Le Green Cottage itself was plumb in the center of Hardelot. This location didn't please Father because, after changing into his swimsuit, he had to walk over half a mile to reach a deserted stretch of beach.

Along the top of the seawall was a mile-long, fifty-foot wide, tiled promenade which was called *la digue*. It was where the older vacationers strolled in all their finery, and if it weren't too windy, the ladies usually carried parasols. Older people believed that a tanned look was unattractive, and therefore stayed covered from the sun as much as possible. But people in their thirties and younger were part of the first generation that thought it fashionable, even healthy, to tan themselves, something they referred to as *très sportif.*

La digue was also used by people of all ages for bicycling or riding on strange contraptions called "*cuisse-taxes*," a uniquely complicated French invention on which two people sat side by side, both pedaling in a recumbent position. A *cuisse-taxe* was really a large tricycle, with two canvas seats side by side and set between the two rear wheels. Two sets of pedals were placed high above the single front wheel, and a very long bicycle chain (in a housing) somehow passed between the two seats on its way to the rear axle. The name "*cuisse-taxe*" combines elements of the words "thigh" and "taxi." A *cuisse-taxe* was rented by the hour and was very popular with young couples, who thought of them as an ideal way to acquire a good tan on their legs, and after a few days, to show off the results of their tanning efforts. They pedaled with their feet at eye-level, so their legs were well positioned to receive the sun and display the tan.

The *cuisse-taxe* struck me as an ingenious and thoroughly delightful vehicle. Sadly, I was never able to talk Mother (by then in her mid-thirties) into renting one. She said it was downright vulgar to be pedaling like that, "with your bare thighs high in the air for all to see."

For smaller children and teenagers, there were two beach activity clubs. Brenda and I belonged to *Le Club des Pingouins*, (the Penguin Club), and the competing club was *Le Club des Mouettes*, (the Seagull Club). Every morning, the regulars of the respective clubs gathered at opposite ends of the beach for two hours of gymnastics and beach activities. After a half hour of fairly strenuous exercise, we played various games or competed in races.

Competitions were usually held within each club, and we were grouped by size (not age) so that kids within any one group could compete fairly. In addition to ordinary races over various distances, there were also relay races, egg-and-spoon races, sack races, pirouette races (cartwheeling all the way to the finish line), somersault races, and races on all fours. Paired contestants also competed in three-legged races and wheelbarrow races. The winner of every race won an inexpensive beach toy.

About once a week, our Penguin Club competed in joint races against the Seagull Club. After such a contest, the club that won the most events had the honor of having its club flag flying beneath the Tricolor on the flagpole at the center of the beach, and it remained there until the next joint competition, a week later. I remember feeling extremely proud after winning two of the events that had helped put our flag on the pole, and I went around accosting strangers at random, pointing out the Penguin Club's pennant fluttering in the breeze and explaining how I had been an important contributor to this triumph.

Late in the morning, the parents of the young participants in these morning activities returned from a round of golf or a game of tennis, and both beach clubs ran late-morning gymnastic sessions for the adults. I liked to stand around and watch the adults groaning and straining as they exercised, and I remember that there was also a lot of laughing and merriment. The instructor must have been something of a comedian as well as an athlete, for he seemed to keep them in stitches. I didn't understand the jokes, which I'm sure were "unsuitable for my young ears," as Mother used to say when adults told jokes I didn't understand, and which she didn't want to explain.

The two beach clubs jointly held sand castle contests, which took place every other week when low tide occurred in mid-afternoon. The contests were sponsored by the newspaper *Le Paris Soir* and were vast enterprises that accommodated each of the numerous age groups separately, and even included a division for adults. Not only were there prizes awarded for each age group but also for "best over-all."

The contests were not limited to sand castle building. Sometimes the contest was for the most artistic *panneau décoratif.* In this type of contest, we built a raised, rectangular panel of compacted sand, usually about a yard square (there were no restrictions as to size). We then decorated our panel with designs or patterns in the sand or with bas-relief sculpture. The works were further adorned with seashells, seaweed, dried-out crabs, cuttlefish bones, driftwood, or any other beach debris, which we had gathered before the contest. Anything was allowed as decoration, as long as it was "of the beach." We also had to provide an appropriate title for our work of art. Adult endeavors usually had humorous or pompous-sounding titles. The titles were written in the sand at the base of each work of art.

By late afternoon, a crowd of spectators in a carnival mood showed up to see the completed efforts of the contestants. After the judging and announcement of the winners, each artist stood by his or her work of art and accepted kudos or kibitzing from parading onlookers. By sundown, the entire collection of masterpieces had been expunged by the rising tide. The disappearance of the artwork caused no great grief, for everyone had other things on their mind as they sat down to superb dinners.

On the day of a contest, the beach club staff was out on the beach by two o'clock, laying down a plaid of lines which they traced in the sand. This grid consisted of squares about ten feet to a side, with six-foot aisles for spectators between each square. The boundaries of the squares were made by dragging a spade on its edge along the wet sand. This left a well-defined mark, which outlined the "canvas" or working area allowed each contestant, and it was understood that no one should step on or destroy these important boundaries. Everything was well organized and laid out for easy comparison among contestants of the same age group. For all their well-deserved reputation for eccentric independence, the French like to have their communal activities well ordered and organized.

After the participants had spent two hours in intense artistic endeavor, a warning whistle blew, announcing that there were now fifteen minutes left for applying the finishing touches. When the quarter-hour was up, a second whistle sounded, the signal for contestants and spectators to withdraw so the judges would have no way of knowing who had done any given work. The judges then ruminated before each work, made notes on clipboards, and argued excitedly among themselves before making their final decision.

In one of the contests, my *panneau decoratif* won—not just for the best *panneau* in my age group—but for the best overall, covering all age groups including adults. I'm sure that allowances were made for age in this award. A press photographer took my picture, using a flashgun even though I was in broad daylight. In my eyes, the flashgun in itself added immeasurable prestige and importance to the event. I stood beside my panel that depicted two squirrels sitting on their haunches. They were facing each other on a branch, each was holding a teacup in its forepaws, and the two were apparently having a conversation.

The panel was entitled "*Le Gouté Chez Les Ecureuils*" ("Teatime at the Squirrels' House"). It was a bas-relief sand sculpture inspired by an illustration in Beatrix Potter's *The Tale of Squirrel Nutkin.* I used brown seaweed to create the effect of rough tree bark and bright green seaweed to suggest the surrounding foliage. I had recruited Raimond to help me carry buckets of seaweed in preparation for adding these details. The saucers the squirrels held were portrayed with flat cuttlefish bones, and the cups with desiccated crab shells. A bent crab claw formed the handle on each cup. The squirrels' eyes were represented by small, black sea-snails, their whiskers by fine dune grass, and they both sported bushy tails made of coarser dune grass.

My proportions, someone pointed out, were a bit off, which probably explains why some spectators asked me, "Well, well, well! What sort of animals have we here?" They obviously had not taken the trouble to read the title, which a member of the beach club staff had neatly written out for me in the sand. The title said it all and caused most viewers to laugh heartily when they read it.

Mother commented that my real inspiration had been the creation of the only entry which departed from the heavily repeated beach, marine or nautical themes from which the judges probably suffered an indigestion, as she put it. Of course, she added diplomatically, my work also had artistic merit in its own right.

The next day, the back page of the newspaper had a picture of me in my bathing suit, wearing a jaunty sailor hat, standing proudly behind my masterpiece and holding my prize, which was a large box of colored pencils. Under it, the caption read, *Jeune artiste fuit l'ambiance de la plage,* (Young artist shuns the beach ambiance). I was not aware this had been my goal or frame of mind. If anything, I embraced and adored the beach ambiance. This journalistic falsehood didn't stop me from basking briefly in my celebrity status, to the despair of Father, who, predictably, thought it was giving me a swelled head. Indeed, all this publicity imbued me with the notion that I was now world famous, at least in the realm of sand sculpture. I was soon disappointed to discover that no one read newspapers at seaside resorts and that I was doomed to continue my visits to public places totally unnoticed.

The beach was unusual compared to most beaches I have seen in other parts of the world. It was extremely wide with very little slope to it, so that at low tide, the water receded over half a mile, leaving a vast expanse of hard, fine-grained, wet sand. This expanse was interspersed with numerous *flaques* (tide pools). The pools varied greatly in size, depth, and position on the beach from one low tide to the next. Most pools were only a few inches deep, and a few were as much as several feet deep. Some were just small ponds, thirty feet across and a few inches deep, while others were occasionally half a mile in length and two hundred feet wide. The pools were formed at high tide by the strong currents of the English Channel, which churned and shifted the sandbars and created low spots that became tide pools.

The idiosyncrasies of the *flaques* could make the beach dangerous to people unfamiliar with them. A cautionary tale doing the rounds and repeated to all newcomers was about a tragic incident that occurred about ten years before I played there.

Young boys at a summer camp for the underprivileged were brought to Hardelot for a beach outing. A convent in Lille, a large city some hundred miles inland, organized the trip. The group had taken an early morning train to Boulogne, where they transferred to the pale yellow trolley, which pulled into Hardelot around twelve thirty. It was a hot, windless day, and the twenty children were anxious to get to the water's edge.

Led by three nuns in full black habit complete with white wimples, the group headed out across that wide, flat beach at a time when all of Hardelot's residents, including the beach's lifeguards, had gone home for lunch. No one ever swam or stayed on the beach during the two-hour lunch hiatus which was, after all, one of the most important events of the day. The nuns and their charges dodged their way through a maze of *flaques*, and finally, after numerous course zigzags executed to keep their shoes dry, reached the edge of the sea. The kids removed their street shoes, waded into the calm sea and splashed about happily as the nuns watched anxiously from shore, occasionally calling out to those who waded out too far. The children had worn their Sunday best for the outing, and none of them was wearing, or even owned, a bathing suit. Young boys always wore short pants in those days, even when wearing their Sunday best.

The nuns stayed on the shore and were probably unaware that to keep their own shoes dry, they were steadily being forced to step back. After about an hour, one of the nuns noticed that the group was stranded on a long, narrow sandbar that had been turned into an island by the rising tide. They immediately called the kids together and decided to march them across the two-hundred feet of shallow water that now separated them from the rest of the beach. They attempted the crossing and turned back when the water became knee-deep. They hoped that if they walked farther along the island they might find a shallower crossing point.

None of the children nor any of the nuns could swim. They made several tries at crossing, but balked each time, returning to the sand bar whenever the water's depth threatened to wet their clothes. If they had persevered in their early attempts, they might well have succeeded by wading through water up to the waists of the smaller children. In the meantime, the tide was rising fast and the span of water they had to cross kept growing wider and deeper. The group was now in considerable disarray and in a state of panic. In the end, some of the older kids and one of the nuns worked up the courage to brave a water depth that came to their armpits and crossed safely. Sixteen children and two of the nuns drowned. The wailing and hysterical survivors stumbled back to the dry sand zone near the *digue* just as the more energetic residents of Hardelot were returning from a six-course lunch.

Father confirmed this horrific story, which had been in all the Paris papers. He remembered it well because he was familiar with Hardelot, though he and Suzy were not summering there at the time. A newspaper article said that none of the children nor any of the nuns had ever been to a beach before. When asked if she knew about the tide, the nun who survived said that she had heard of the term but had no idea what a tide was. At that time in France, going to the seaside for recreation was practiced mostly by the wealthy and was still a relatively new phenomenon.

The fact that this incident happened does not mean that the beach at Hardelot was seriously dangerous. The accident occurred where most people didn't usually swim. People were deterred from swimming at low tide by the long walk required to reach the water's edge. And once they reached it, they had to wade another quarter mile before the water was deep enough to swim. Rather than walk so far, swimmers waited until it was closer to high tide, when the water's edge was a hundred feet from the row of cabins and the tide pools were completely obliterated. If, through inattention, someone found himself out on a sandbar island formed by the rising tide, there was no problem if he or she were willing to wade, or in rare cases, swim a short distance. Unusual conditions played a key role in causing this extraordinary tragedy. It was one of the hottest days of the year, so the kids were impatient to reach the water's edge. An exceptionally low tide coincided with a time when the beach was completely deserted and lifeguards were off duty. These factors and the helplessness and ignorance of the nuns all combined to bring on the disaster.

But low tides and tide pools also provided all kinds of fun. The *flaques* that remained at low tide were home to a huge population of small shrimp and crabs. The local *bazar* (general store) sold special nets with which to catch the little creatures. These semicircular shrimp nets had a straight edge formed by a beveled board. This sharp-edged board "chiseled" a thin layer of sand from the bottom of the tide pool as it was pushed along by means of a pole fixed at the center of the board. The shrimp and some of the fine sand beneath which they hid were lifted by the chisel board and passed into the netting that trailed behind the board. The collected sand passed through the netting, leaving the shrimps therein. A semicircular hoop attached to the ends of the chisel board (and to the handle at its center) held the net open. At the *bazar*, they sold nets in a wide assortment of sizes, so that everyone could savor the primal thrill of the hunt, from the tiniest toddler to the largest of adults.

The shrimp were abundant and were caught on a much larger scale by professional shrimpers, who usually filled their baskets by nine in the morning. Then, with their bushel-sized baskets heavily loaded with thousands of shrimp, they boarded the pale yellow trolley back to Boulogne. There, the shrimp were packed in crushed ice and shipped by rail to fish markets in all the major cities of France. These little gray shrimp were delicate and clean tasting, with shells so thin that people usually ate the whole tail without removing the shell. Shell removal was a tedious process performed only on the biggest shrimp whose shells had grown thick enough to be unpalatable. At the time, I was convinced that my tummy converted the tiny shrimp shells directly into fingernails and wondered how people who didn't eat shrimp managed to have any fingernails at all.

The professional shrimpers were middle-aged women who wore rough, ankle-length denim skirts that dragged in the shallow tide pools and were always wet up to the knees. The women worked barefoot and used shrimp nets four feet wide. They pushed the big nets from one end of a long tide pool to the other, then lifted a net so full of shrimp that it often took them ten minutes to round up their catch and toss them into a basket left on the beach nearby. To keep the shrimp from jumping out and escaping when the basket was nearly full, the fisher-women covered them with seaweed. The shrimp "jumped" by snapping their tails. The damp seaweed also kept them alive and fresh.

On days when the professional shrimpers hadn't already fished the *flaques* in the early morning, I pushed my own tiny ten-inch-wide shrimp net across the tide pools in a state of high-pitched excitement at the prospect of a catch. Standing in a six-inch-deep tide pool, I could barely make out the shrimp as they darted around the *flaque* in search of food, six to ten feet from me. When I moved closer, the shrimp quickly vanished as they propelled themselves backwards into the sand by a flick of their tails. All I had to do was to push my net across the place where I had seen them disappear and lift the net to find them skipping frantically on the netting, sometimes as many as half a dozen if I was lucky. I then ran back to my sand pail at the water's edge. A small skirmish would ensue between me and the three or four shrimp I had caught. They were jumping all around my net in an attempt at escape. Many of them succeeded and disappeared quickly into the damp sand before I could recapture them. Because the big shrimp were usually the successful escapees, my catch consisted mostly of the tiniest ones.

Instead of seaweed to keep them fresh, I kept my pail full of seawater and added some sand, which settled to the bottom and was intended to make them feel more at home. After a satisfying hour of shrimping, I scampered home with water from the full pail slopping down the side of my leg. Françoise, always happy to cook anything, greeted me with enthusiasm. Some twenty to thirty of these minuscule morsels were served on a small side dish beside my main course at lunch. I would then ceremoniously bestow some of the larger ones to various guests, who accepted them graciously.

The miraculous aspect of this sport was that each high tide seemed to replenish the supply of shrimp, and their number never appeared to diminish as the season wore on, or from one year to the next.

The sand in Hardelot, when wet, was ideal for building sand castles because it was extremely fine and stuck together nicely when wet and compacted. The damp sand lent itself well to carving with a toy spade or trowel, so that older, more sophisticated kids (and quite a few adults) built elaborate sand sculptures and finely detailed edifices.

The best place for building a sand castle was beside a tide pool. There, I could dig canals or moats around the castle, complete with bridges made from driftwood. I usually carried a small toy car along with my trusty spade and sand pail as I set out for the beach, so I could "drive" my car over the bridges, then through tunnels into the courtyards of my castle. Sometimes, a friend's toy boat would come steaming up my canal to pay me a visit.

The best fun of all was the building of dams. I, or one of my friends, ran around the beach at low tide looking for other kids interested in building a dam. It took a large team of enthusiastic workers for the dam to be successful. Since the beach at low tide was well populated by kids building castles, shrimping, or playing with toy sailboats in the tide pools, it wasn't too hard to assemble a good crew of workers.

The first stage of dam building was to create a fast-flowing river by digging a canal linking a decent-sized pool higher up the beach to a pool at a lower level. This canal sometimes stretched as much as a hundred yards in length; canals of such length were possible because dam building volunteers were usually numerous and the canal was initially just a few inches wide. The upper pool had to be large enough so that a strong and sustained flow of water soon traveled down the canal, widening it by erosion as the water raced through.

Once started, the flow in the drainage canal grew surprisingly fast and could create havoc. Tide pools the size of a football field could be drained in less than half an hour, leaving a desolate landscape of castles with dry moats, bridges over rivers and canals that were no longer there, and Lord knows how many little shrimp homeless and destitute. Sand castles along the edges of the lower pool could also be threatened by a danger of the opposite sort: rising water levels caused flooded castle courtyards, put drawbridges under water or caused them to float away. An unexpected rise in water level could also cause mothers and governesses, deep in conversation or engrossed in a novel as they sat in "sand-chairs" nearby, to find themselves, mysteriously, sitting in two inches of water.

When this crisis was imminent, the real fun and challenge was upon us. Immediate action was essential to avert the impending catastrophe just described. The cry went out for more help, and other kids on the beach gladly joined in the heroic endeavor and were instantly converted into dedicated dam builders.

We dug furiously, building two high mounds of sand opposite each other, one at each edge of the rapidly flowing canal that had grown to about three feet wide. When the dam builder in charge deemed the mounds high enough, he gave the signal for both teams simultaneously to push their mounds into the raging torrent. This action stopped the flow and gave us time to do some fast digging to build levees (dam extensions) on each side of the temporary plug.

The thrill and challenge of the game was to see if we could build up the levees extending outward on each side of the original plug, and stay abreast of the rising water level behind what was now officially *le barrage* (the dam). When the team was large and experienced, the water depth behind our dam sometimes reached two feet and the outward extensions could be thirty feet long on each side of the plug. The whole enterprise usually took the shape of a horseshoe.

We never won this valiant battle against the forces of nature. Eventually, the water behind the dam rippled over the crest of the construction work and triggered a spectacular dam rupture. The water raced through the ever-widening gap in far more copious flow than before the plug was pushed into the canal. Inhabitants in the vicinity of the lower tide pool now really had to scramble to avoid the arriving tidal wave. By this stage, however, the morning was usually spent; the noon dinner bell was sounding, we knew there was other more important business at hand, and we had to leave the little shrimp to fend for themselves and find new homes in the lower pool.

Because the wet sand presented such a hard, flat surface, all sorts of vehicles rolled happily on the beach, as racing cars do at a similar beach in Daytona, Florida. Many people carried their bicycles over the strip of dry sand near the seawall and, once on the hard wet sand, rode them great distances, sometimes in organized races.

Tweet occasionally took me out to the farthest reaches of the beach at low tide where we had a grandstand view of sand yacht races. The events were conducted on this remote part of the beach so that the speeding craft would not endanger the mob of children playing on the rest of the beach.

A sand yacht is simplicity itself and consists of a light wood frame, three wheels, two seats, a steering wheel, a stayed mast, and a triangular sail with a boom. The frame consists of two main beams which cross, giving it roughly the shape and proportions of a crucifix. The two steerable front wheels are placed at the ends of the shorter crossbeam, and a single wheel trails at the tail end of the longer beam. The mast stands where the two beams cross. The two rudimentary canvas "bucket seats" and footrests are mounted, one on each side, at the aft end of the longer beam, near the back wheel. And because a sand yacht has no brakes, a rubber-bulbed *klaxon* (horn) is needed to warn beach strollers of the sand yacht's silent, fast, and unstoppable approach.

These *Char-à-voiles*, or, translated literally, "sailing chariots" could reach speeds as high as sixty miles an hour in strong winds, though few people sailed them on such occasions. On weekends, at low tide, we could gaze north or south across miles of deserted sandbars and see what looked like a cluster of white butterflies, quivering as they hovered on the horizon's mirage. What we were seeing were thirty or more sand yachts in close formation, their speed, towards or away from us, arrested by distance. Before long, they sailed silently past us at great speed, bound for a distant marker on the opposite horizon.

In a stiff breeze, the windward wheel of the two front wheels of the sand yacht lifted into the air. If this wheel stayed off the ground for long distances, the driver, by holding his sail close hauled, was achieving peak performance and mastering a delicate balance between the highest speed possible and tipping over. Spills were frequent, but I never heard of anyone being hurt, in spite of the fact that they wore neither helmets nor any protective gear. A spill didn't disqualify the racer, who usually wasted little time righting the craft and hopping back on to continue the race.

Tweet was absolutely fascinated by sand yacht races. I could depend on her to escort me to one whenever I reported to her that a race was about to take place. I think Tweet may have been more interested in the young men who raced than the racing itself, for she used to hang around them afterwards, listening to them talk of their racing exploits and mishaps, and often joined in their camaraderie. Meanwhile, as the sand yacht sails flapped or fluttered loosely in the wind, I was content to sit in the driver's seat of one of their chariots. Crouched over its steering wheel, I pretended I was breaking a new speed record.

On calmer days, Father occasionally rented a sand yacht, and I was sometimes allowed to ride along with him for the thrill of my life. My job on these rides was to man the *klaxon*. Father was extremely nervous, especially about the tide pools, which sand yachts usually crossed easily, creating great splashing and plumes of spray. Some of the pools close to the sea's edge at low tide were sometimes bordered by a sharp drop-off and were considerably deeper than the usual depth of six to ten inches. This made crossing them, particularly at speed, an exciting and wet experience. Occasionally, sand yachts tipped over in mid pool, which happened when they became bogged down in the pool's soft sandy bottom or when a wheel on one side encountered unexpectedly deep water. Father was so apprehensive of these situations that, much to my chagrin, he never chanced crossing a tide pool in a speeding sand yacht. I had to settle for some fairly tame sailing and just witness the more dramatic spills from afar.

Within the confines of Le Green Cottage, life was as well ordered as it was out on the beach. With a houseful of guests throughout most of the summer, being well organized was the only way to avoid disrupting Raimond and Françoise in their busy day.

In the morning, Raimond brought to each bedroom a jug full of very hot water to be mixed in a washbasin with cold water from another jug that was already in each room. Only the master bedroom had both hot and cold running water and a drain in the washbasin. Françoise brought my parents and our houseguests a cup of coffee or tea, and for Brenda and me she brought freshly pressed grape juice. These beverages arrived around eight o'clock or whenever Mother had decreed reveille for the household. Half an hour later, we were expected to show up for a formal sit-down breakfast.

Raimond rang a dinner gong five minutes before each meal, including breakfast. Being late for meals was considered extremely bad form. The reason for this punctiliousness was that the day's activities for every member of the family, houseguest, and servant had been carefully planned and coordinated the night before. A planning conference was part of the dinner conversation, and the pertinent details were silently noted by the ever-present Raimond. The activities of the next day might be playing golf or tennis, loafing on the beach, sightseeing at the fishing harbor in Boulogne, or shopping the elegant boutiques of Le Touquet. The two towns were each about 20 miles away. Sometimes, Mother organized an afternoon drive to Cap (Cape) Gris-Nez, France's closest point to England. There, we could see derelict gun emplacements built during World War I to stop German warships from using the Channel to reach the open sea. On clear sunny days, we could see the white cliffs of Dover shining brightly twenty-two miles away.

After breakfast, people went off in various directions to their chosen activity. For those at the beach, where wristwatches could come to a permanent and grinding halt due to sand intrusion, the lifeguard sounded a loud bell at twelve-thirty. This indicated he was going off duty, but more importantly, it signified that lunch was imminent and that it was time to hurry home. By one o'clock, the beach was deserted, and everyone was sitting down expectantly at the dinner table, like theater-goers waiting for the curtain to rise. While this must sound very regimented, which of course it was, no one seemed to object, and everyone took it in stride as a small price to pay for a large choice of pleasant activities interspersed with exquisite *repas*. The meals were convivial affairs with people taking turns humorously recounting the day's activities or commenting thereon. Each telling was followed by light-hearted banter, joking and much laughter. I used to watch Raimond working hard to restrain his laughter whenever someone told an especially funny story. He thought, perhaps correctly, that he wasn't supposed to laugh.

By dinnertime, things became less tidy. The end of cocktail time was sometimes subject to the vagaries of neighbors, who were occasionally asked to "come over for a drink." An invitation phrased this way clearly meant cocktails only. But some guests, perhaps hoping that they would be invited to enjoy one of

Françoise's superb dinners, clearly violated this well-established protocol. It then turned into a waiting game, because the meal had been planned and the table set for eight, not ten people, for example. It took very special circumstances for Mother to capitulate and jostle Françoise's well-planned preparations. Françoise was surprisingly patient and flexible at this hour. It was clear she understood Mother's predicament. But at lunch time it was another story. The difference was that after doing the lunch dishes, Françoise always took a long nap, and understandably, encroaching on this well-deserved rest was more than just frowned upon.

During the day, Raimond was not always needed at the villa, and on these occasions, he sometimes joined me in whatever activity I had planned at the beach. When this happened, Tweet could join Mother in a round of golf or tennis if Françoise could be talked into baby-sitting Brenda. Much as I loved Tweet, I especially enjoyed Raimond's company because, among other things, he brought along an adult-sized spade, so the scale of our castle and dam building increased tenfold. Raimond seemed to enjoy all of my beach activities and, as we set out, I could tell by his wide grin how much he anticipated the pleasure of these outings.

Raimond also came shrimping with me. He brought his very own four-foot-wide shrimp net and a full-sized pail on these expeditions. Once we reached the beach cabin, he took off his shoes and socks and carefully rolled up his neatly creased trousers, exposing his white calves and feet. He retained the black bow tie and the black and yellow-striped waistcoat he always wore, but rolled up his shirt sleeves and worked carefully so as not to splash or soil his clothes. These elaborate precautions did not prevent him from being a vigorous and prodigious dam builder and shrimper. The two of us usually returned with enough of the larger shrimp for a generous hors d'oeuvre worthy of ten people. As usual, Françoise greeted our return with exclamations of pleasure. She was obsessed by cooking and could be depended upon to make a bold culinary assault on anything that was remotely edible. The sight of a bucket of little gray shrimp in need of cooking sent her into paroxysms of delight.

The end of dinner always fell well past my bedtime. However, I was allowed to sit with the grownups at the dinner table for the time it took me to consume a bowl of soup and a small side plate of something else specially prepared for me. Having finished my little repast, I was expected to kiss Father, Mother, and Tweet goodnight, then make a silent, discreet exit and go to bed without protestations. This usually occurred at about the time the adults were being served their main course. I once did protest the advent of this preordained departure, and my penance was to be served my dinner in the kitchen for a whole week. There, I didn't even have the solace of Raimond's company. He was much too busy serving, or standing behind Father, keeping a watchful eye on the needs of the diners. Françoise was also very busy, putting servings on plates and the finishing touches on her various dishes. Brenda, barely four years old, had long since been put to bed, so it was a lonely punishment and one I never suffered again.

Bastille Day, 1935, was the most special of many memorable Bastille Days because on this date, I was allowed to remain at table for the entire dinner, until ten o'clock. After the dessert course, consisting of a hastily served *méringue glacée*, the diners adjourned to the veranda for the demitasse and to watch one of the most spectacular sights I can remember. I suppose, though, that I was already a bit intoxicated by the thrill of staying up so late. The sight of those blazing, whirling, bursting colors of the firework display over the tennis courts in front of our house was a moment of utter perfection and total bliss.

The day after Bastille Day, Father left on his first trip to America with Aldridge, his boss at Anglo-French. Upon their return from this trip in late August, Father and Aldridge were met by Aldridge's chauffeur at Le Havre, where they disembarked. Since it was a Friday, they drove straight from Le Havre to Hardelot and arrived in Aldridge's magnificent, brand new, bottle-green Rolls Royce convertible. Within minutes, it seemed as though half of Hardelot was crowding around this graceful, gleaming car. Raimond decided that the Rolls Royce should be moved into the garage to give it some respite from the curious onlookers. This, unfortunately, proved impossible. The garage was found to be a foot short. The rear end of the Rolls Royce protruded ignominiously from the open door like a fish's tail from a heron's beak, as Mother described it. Worse yet, the chauffeur could not leave the car because he could not open the car door within the garage's narrow confines. This produced great mirth and some derision from the gathered onlookers. They raised a great cheer as the car was backed out, presumably pleased that the object of their admiration was not to be removed from their sight. The car remained out on the street where every passerby seemed determined to touch and caress it to see if it was indeed real. The following morning, Raimond was up at dawn polishing off the numerous fingerprints that now adorned the Rolls. Fortunately, the novelty soon wore off, and the car was eventually left alone.

Aldridge stayed only a few days. Part of the reason for his visit to Hardelot was that his divorce had been settled. This news was a great disappointment to Brenda and me for it meant that Tweet was returning to London with him. We both adored Tweet, and fortunately, she came back for a week every summer thereafter, permanently designated as "our most favorite houseguest."

Something which obsessed and bothered me all that summer was the fact that I never wore long trousers. When I asked Mother if she would buy me a pair, she told me they did not make them for five-year-old boys. I think her reply was probably correct, in France anyway. This struck me as grossly unfair, and I became convinced something should be done about the situation. I pondered the problem for quite some time, and by mid-summer, I finally had a clear picture of how I would set about putting things right. However, it did involve sewing, an activity that had recently left a rather bad taste in my mouth after I had been expelled for "sewing astray" at that first school I attended. Somehow, the excessiveness of that expulsion only stiffened my resolve; the fact that I might redeem my honor and show the grownup world that I could sew responsibly added further merit to the undertaking.

I set about looking for suitable material, and in a cupboard in a little-used guest room, I found some material that was predominantly dark blue and had a pattern of small yellow flowers. The piece had curtain rings along one edge but appeared big enough for my purposes, though I wasn't exactly pleased about the flower pattern. It would have to do. I sneaked into Françoise's room, where I found a pair of sewing scissors, a needle, a thimble, and a spool of white thread on her dresser. These items I commandeered each day, taking care to replace them carefully after every sewing session exactly as I had found them. The jig would have been up if she had noticed anything missing or out of place.

First, I cut off the strip where the curtain rings were attached and then cut a rectangle I deemed to be the correct size. The width of the rectangle had to be equal to my waistline, plus a little extra for a seam (I didn't know the term "seam", but I had noticed the detail on my existing shorts and understood the concept). The length of the rectangle quite clearly had to be the distance from my waist to my heels.

Cutting in a straight line proved to be a nearly insurmountable challenge. In fact, I cut into the curtain so erratically that the piece was rendered useless. Fortunately, there was a second curtain in the cupboard. Before launching into that piece, I did a good deal of practicing on the botched curtain. Also, I put to good use a yellow pencil from the box of colored pencils I had won. I used the edge of a drawer (from a dresser in the guest room) as a ruler and found that having a well-defined yellow line to follow on the blue material made cutting in a straight line more or less feasible. My cutting still wasn't truly straight, but at least I could spot my "wanderings" before the whole piece was irrevocably ruined. My labors eventually produced an acceptable rectangle, if I were willing to overlook its wiggly, jagged edges.

I folded my rectangle in two, and sewed together the two edges opposite the fold line to produce a "tube," the girth of which was my waistline. That done, I laid my tube flat on the floor, folded it lengthwise at its midpoint, and stamped and danced hard on the new fold so as to make a distinct crease. I then opened the flattened tube on the floor once more, and marked with my yellow pencil the crease that my dancing and stamping had created. I had thus bisected the piece. Again, I didn't know the terms "bisect" and "crease" but understood what they were meant to achieve. Then came some more sewing. This time, the track of my stitchery was up that bisecting yellow line, but about half an inch to one side of it. At first, my stitches were small and almost neat, as if done by a sewing machine, but I soon lost patience, and the stitches grew gradually larger as I worked my way up the piece. Eventually, my stitchery was closer to basting.

When I had progressed all but about four inches of the full length of the tube, my stitching made an abrupt and deliberate U-turn. This crucial point was to be the crotch of the trousers, and the four-inch length I mentioned was my estimate of the distance between my belt line and said crotch. I now proceeded to sew back down the yellow line, but half an inch on the other side of it. Two weeks later, when I had completed this last step, all that remained to be done was to take a pair of scissors and ever-so-carefully cut my way up the yellow line to the crotch point where I had made the U-turn—*et voilà!* I had myself a pair of long trousers. The whole job had taken me about a month.

If this seems an excessively long time, the reader must remember that it was a covert operation. I didn't want to arouse suspicion by spending long periods of time in that unused guest room. Besides, I had other important work to do. There were sand castles and dams to build, sand yacht races to watch, whole mornings taken up in gymnastics, and shrimp to catch. Also, I had to steal and return the sewing implements each time, which had to be done with time-consuming stealth. I often had to wait for Françoise to finish cleaning rooms in the surrounding area before the coast was clear.

Last but not least, there was the problem of needle threading. I had seen Mother do it and therefore knew it was something that was humanly possible. Nevertheless, I found the task incredibly difficult; some days I never started any actual sewing because I couldn't thread the beastly needle despite innumerable tries. I eventually found a way around the problem, but I soon found it was far from the ideal solution.

When, after days of trying, I finally succeeded in threading the needle, I cut off a piece of thread about ten feet long. I was reasonably sure this was enough thread to see me through the entire project without ever having to thread that wretched needle again. The drawback to this method was that with each stitch, I had to place the empty dresser drawer on my work, so it would stay put as I walked the needle across the room, pulling my thread through the material. I had to spend considerable time untangling the thread after each stitch as the extra amount seemed to have an innate tendency to form a rat's nest every time I turned my back on it. Though awkward, this method was still easier than threading a needle each time I started work and, being the lesser evil, I persevered with it. Fortunately, Françoise had numerous needles in her pincushion, so I didn't see the need to return the needle each day with all that thread attached to it. That would have been a major problem in itself, not to mention how suspicious all that loose thread would have looked on Françoise's dresser. In its second week, the project had all the earmarks of a bad dream, and I seriously considered abandoning it, but somehow I found the courage to persevere.

When I completed my Herculean task, I took stock of what I had achieved. The waist and crotch were extremely tight, but usable, if only barely. That was precisely the problem, for as I discovered by looking in Mother's double mirror when no one was home, I was exposing more of my cleft than I considered decent. That four-inch allowance for the waist-to-crotch distance had been at least three inches short of what was needed. Not to worry, I would solve that problem by being careful not to turn my back to my audience.

The white thread on the dark blue material was an unusual design accent, as were the jagged and unhemmed cuffs and waistline. The flowered pattern for men's garments was still a few decades off, so that, too, was a fashion novelty. All these minor shortcomings seemed trivial in comparison to the achievement as a whole. I was especially proud of the fact that I had managed it without sewing myself to some piece of furniture, which was remarkable, considering the important role that the dresser drawer had played in my project.

I carefully planned my entry into the world of fashion. Lunch seemed to be the best time for a grand entrance. Everyone would be there, seated, and in an expectant mood as they waited for Raimond to start serving. With some careful maneuvering and timing I could be the last to enter the dining room before Raimond appeared with the platters. They would all see me enter and gasp with surprise and admiration.

I waited in the vestibule until the right time and walked into the dining room with studied nonchalance, striving for an effect of self-assurance, elegance, and ostentation, all at once. By the time I had reached my chair, I was dismayed to discover that no one had noticed me. I immediately muttered to myself, "*Zut!* I forgot something!" and walked out of the dining room backwards to conceal my partially exposed cleft. Once out of sight, I immediately re-entered the dining room, this time making a loud sound somewhere between a cough and a clearing of the throat to draw attention to myself.

Father, who was closest to the door, looked in my direction. To avoid interrupting a guest who was discoursing volubly, he said under his breath to me, "Alan, this is lunch and not a masquerade ball. Now go to your room, take that silly thing off, whatever it is, and come back properly dressed." I wasn't to be thwarted and at some risk to my semi-exposed behind, I kept on walking past Father to my chair, certain that Mother would notice me, proclaim the magnificence of my attire, and thus vindicate my efforts.

She did notice, and after a pause to take in what she was seeing, burst into laughter. Soon, the other guests noticed me and joined in the merriment. With my tail between my legs, I retired to the kitchen.

There, I explained to Raimond and Françoise what had happened. Raimond was immediately sympathetic and, without cracking a smile, said it was a pity they couldn't appreciate the trousers for what they were, *un vrai chef d'oeuvre*, a true masterpiece. Raimond was turning out to be the best friend I ever had. He even soothed Françoise, who was out of sorts over my having used her sewing stuff and over my going into their room, which was strictly off limits to me. Françoise then gave me my plate of food, which I ate at the kitchen table as she interrogated me further about my tailoring travails.

After eating, I found that the large meal had only made the tightness of the trousers worse. For a panicky minute, I thought I might never be able to get them off and that I was cursed with having to wear them for the rest of my life. But a prolonged and painful struggle finally saved me from this dreadful fate. I put on my bathing suit for an afternoon of sand castle building and asked Raimond to put the ill-fated trousers in the garbage bin. Since then, I've never been keen on sewing, nor have I tried to be in the vanguard of fashion.

Le Green Cottage (slightly right of center), Hardelot villas, 1935

Tweet, Brenda, Alain, Aldridge, and Dan, Hardelot, 1935

CHAPTER 4

An English Governess and a Golfing Dog

The end-of-summer trip back from Hardelot to Ville-d'Avray was a long drive in Mother's slow, low-powered Talbot. So before we left Le Green Cottage, she went to the shops in central Hardelot and purchased a *baguette*, some ham, cheese and tomatoes. These picnic ingredients, along with some plates, goblets and a few eating implements were packed into a picnic basket, which was then jammed into the already overloaded Talbot. Brenda, Mother and I wedged ourselves in and pushed off by nine in the morning.

Around noon, Mother turned off the main road onto the first promising side road and drove until we all agreed on a bucolic spot overlooking the gently rolling hills of the Pas-de-Calais. All around us, small fields of wheat, oats, flax, barley, rye, and hay, contoured in bands and rectangles, formed a patchwork quilt of different hues. The settings for Mother's picnics were always wide open landscapes, which she particularly loved.

Sitting on an old blanket, surrounded by deep grass mottled with wild poppies, we savored our picnic and were lulled into a trance-like state by the steady twittering of a skylark as it fluttered erratically in the sky above us.

After a brief postprandial nap, we continued our leisurely drive across this grand landscape, with Mother pointing out things of singular beauty or special interest. If they were crops, she would explain how they were used. If they were castles, churches, or cathedrals, such as those at Amiens or Beauvais, she told us their names and main characteristics. Or she would provide us with the lore and history of the locale we were passing. I believe she must have studied the route beforehand for she was a steady fountain of knowledge on every trip. I loved this running commentary which was never dull and was her ingenious way of keeping us from getting restless during the long journey.

Raimond and Françoise left the day before we did, riding in the larger, faster Peugeot with Father. He always managed to make the daytime drive in about four hours, which gave Raimond and Françoise plenty of time to unpack the car and finish an inventory at the house in Ville-d'Avray before we showed up. The latter chore was needed at this house, too, because it had been sublet for the summer.

In those days, Ville-d'Avray was still *dans la campagne*, in the countryside, even though it was only fifteen kilometers from central Paris. Ville-d'Avray had no beaches or mountains, but apartment-dwellers from Paris found it an ideal and convenient summer refuge from the city's bustle and clatter, replete with trees and flowers, suffused with birdsong, and blessed with rural tranquility. Father, who remained and worked in Paris a good part of the summer and who couldn't stand being alone in Ville-d'Avray, stayed at a comfortable hotel near his office in Paris.

Every weekend, Father drove from Paris to Hardelot on Friday nights, preferring to drive at night when the main roads were free of local traffic. Horse-drawn farmers' carts were still the major cause of delay and clutter on main roads in the daytime. At night, the only congestion consisted of rabbits and hares, which populated his headlight beams and often joined him for the rest of the journey, dangling from the car's radiator grille. Françoise welcomed the arrival of these unexpected riders with her usual excitement and promptly converted them to a *civet de lupin* (rabbit stew) for Saturday lunch.

Father once made the 280-kilometer trip in three hours. This was before the days of the *autoroutes* (super highways), and included stretches through the centers of many small towns with crooked streets and complicated intersections. But main roads between towns were dead-straight, and Father thought nothing of driving at 150 kilometers an hour. High-powered, superbly sprung cars, such as Peugeots equipped with steel-belted Michelin tires, were already available in France in those days, so the trip was not as reckless as it sounds. In Mother's Talbot, or later, in her Simca, the trip took us about eight hours.

Our return to Ville-d'Avray was a shock to me. After the bright, sunlit, open spaces of the seaside, Ville-d'Avray seemed dark and closed-in, as if it had grown old and fusty over the summer. The foliage, light green and lacy at the time of our departure in June, had grown dense and was now a dark shade of green. The effect was heightened by the fact that we arrived in the late afternoon, after the sun had dropped below the tree tops, but before dark. The contrast was striking and made me morose. I recovered the following morning with the arrival of sunlight in the garden. A temporary gardener had been hired for the summer, and many flowers were still in bloom. The well-trimmed lawn, mottled with sunlit patches, glistened under the morning dew.

I returned to the Cours Boutet de Monvel that autumn and discovered that the homework load had increased from three hours to four hours a day because I was now in a higher class. It's hard to say who was more dismayed by the increase, Mother or I; she spent as much time coaching me as I did on my homework. Tweet's departure had left a gaping hole, and the hunt for a governess once more went into high gear.

To our collective amazement, it was Father who was the first to bring one in. He returned from a business trip to England in the company of an English governess whose advertisement he had seen in the *London Times*. Miss Parris was a grim-faced, graying, grumpy, older woman who had sought the position because she wanted to learn French.

Right from the start, things didn't go well with Miss Parris. The biggest problem was that she knew absolutely no French, so she was no help to me with my homework assignments. Then, Mother and I found life easier if we spoke English to her, which meant that she was not achieving her own goal either.

On one occasion, Mother couldn't go to the Cours Boutet de Monvel with me and wrote out detailed directions for Miss Parris on how to get to the school by train and bus. Fortunately,

I had previously done the trip by train with Mother on a day when her car was being repaired. As it turned out, Miss Parris' sole responsibilities on this excursion were to be in charge of the money and to pay for the train and bus tickets. When we reached Paris, I had to show her where to exit the vast Gare Saint Lazare and where to take the bus. Luckily, Miss Parris had the bus number in the instructions because that was the one thing I didn't remember. But I knew where to get off the bus and from there, the way to the school.

At the school, Miss Parris was unable to understand a word of the verbal instructions given to the parents. We didn't discover this problem until we reached home, so I enjoyed a brief respite from homework for two days until Mother made a special trip to the school to get the information we needed.

On the way to the bus stop for the return trip (on the day she escorted me), Miss Parris and I walked past a *vitrine* (shop window) with the most exotic display of pastries I had ever seen. Mother and I regularly passed this *patisserie* on our way to and from the Place de la Madeleine where she usually parked the car while we attended the Cours Boutet de Monvel. She had repeatedly turned down my suggestion that we go in and enjoy *un petit goûté* (a spot of tea). I had long suspected that the reason for Mother's refusal was that she didn't want to reward me for an afternoon of daydreaming and embarrassing her in class.

I now told Miss Parris that Mother regularly took me into the *patisserie* for tea and pastries because she felt I needed sustenance for the long trip home. Miss Parris, who was by now completely in my thrall, dutifully led me into the establishment and allowed me to choose a superb pastry and did the same for herself as she ordered tea for the two of us. Dear Miss Pariss complimented me on my choice of a fine tearoom as we enjoyed a delectable *goûté*. But she almost fainted when the waiter brought *l'addition* (the bill) for our little regalement. She barely had enough money to cover it.

At home that evening, we learned that Fauchon's, the establishment where we had our tea, was the most luxurious and expensive patisserie and tearoom in all of France. When Mother heard about my little caper, she was much amused and congratulated me for my ingenuity and refined taste, but Miss Parris knew I had played a trick on her and was greatly peeved, even though Mother reimbursed her for my extravagance.

Soon after this incident, Miss Parris complained she was not learning any French, and after six weeks with us, she handed in her notice. Brenda and I had never warmed to her, and were not unduly saddened by this news. After she left, Mother insisted on giving Brenda and me an extra thorough scrubbing during our regular evening bath, and mentioned that she had recently complained to Miss Parris that she never washed behind our ears (and other places) at bath time. Mother claimed that the rebuke had been the straw that broke the camel's back, and had led to Miss Parris' departure. I, on the other hand, felt sure that *l'affaire patissière* had been the straw in question.

My parents wanted Brenda and me to speak both languages. They achieved this more by accident than by design: Father always spoke English to us, and Mother always spoke French. During the years we lived in France, Mother almost never spoke English to Father, and he seldom spoke French to her; this was true even when their conversation went back forth at a rapid pace. I believe they had conversed this way since they first knew each other. Their bilingual communication took place even when Brenda and I were not involved, and the custom did not end until the 1940s when our family found itself in an English-speaking country. Father spoke French to Raimond or Françoise, and did so very well, though with a trace of an accent.

At school, the one subject in which I did moderately well was arithmetic; at last we were working with numbers from nine to ninety-nine. We were now doing additions with carry-overs, subtractions, and even divisions (without remainders), but always with numbers and answers less than ninety-nine. I enjoyed this, but was continually chastised for lack of neatness, about which Mademoiselle De Monvel was a real stickler.

Despite rather poor performance, I believe I was learning and discovering a great deal just riding in the car to Paris, or riding the train and the bus on the way to school. The everyday comings and goings of Parisian life fascinated me, as did the appearance of the buildings, the bridges, buses and railways. I was so taken with all I saw that I drew a picture of the two routes we took to school, showing a tunnel for cars and another one for trains. My "map" included the bridges and barges we saw as we drove along the Seine, the treeless streets, and the tree-lined *Grands Boulevards*. These details were clearly, if whimsically, portrayed in my drawing which Mother praised lavishly. But Father criticized it for being "rather badly not to scale." It bothered him that the little village of Ville-d'Avray was shown as being larger than Paris itself. I was only five at the time, and I don't recall being hurt or discouraged by Father's critique.

It was left to Mother to explain the concept of scale to me. She was very good at explaining things of this kind. She also told me that Father's comment was prompted by his desire to help me in my next map-making effort and that he was really quite proud of me. She also warned me that Father was basically opposed to praising me in any way whatsoever. "He thinks it will give you swollen head," she explained in English, there being no workable equivalent in French. This was her way of saying "give me a swelled head." I didn't know the meaning of the idiom at the time, so, with some alarm, I took it literally. Since I believed Father was the wisest of men, I was sure he knew whereof he spoke, and resigned myself early on to the fact that I would never get praise from him. But I wondered why praise from Mother didn't produce the same disastrous deformity.

As a result of Father's criticism and Mother's elucidation of the subject, I became obsessed with the matter of scale. I don't mean that I had a precise numerical sense of scale. But I certainly understood that a toy soldier could not, by any stretch of the imagination, get into a Dinky Toy car that was not even as long as the soldier was tall. On this basis, I refused to allow toys of different scale to coexist in whatever game I was playing. I became a purist when it came to scale.

Something which was causing me some concern was my gondola. I still enjoyed poling it about the garden but felt quite limited by the fact that I could only pole it on the paths of the garden that were level. Poling up even a slight hill was out of the question. Each time I lifted the pole to move it forward, the gondola rolled backward and lost all the ground gained on the previous push. Since not much of the garden was level, something had to be changed so that I could take my gondola all over the garden, which was criss-crossed with well-laid-out paths that didn't always run level. An easier method of propulsion was also needed. Even on level ground, the poling routine, though romantic and charming, was exhausting.

It soon became obvious to me that the solution was to turn my gondola into a locomotive, for locomotives are not propelled by poling, and I could just push it along as I pretended to be a locomotive driver. I visualized how the change could be made by using an old barrel. Like the perambulator from which the original gondola had been created, a barrel, no longer used, had been cast aside in the chicken coop. As usual, Raimond was willing to listen to my plans. In short order, the transformation was in progress. The old barrel was mounted on top of the gondola's "hull" to become the locomotive's boiler. A tin can was attached on top of the barrel for a smoke stack. The pram's push handle was restored to its original location to make it easier to push the locomotive. Various details such as pistons, connecting rods and train lights were painted on the former gondola hull and the barrel to complete the effect of a "loco," as we called locomotives in those days.

The initials "P.O." (short for "Paris-Orleans," one of the important rail lines of the time) were added in bright red letters to the loco's boiler, which was painted with shiny black enamel to match the original gondola's color scheme. This lettering caused a minor, though brief, argument between Raimond and me. I was an ardent fan of the "P.L.M." (Paris-Lyons-Marseille) railroad, and wanted those three initials. Raimond countered that the P.O. railroad was the one he and Françoise took to visit their son in the Pyrenees, and that was why he wanted those two letters. I could see the futility of trying to match that argument, so I quietly capitulated.

This impressive locomotive pleased me no end, and I could now push it on any remote loop around the garden, level or sloping. One drawback to my new loco design was that Brenda could no longer ride as a passenger, though some of her dolls were small enough to be jammed in the space between the barrel and the original pram "hull." But Brenda objected to this unseemly treatment of her dolls. It was probably just as well that she had no interest in rail travel. The new loco was much heavier than the gondola, and I could barely push it up the steepest path in the garden. I continued my travels with the P.O. loco alone, quite content as I chuffed and puffed my way up the inclines.

That autumn, another character made his appearance on the scene. Jock was a Scottish cairn terrier, already mostly gray in his middle age, and a wise little mutt. Cairns are a fairly rare breed of dog. The best way to describe them is to explain that "Toto," Dorothy's dog in the film "The Wizard of Oz," was a cairn. We almost failed to acquire Jock. He had been sent to us by rail in a crate that was incorrectly addressed and routed. He was shipped to the wrong station and when we went to meet him at the agreed-upon rail destination on the day of his journey, he didn't arrive. Mother initiated a major search for him, which lasted several days and took us to nearly every rail station in and around Paris, much to my delight. We eventually found Jock, but not before some kind-hearted old stationmaster realized that the little dog's food supply had run out, that he needed water and a long stroll, preferably along a tree-lined street. Mother had a hard time prying him from the stationmaster who had grown extremely fond of him, but when it was apparent that Jock responded enthusiastically to the call of his name, the old man tearfully released him to us.

Jock was no ordinary dog—but then, few family dogs are. Beyond that, however, Jock had some extraordinary traits due to the training he had received from his former master, a British golf pro at the Hardelot Golf Club. Jock was the only dog who was ever allowed on the course in Hardelot, and it was because the pro had taught him golf etiquette.

First and most importantly, if he were anywhere near a golfer about to take a swing at the ball, Jock immediately sat down and remained motionless, even stopping his panting on a hot day. Second, he never chased balls or picked them up in his mouth. But upon being given the command "find the ball, Jock!" he would set off in a determined way to locate a ball that had gone into the rough or out of sight. Upon finding the ball, he sat patiently beside it until the ball's owner said something like, "Well done, Jock!" My parents never lost a ball when Jock was along. Third, Jock never chased rabbits nor ran about freely on the course. He scampered along in a business-like way directly behind Mother or Father during the entire game. His reputation as a golf dog was known at any club where the pro had played. At the Saint Germain Golf Club (not far from Ville-d'Avray) Jock was immediately allowed on the course with my parents on the basis of a reputation that preceded him. They had heard of his prowess as a golfing dog, were anxious to see him strut his stuff, and welcomed him with some fanfare.

The golf pro who had trained Jock and who gave him to Father was returning to live in England after many years of teaching golf in Hardelot. The pro didn't want to subject Jock to the six-month quarantine which England imposed on all dogs arriving from overseas as a precaution against rabies. (England was completely free of the disease at the time.)

A dog usually attaches itself to one member of the family who becomes its master, and there was no doubt that Jock's master was Father. This was surprising, since Father never fed him and was seldom home. Whenever Father was home, Jock stayed as close to him as possible most of the time. When Father drove off to work, Jock was always present to see him off, watching the car for some time as it disappeared, as if to make quite sure Father was really leaving. But as soon as Father was definitely gone, Jock turned his loyalty to me and shadowed me whenever practicable, probably because I petted him and talked to him a great deal. Jock also got on well with Raimond who fed, bathed and brushed him. Jock had a wiry, grayish-black coat, the softest, velvety, jet-black ears, a somewhat bushy tail that stood upright in the shape of a crescent moon, and from the back he looked as though he had on little Cossack pants. In Condette, Jock loved to chase after the many wild rabbits and a fox who resided somewhere in our garden, but he never chased the chickens or the odd tame rabbit that scampered about freely in our neighbor's barnyard when we visited there. He had an uncanny sense of right and wrong. He was so well behaved that we seldom went anywhere without him, and he quickly became a much loved member of the family.

CHAPTER 5

Serious Smuggling and a Miraculous Catch

At the Cours Boutet de Monvel School, the mating antics of the pigeons on the roof of the American Embassy continued to distract me. The teacher, Mademoiselle de Monvel, wasn't much help in holding my attention. Her manner of teaching was dry and unexciting, which was also a fair description of the way she looked. She wore no make-up to improve her somewhat sallow demeanor, her graying black hair was pulled back tightly into a bun, and her attire was always an unadorned, black dress. I can still hear Mademoiselle de Monvel's monotonous and incessant voice, and I remember Mother commenting that she never smiled.

According to Mother, I had always had a tendency to be a daydreamer, and it was at the Cours Boutet de Monvel that my notoriety in this regard was confirmed. After a week spent drilling me on all the answers related to my homework, Mother was forced to sit at the back of the classroom and watch me make a fool of myself. Mademoiselle de Monvel progressed along the row of students asking questions about the assignment, and when it was my turn to answer, I was stymied because I had been looking out the window at the pigeons and had not even heard the question.

The teacher frequently scolded me for daydreaming, accusing me of being *dans la lune,* an expression that made no sense to me, even after I asked Mother what it meant. "When you are 'in the moon,' it means that you are not on earth with the rest of us," she replied cryptically. That didn't help much, but the thought that I could actually be "in" the moon started me on one of my more memorable daydreams.

I had already learned from Raimond that the moon was a ball, and quite naturally I assumed that it was hollow, like a rubber ball, especially since it was apparently possible to be "in" the moon. Why not have such a ball, or moon, hang from the ceiling of the classroom? I pictured it in my mind as being quite large, somewhat bigger than I was tall, and bright yellow like the round, glowing full moon I occasionally saw from my bedroom window as it rose through the bare branches of our linden tree in winter. My moon would have a small trap door in its base, like the trap door to our attic, and a rope ladder would hang from the trap door. There would be a small school desk and a chair inside my moon, which would be equipped with two porthole windows. From the outside, the portholes would be the moon's eyes and the trap door its mouth.

When I felt like being *dans la lune*, I could go up the ladder, pull it in behind me and would then be able to daydream all I wanted without incurring the displeasure of the Mademoiselle de Monvel or Mother. Through the porthole windows I could keep an eye on what was going on in the class below, paying attention only if I found it interesting. I could easily slip down the ladder—back to earth—for something that really intrigued me, such as what came after ninety-nine.

I felt a strong urge to make a drawing of my moon, and even took a yellow coloring pencil to school with me on the day I decided to put my moon on paper. I was almost finished with my sketch when Mademoiselle de Monvel walked down the row of desks to mine and asked me what I was doing. Despite her cross look, I was sure she would be impressed once I explained my drawing to her, so I enthusiastically launched into a complete review of my design. I even pointed out a little stickman sitting inside the moon, telling her it represented me, and explained the reason for my being there.

She listened without interrupting as the class grew more amused with each new detail I provided. I was playing to an audience and discovering that I enjoyed the role. Surprisingly, the teacher allowed me to continue, probably to make sure she was uncovering enough evidence to justify a real tongue-lashing.

While the class and parents at the back were amused, Mademoiselle de Monvel, who always took herself very seriously, was definitely not. After I finished my detailed explanation, she chastised me at some length for wasting class time. I was unrepentant but kept silent. I had already discovered the futility of trying to reason with adults when they were in a chastising mood. Besides, wasn't she the one who had initiated the wasting of time by interrogating me?

Sometime during that second year at the Cours Boutet de Monvel, we passed ninety-nine and now swam more freely in the great wide ocean of all numbers, so I must have descended from the moon, at least until I had learned the rules for counting to *any* number. We also launched into long division and multiplication problems involving numbers with more than two digits. That, too, must have kept me from being *dans la lune* much of the time.

In early spring of 1936, I came down with what the French call *une appendicite á chaud,* an inflamed appendix. The first day, Docteur Narnier thought my pain was just indigestion. The next day, the pain was much worse, and the doctor announced that my appendix had ruptured and that immediate surgery was the only way to save my life. French law at the time decreed that surgical operations on a child were not allowed without the father's consent.

The problem facing Mother was that Father was in Warsaw on a business trip. Over the next ten hours, she made numerous unsuccessful attempts to reach him by phone. There was only one tenuous "trunk line" to Warsaw, and there was a queue of callers ahead of Mother. She pleaded with the operator who said that she had heard "that old story before." When Mother attempted to send a telegram, the telegraph operator warned her that the Poles exacted a ridiculously high excise tax on telegrams, and there was little assurance that the telegram would even go through. Mother sent off a telegram anyway. As the day dragged on, Mother kept on trying to reach Father by phone. Docteur Narnier, who had to hear my father personally instruct him to operate before he could proceed, now joined the vigil full time and kept reminding Mother that if he didn't receive the permission soon, it would be too late to operate.

By four in the afternoon, I was delirious and shaking with fever. Still no word from Warsaw. Mother, true to form, once again took the bull by the horns. She asked Raimond to carry me to the car, and ordered the doctor to stay where he was. For good measure, she instructed Raimond to stand guard over Docteur Narnier and see that he did not leave our house until the permission arrived from Warsaw, even if it meant putting the doctor up for the night.

Decades later, as Mother told me the events of that day, her voice was still edged with tension.

"Raimond carried you to the garage and Françoise was sitting with you in her arms behind me in the car. Then I was driving with a break-necking speed towards the nearest-by hospital which was in Versailles with my hand pressed on the *klaxon* all the time. Raimond knew I was doing this, so he tied a high wooden pole with a white flag and the red cross nailed on. The pole was right on the front bumper so all the cars around would see it waving in the wind of my speed and letting me drive through them," she said. "I was pushing on the klaxon and going right through red lights even without stopping for them, and all the traffic of the rush-hour in the afternoon was dividing itself for me to pass as I went by. Without Raimond's flag you would not be living here right now!

"Françoise was always very nervous with us in the car whenever she drove in the back seat anywhere, but now she was sitting there, holding you tightly in her arms in all the turnings, crying some torrents of tears over you who was like a son for her, and not seeing I was driving like a madman which would be making her more nervous even if she was not so occupied with you.

"Docteur Narnier was a Doctor with only a narrow brain [narrow minded] and had no imagination and no *intiateeve*," Mother continued. "He thought it was no use and a wasting of money to take you to the hospital before getting the permission of Dan if anyway you're dying before the phone call arrives. He told me to my face that I am crazy and that you might not be living when Dan phones me, so why take you to the hospital if you were going to be dead there? And it was very expensive to die in a hospital even if they do nothing on you, he said. I told him right back in his face that I would be suing him if he was leaving the house before the call of Dan arrives. If I had not done this and we lose all that time waiting for the permission to arrive, you would be dying with the permission in the car on the way."

After I was admitted to the hospital, Mother phoned Raimond at home and heard that Father had found her telegram in his hotel room after a late dinner and had been able to get a trunk call through to Ville-d'Avray. With the needed approval, Docteur Narnier had already called Docteur Moronguet, the surgeon who would arrive at the hospital shortly.

"Thank God in Warsaw they are always running three hours in front of us or else Dan would have been too late. He was in the middle of the night over there, with all the phones empty for him," said Mother, in her marvelously convoluted way.

Mother donned a surgeon's mask and escorted me as the hospital attendant pushed my wheelchair into the operating room. She said that the operating room had once been a vaulted wine cellar. The brick walls and curved ceiling were painted white, which was the only concession toward making the place resemble a medical facility. The operating table was a sturdy, blood-stained, wood table over which they were draping a bed sheet as I was wheeled in. The room's only lighting was an extremely bright, bare light bulb hanging over the operating table.

"At least the white walls were shining some light onto your tummy when he leaned over you," Mother said, and added, "I don't know how he saw what he was cutting inside you." But what appalled Mother even more was the lack of any heating. She described the room as "glacial," and said, "I could see your little bare body shivering like a madman before they put the asthetic [anesthetic] on your nose, and I asked them if there is not a blanket they could put over you. They said no—the hairs of the wool would go into the cicatrice [scar] and would be infecting you. Then they just put this handkerchief on your nose and poured a whole little bottle of asthetic over you."

Docteur Moronguet said that another hour's delay would have been fatal. Mother, who stayed in the operating room and saw the whole thing, said the surgeon was very neat and that the operation only took about fifteen minutes.

When I came to the next morning, I was coughing profusely, and my fever had not abated, to the consternation of everyone. I now had what they called "double pneumonia," complicated by pleurisy. This, they said at the time, was because of exposure to cold during the application of the chloroform.

I remember almost nothing of the next several days because I was so gravely ill, but I can't blot out from memory a series of dreadful sessions with a nurse, who was also a nun. Twice daily she glided silently into my room beneath a gigantic white wimple, carrying a large, white-enameled pail containing something that looked and steamed like a fresh cow dropping on a winter's day. The item in question was "*un revulsif,*" or, as the nun referred to it with sadistic glee, "*un bon cataplasme*" ("a good and strong mustard poultice"). She seemed to take particular pleasure in announcing to me that it was time for this primitive and painful procedure, as if the dread and terror that those words struck in me were a necessary part of the treatment. For readers unfamiliar with this medieval remedy once used for a wide range of ailments, it consists of a gruel of ground mustard seed, an extremely hot variety, folded into several layers of gauze cloth. Some kind of salt was added to make its action more powerful. This repulsive, khaki-colored wad was placed in a pail of water and brought to a boil in the convent's kitchen. The nun, using rubber gloves and tongs oo ac not to burn herself, then flung this scalding hot pad onto my bare chest and held it there with a thick towel as I shrieked in pain. After a few minutes, she lifted my torso and slipped a second one underneath my back so that I was now sandwiched between the two scorching wads. "It's important to get as much lung coverage as possible," she explained officiously.

The pain was excruciating and did not fade as the pads cooled, at which time the mustard took over, literally burning the skin by chemical action. There was also the revolting, acrid smell of the mustard just below my nostrils. I believe the mustard vapors were meant to penetrate my lungs and to cause further "burning" there, too. Like a hollow log, I was burning from within and from without. My shrieking usually attracted the Mother Superior to my room. She ordered me in a stern voice to be quiet, or she would punish me. She accused me of waking up every patient in the ward and advised me, "*Il faut apprendre à souffrir pour le Bon Dieu*" ("One must learn to suffer for the Good Lord"). This did nothing to quell my wailing, for what greater punishment could she possibly inflict than the one I was already enduring?

After twenty minutes, the nun removed the poultices and applied warm olive oil to ease the burning of my skin. Nevertheless, it remained red and sore for several days after the last application. Eventually, my fever slowly subsided. During this time, Mother was at my bedside night and day. Then, a new crisis arose. I was not eating or drinking any of the beverages (water or orange juice) offered to me. It was Mother who correctly diagnosed the problem. The dreaded mustard poultices were always administered about an hour before both lunch and supper, and upon completing the treatment, I was in such a state of nerves and terror that eating was out of question.

Mother explained her theory to the nun, who declared that she wasn't about to change the scheduling of her ward duties to accommodate my whims. When Mother told Docteur Moronguet about the matter, it was evident that he did not want to tangle with the nun, who was a surly, vindictive woman, feared by everyone in the ward. He ducked the issue by explaining that he had no say in the hospital's scheduling unless it was "a matter of life and death." At that point, Mother exploded. "Don't you think my son's life will end in death if he does not eat soon? Is that not a life and death matter? My son has not eaten in a week with all these dreadful *cataplasmes!*" she shouted in outrage.

The surgeon certainly knew about my pneumonia and the pleurisy, but he did not know about the mustard poultices. He explained that he had ordered a twice-daily *revulsif* and that, although mustard poultices came under that heading, he had assumed the sisters would use a modern type called *ouate thermogène*.

The nun grumped that *ouate thermogène* was for sissies and was too mild to do any good. Nevertheless, she grudgingly made the switch. It was a huge improvement, chiefly because it didn't smell of mustard and did not burn my skin quite as much, though it still felt extremely hot and left my skin red from its mysterious heat. The stuff came in the form of a large apricot-colored pad of cotton wool. The sister unrolled this dry pad from its wide "jelly roll" paper packaging and, using scissors, cut a piece the right size for my chest. The pad was activated by sprinkling it with eau-de-cologne that was applied liberally to the pad and to my chest with an atomizer. Then, mysteriously, the pad felt extremely hot when applied to my cologne-doused skin. The heat was purely chemical. I didn't like the treatment, but it was such an improvement over the mustard poltice that I accepted it without becoming panic stricken and without shrieking. With the change in treatment, my appetite returned.

One day, Raimond came to visit me in the hospital. "You know the black P.O. locomotive?" he asked cheerfully. (The gondola-to-locomotive transformation had been implemented only a couple of months before.) "Well," he continued, "while you were gone and not using it, I took the opportunity to repaint the entire locomotive in royal blue, and to change the P.O. insignia to a P.L.M. insignia. I did the lettering in yellow to look like the gold lettering used on the real P.L.M. locomotives. I think it's a big improvement and I know you will like it." The speed of my recovery started to match that of the real P.L.M. express trains.

When I returned home from the hospital, Mother made me drink a small glass of beef blood three times a day as a treatment for anemia. I don't know if this was real beef blood. Purchased at an apothecary, it looked and tasted like blood, but it didn't clot; Mother maintained that it was real beef blood, somehow sterilized for medicinal use. I dreaded taking the stuff, but it must have worked, for I soon regained a healthy color, though none of the weight I had lost.

While I was still convalescing, Mother took Brenda and me to visit our grandparents in Brussels. She hoped that during this sojourn I would regain some weight, as my grandparents' household, and indeed Brussels itself, were both known for superb food. Not that Françoise's cooking was in any way inadequate. It was more the style of eating that was different. In Belgium, at least in those days, people ate richer foods and larger quantities at each meal than did the French in general. The Belgians were more *bons vivants* than the French, according to Mother.

For good measure, Françoise offered to make a batch of *pâté de foie gras aux truffes* (goose liver *pâté* with truffles) to take with us to Brussels. This was something else with which Mother was plying me, in the hopes it would fatten me up. *Pâté* is loaded with fat and rich in iron, and she genuinely believed that by eating a goodly portion of it everyday, all my dietary needs would be addressed. *Pâté* had become one of Françoise's great specialties, and her *pâté* was much prized by my gourmet grandparents. This delicacy was, of course, available in Brussels, but every *pâté* is the unique creation of the chef who makes it, and Françoise's *pâté* was quite exceptional.

It's possible Mother may have thought that she could not ask her parents to buy this premium-priced delicacy especially for me. Or perhaps she just liked the idea of presenting her parents with this special gift. But there was another reason why Mother accepted Françoise's offer.

On a previous trip to Brussels, Mother had been made to pay a substantial customs duty on a *pâté* she was carrying. The experience had left her seething with resentment. "The customs duty was three times what I would have paid if I had just bought the *pâté* in Brussels!" she had exclaimed when telling us about the outrage. It was clear she wanted to even the score by outwitting the customs officials on this trip. As a teenager in Brussels, under the German occupation during World War I, Mother had been involved in food smuggling for the sake of having something palatable to eat. Any border crossing seemed to stimulate this once important instinct in her and allowed her to savor once more the thrill and excitement of smuggling.

Françoise prepared her two-kilo *pâté* in a heavy earthenware crock, which itself would be no small or trivial thing to conceal from a customs officer. For those who might wonder why the *pâté* had to weigh all of two kilos, hardly a small portion when it comes to *pâté*, I must explain that two kilos was the size of the *pâté* produced by Françoise's recipe, and that jostling Françoise was not something one did lightly. Besides, a smaller *pâté* would hardly present the challenge Mother craved.

It just happened that Uncle Hill (Major Hill, Father's army friend) had given Brenda a rather unusual doll. It was a large doll that was mostly pale blue plush on the exterior, rather like a teddy bear. But instead of a teddy bear's head, the doll's almost spherical head had a plasticized cloth circle where the face should have been, and on this smooth surface was imprinted a little girl's smiling face. I thought this doll was nothing short of grotesque, especially in profile, but Brenda adored "Collinette," as the doll was called. Brenda had named the doll after Uncle Hill; *colline* is the French for hill.

Collinette was no ordinary doll in certain other respects. Her limbs and head were stuffed and fairly rigid, but Collinette had a zipper down her back, her body was limp and completely empty, and this cavity was nicely lined. The purpose of this empty space was for Brenda's pajamas in daytime. When thus filled, the doll assumed some semblance of a human figure. From Mother's point of view, Collinette's virtue lay in the fact that her interior cavity was large enough to hold the ceramic terrine in which the two-kilo *pâté* was cooked.

For the trip to Brussels, the terrine containing the *pâté* and its lid were tied together with string. Thus secured and wrapped in wax paper, the whole package went neatly into Collinette's capacious interior. Brenda clearly didn't like the idea, and wondered what would happen to her pajamas, but Mother assured her that Collinette would survive the trip in pristine condition and that her pajamas could travel in a special doll suitcase she would buy for her. Brenda was placated and Collinette was enlisted as a major participant in Mother's smuggling caper. The plan seemed simple enough, and foolproof.

On the day of the trip, Mother found that little Brenda, only four years old, could barely lift the *pâté*-stuffed Collinette, let alone carry her any distance. Furthermore, the crock was so bulky that Collinette's already none-too-graceful outline was further distorted, making her look as if she were "with child" and carrying it rather low. Fortunately, among Brenda's other treasured possessions was a small baby carriage intended for her dolls. With a bit of squeezing and pushing, the corpulent Collinette could, with some effort, be wedged into the baby carriage.

The flimsily built toy pram wobbled precariously under its heavy load as Brenda valiantly trundled it along the railway platform at the Gare du Nord in Paris. When we reached our railway carriage, Mother and I, each holding one end of the pram, struggled to lift it into the compartment. Lying there in her baby carriage and looking up at us with her jovial face, Collinette seemed all sweetness and innocence. Waiting in the carriage for the train to depart, I prayed silently that the customs inspector would view her the same way.

As our train sped towards the Franco-Belgian border, the little pram rolled uneasily back and forth in the compartment's aisle with each lurch of the train. Collinette continued to stare blissfully at the ceiling and didn't seem to mind. Brenda, wearing a dark green velour coat and shiny patent leather shoes, carefully rearranged the doll blanket around Collinette, and said a few soothing words to her baby. With the doll blanket over her lower half, Collinette's distorted shape didn't show. Luckily, we had the first class eight-passenger compartment to ourselves. Mother, in an elegant blue matching skirt and jacket, appeared calm as she read a mystery novel. For a while, I was content to watch the passing scene, but as the trip progressed, I began to eye Brenda nervously. She didn't seem convinced that all was well with Collinette and started to fret over the doll.

I don't think Brenda understood the high stakes of the game. I, on the other hand, had overheard Father warn Mother about the foolishness of this venture. "If you're caught smuggling, you'll have far more to pay in fines and other problems than if you simply paid the customs duty," he had warned her. As a result of my eavesdropping, I was well aware of the situation we were in.

I was, in fact, highly anxious that Mother might end up in jail if she were caught, and I also worried because I was involved in what sounded to me like a major crime.

At one stage of the journey, Mother took us to the toilet. As we walked along the carriage corridor, I peeked into the various compartments through their windows and happened to spot the dreaded customs inspector at his wicked work. He was dressed in a black uniform and wore an imperious-looking visored cap. He reminded me of Mother's descriptions of the occupying German officers in the war. On the return trip to our compartment, I once again glanced into the compartment where the inspector seemed to be scolding some poor woman who looked as though she were pleading with him. My worst fears seemed to be upon us.

We were on an express train, so the customs inspectors had boarded in Paris. Knowing they were on a three-hour journey, the inspectors took their time as they advanced methodically through the train, spending considerable time in every compartment, opening all suitcases and searching each one thoroughly.

It wasn't long before the customs inspector opened the door to our compartment. At that precise moment, Brenda decided it was time to take Collinette out of her pram and started a struggle to un-wedge the well-ensconced Collinette. Brenda's unsuccessful struggle gave me time to grasp the danger we were in. I jumped from my seat and finished the job of removing Collinette from the little carriage, making sure I stood between the baby carriage and the customs inspector so that he could not see the doll. I seized Collinette below the waist and, with my arms encircling the doll so that her incriminating tummy was well concealed, I sat down in the seat closest to the window and farthest from the compartment door. There, turning towards the window so that Collinette was even less visible to the inspector, I started extolling to her the beauty of the passing landscape, which consisted mainly of coal mines, dross heaps, grimy factories, and slum dwellings.

Brenda was not a bit pleased by any of this and soon initiated a determined effort to pry Collinette from my arms. I held on firmly. In the meantime, the surly customs inspector scrutinized Mother's passport and started to ransack her suitcase. The inspection must have lasted a long time, for he pulled almost everything out of the suitcase, unfolding garments and prodding into everything. Meanwhile, the struggle between Brenda and me raged on. Brenda was tearing and pulling at anything she could grab. She was hitting and scratching me as she berated me through a veil of tears. But I clung tenaciously to the doll.

When the customs inspector had gone through all of Mother's belongings, he turned his attention to me and said crossly, "Come on now! Let her have the doll!"

There was what seemed to me like an interminable silence, during which Brenda stopped crying, and the inspector glowered at me accusingly. Finally, for lack of anything else to say or do, I blurted out a bald-faced lie.

"But it's my doll!" I protested. Before Brenda could interject, Mother quickly said, "My son is right! He loves dolls—he always has—that's why I didn't stop this quarrel sooner. My daughter is always pestering him and trying to take his dolls!" The customs inspector stared at me suspiciously for some time, then turned and left our compartment mumbling to himself and shaking his head.

As soon as the inspector was out of sight, I put Collinette back in her pram. Brenda now insisted that her doll didn't look comfortable in her pram and needed cuddling. And she protested loudly that Collinette was *her* doll. Mother tried to explain the delicacy of the situation to her, and although I don't think Brenda understood, she eventually resigned herself to leaving Collinette alone. With the inspectors on board until we reached Brussels, our situation was still tenuous.

My prolonged state of high anxiety, Brenda's clawing and pummeling, and my sudden, unexpected blurting out of a huge lie had taken their toll. I was in tears and badly in need of reassurance. Between sobs, I managed to tell Mother how much the lie was gnawing at me, and that I didn't think I could continue to lie if the inspector were to return.

Mother moved over so that she now sat next to me and put her arm around me. In hushed tones, she tried to reassure me. I heard her say, "During the war, I found it necessary to tell lies to a bunch of bandits and bullies to keep from starving." Turning suddenly petulant, she said, "These customs inspectors are no better than those terrible *boches!* The nerve they have to paw through my lingerie—and those enormous duties they demand from us—the nasty brutes!" Then, calming down, for she was obviously shaken by her own rhetoric, she added, "You were being loyal to my cause, and you were absolutely wonderful! Alain, I'm very proud of you! You told a white lie to save us all, and it was the right thing to do. A white lie is a lie told for the greater good. So don't worry yourself anymore about this matter."

When we reached Brussels, Collinette's painted smile seemed to be a knowing smile, and once in Brussels, she was restored, none the worse for wear, to the more mundane task of pajama storage.

My grandparents greeted us and Françoise's delicious *pâté* with delight. Mother got her revenge for that levied duty and a double dose of the excitement she apparently craved. However, I think she was genuinely contrite, if not ashamed, about what she had put us through, though not about the smuggling *per se*. She asked Brenda and me not to tell anyone about this incident. Yet, for the rest of her life, every time she crossed an international border she couldn't resist some new (and minor) smuggling escapade to prove to herself that no authority could tell her what she could and could not do.

Brenda and I loved to visit our grandparents, who doted on us while Mother went out visiting old friends and the haunts of her youth. This was the last visit to Brussels during which I would see Granny in good health. Later that year, she fell down a flight of stairs and broke her spine. At that time, there was nothing the doctors could do to heal or help her. Over the next three years, Mother took her disabled mother to see all the best specialists in Paris and London, but to no avail. Granny remained a total paraplegic for the next fifteen years, until she died at the age of seventy-six.

Even before the accident, Granny was a frail-looking woman. She was a sweet and affectionate soul, and after her accident, patient and uncomplaining about her continual pain. She continued to read to us children, even though she sat completely bent over in her wheel chair. I still remember Granny's gentle voice as she asked me to turn the pages of the book she was reading to me. We used to lay our children's books on the floor in front of her. She looked down and could not raise or move her head from this position. She had also lost the use of her hands, so that she had to be fed, and lifted into her bed, still bent over with her face barely a foot from her knees.

Grandpa was an energetic and high-strung man, well informed about what was going on in the world, an enthusiastic "modernist" and optimist, who was sure that technology (such as it existed then) had, or soon would have, a solution for everything, including his wife's injury. Despite his high-energy nature, he was a gentle, affectionate man, soft-spoken, modest and considerate.

My grandparents' house at 109 rue Berckmans, in Brussels, with its huge rooms and high ceilings, was a veritable palace. The house had five stories, sweeping staircases, grand fireplaces, and massive crystal chandeliers. It seems strange that such a luxurious mansion should find itself across the street from two small, "half-basement" business establishments. Both shops were among the special delights of our visits to Brussels. One of them was a first-rate toy shop, and the other, the best place to buy chocolate truffles in all of Brussels, which at the time was the chocolate truffle capital of the world.

My grandparents' house had a fair-sized back garden separating it from a second building that housed a large artist's studio. It was in this studio that Grandpa had his architectural office. A tunnel-like greenhouse linked the two buildings at the main floor level. The "tunnel" was really a bridge since the garden separating the two buildings was at the kitchen level, one floor lower. Grandpa cultivated muscat grapes on an elaborate trellis so that the vines lined the two walls and ceiling of the greenhouse. Grapes grew in profusion a good part of the year.

The main house was pierced by a large entrance hall at the same level as the greenhouse bridge. Since the greenhouse was kept at the same temperature as the house, no door was needed where it met the entrance hall. Upon entering the front door, one looked down the long entrance hall and straight into the green luminosity of the hothouse tunnel. Clients arriving to visit Grandpa in his studio were thus ushered through a marbled hall hung with fine paintings, and continued on through a verdant tunnel from whose foliaged walls and ceiling hung huge bunches of muscat grapes. I can still see those plump, amber grapes all aglow, backlit by the morning sun.

I remember the rooms of the house as sumptuous, with twelve-foot-high, floor-to-ceiling windows overlooking the street in front. The main floor of the house consisted of two huge rooms: a living room at the front and a dining room that opened onto a glassed-in "sunroom" at the back of the house. The sunroom, much like a greenhouse itself, overlooked the courtyard garden one floor below. Each of the two main floor rooms had a large fireplace, an immense crystal chandelier, and a room-sized oriental carpet. Above the marble mantle piece in the dining room was a six-by-ten foot oil painting entitled "*L'Abondance*." The painting had been done around 1830, by Grandpa's grandfather, Antoine. It represented four cherub-like, naked little boys frolicking in and around a mountainous pile of grapes interspersed with other ripe-looking fruit: melons, apples, cherries, pears, peaches and plums. The young children portrayed were modeled by the artist's sons, and were painted life-size.

Four of the five floors of the house were equally luxurious and well appointed. I never saw the fifth floor because it was exclusively the servants' domain, and I was not supposed to go up there. A very large dumbwaiter connected all the floors to the kitchen in the basement. With the basement windows set high and near the ceiling, the basement should more correctly have been called a half-basement. The latter included the kitchen, a pantry, a larder, a wine cellar, a servants' dining room and a "common room" for their use. All were spacious and well-equipped rooms.

In 1936, with just my two grandparents living upstairs, the servant staff had been reduced to Georgette, Philomène, and

Matilde. These three elderly spinsters had their rooms on the fifth floor. Before World War I, when Mother and her two sisters were still young girls, there was also a manservant, who served as both gardener and butler.

One of our activities in Brussels was walking a short distance down the gently sloping rue Berckmans to the Avenue de Waterloo. In Brussels, this avenue was about the equivalent of the Champs Elysées in Paris, a broad, tree-lined boulevard with wide sidewalks, elegant shops, restaurants and sidewalk cafés. 109 rue Berckmans was also close to several fine museums, including the Palace of Fine Arts, where paintings done by my great-great grandfather, and statues sculpted by his son, Jules, were on display. Mother was very proud of her heritage and took us to see these works every time we went to Brussels.

When the adults went off somewhere, Brenda and I were left in the care of Georgette, the "first cook." Georgette had been in my grandparents' household since they were first married. She was in her seventies, and still spry and active in the running of the household. She had a jovial demeanor, and her face reflected her good-natured approach to the world and a life filled with kindness. She had a special fondness for me because she had spent a year helping Nurse Khondakov take care of me when I was a baby and Mother was away in Africa. Now that I was six, Geogette let me hang around the kitchen as she cooked and, like Françoise, she allowed me to "help" her with minor kitchen procedures.

Four years later, in 1940, when the Germans invaded Belgium, Georgette, who had no other family, stayed on with my grandparents. Philomène and Matilde went away to live with their own families in the countryside, where food might be more plentiful. During World War II, Georgette was active in the underground resistance movement despite her advanced age. In the servants' rooms, she ran a "safe-house" for Allied airmen who had been shot down over Belgium. The fifth-floor rooms were ideal for this purpose, having the advantage that if a search of the house were ever initiated by the Gestapo, the flyers could escape over the rooftops. Georgette had gained ample experience in the art of smuggling black market food during World War I, and thus managed to provide food for the airmen, some of whom were wounded.

Georgette tended the wounded herself. Calling a doctor was too risky and therefore out of the question. People suspected of underground activities were interrogated and tortured by the Gestapo until they revealed what they knew. The usual way to get a person to talk, and one that seldom failed, was to have the prisoner watch the torture of a close family member. The penalty for participating in the underground resistance movement was death by firing squad. The fewer the people who knew about underground activities, the safer it was for everyone. No one was told anything that he or she didn't absolutely need to know.

The flyers stayed at 109 rue Berckmans for a few days, or sometimes months, until they were fit to travel and properly equipped to do so. Then, they were moved from one safe-house to the next in a chain of safe-houses and eventually reached a place where it was possible to arrange a crossing of the Channel back to England. Civilian clothes and fake identification cards had to be procured for the flyers before having them attempt the move to the next safe house. All of this required great ingenuity and extreme stealth.

My grandparents were not part of this clandestine operation, and were never told about it. There was nothing they could add to what Georgette was already doing for the flyers, and they might have ended up being interrogated by the Gestapo. All these details were revealed to Mother after the war by Katrine, a neighbor, who was part of the same underground "cell" as Georgette. But Granny (who survived the war) added some details to the story. She told Mother that Grandfather was well aware that Georgette's household expenses had increased dramatically since the arrival of the Germans in Brussels. The money Georgette requested weekly for household needs grew beyond reasonable bounds, and since he was sure that Georgette would never do anything dishonest, he never questioned the increase, surmising that Georgette was somehow contributing to underground activities. He also knew better than to ask questions.

Two years into the German occupation, Grandpa died very suddenly of unexplained causes. Katrine said that Georgette had obtained (on the black market) enough "special" food for a small celebration of his seventy-third birthday. She maintained that the Gestapo had intercepted the black market food and had somehow laced it with poison in an effort to put an end to such contraband. She cited as proof the fact that Grandpa was in sound health on his birthday, and that on the following day, he awoke with violent stomach convulsions which were quickly followed by his death. All the symptoms of poisoning were present, Katrine insisted. But of course, there was no going to a doctor or to the authorities, no autopsy. Pursuing the subject, Mother pointed out that her mother and Georgette had both participated in the modest celebration and had suffered no similar symptoms. Katrine stood by her theory, explaining that through the underground network she had heard of several similar cases elsewhere in Brussels at the time. She also postulated that the poison might have been in the form of a micro-capsule, localized in a small portion of the food and thus would have affected only the person who ate that portion.

A week or so after Grandpa's death, the Gestapo banged at the front door, forced it open, and, armed with sub-machine guns at the ready, marched in, twelve strong. This was described to Mother by the toy shop owner, whose shop was across the street and who saw the Germans arrive at 109 rue Berckmans and break down the door. Without saying a word to Granny in her wheelchair in the dining room, they searched the house. Granny told Mother that she thought that Georgette had probably tried to hide in the dumbwaiter, for she heard the soldiers struggling with the dumbwaiter which seemed to be stuck. When the men finally succeeded in bringing the dumbwaiter to the level of the dining room, Granny heard both their exclamations of satisfaction and Georgette's terrified whimpering. They dragged Georgette away and finished searching the house but apparently found nothing else. No one ever saw Georgette again. No funeral was held until the end of the war, when it was finally confirmed that she had been shot by a firing squad. She is honored in a group memorial dedicated to those killed while working for the underground movement in Brussels.

Katrine said she had heard the commotion and had fled the area because of her association with Georgette. Two days later, she worked up enough courage to return to the neighborhood, not knowing what had happened or what she would find. She entered 109 rue Berckmans via a communal garden gate, and found Granny still in her wheel chair where she had waited patiently and in helpless silence for two days. Granny was taken to a convent where she was well known as a lifelong benefactor of the order. She lived there in the care of the nuns for another nine years. She was alert, able to read, and to converse intelligently with her visitors until her death. The nuns said she lived in a state of continual pain, and that she categorically refused any kind of a pain-killer, and never uttered a single complaint.

When Mother brought Brenda and me to rue Berckmans before the war, Georgette used to play with us when she could find the time to do so. We loved her attention because she was a happy soul, young at heart, with a good sense of humor, and a generous nature. Later, when I was old enough to appreciate her venerable age, I marveled at the way she had gone up and down stairs while playing these games with us. She ranks among the people I hold most dear.

On our return to Ville-d'Avray in early May, I was well enough to play in the garden, but I was still too weak to push the newly repainted locomotive up the sloping paths. My locomotive stayed parked in the low spots of the garden until Raimond had a minute to push it up the hill for me, which he did about four times an hour when he was working in the garden.

I returned to the Cours Boutet de Monvel about a month before the end of the school year. I had been away for over two months due to my illness and the trip to Brussels, so my performance in class was even more dismal than it had been the rest of the school year. It was a two-year school, and at the end of the second year, they held a prize-giving and graduation ceremony.

An assortment of toys was laid out on a table at the front of the classroom. Mademoiselle de Monvel called each child in turn to the table to choose a toy. The order in which we were called for the collection of our prize was based on our scholastic standing. To no one's surprise, I was the last one called up to the table.

What did come as a surprise was that there was actually a choice of toys left when my turn finally came. One student was absent, so there were two items. The prizes available to me consisted of a forlorn little toy car, cheaply and poorly made of stamped sheet metal, or a boxed tea set that one of the little girls in attendance might have chosen for her dolls. I stood there contemplating this pitiable choice for some time. I really wanted neither.

Finally, I grudgingly chose the dolly tea set. The class and the parents at the back of the room had been watching these proceedings with some interest, since I had a reputation for being the class character. Mademoiselle de Monvel couldn't resist making fun of my situation and said, "Well, Monsieur Alain, are you planning a tea party for your dolls?"

There was a burst of laughter, and when it subsided, I explained my choice. "No. The car is not to scale with my electric trains *et a l'air d'être de la camelote* (and appears to be a piece of junk). I have a little sister who might perhaps enjoy the tea set for her dolls."

I doubt that any of the students knew what "scale" was, but I don't think the word was lost on the parents at the back of the room, several of whom did some subdued clapping. Among them was Mother, who, for once, in what must have been a rough year for her, now seemed proud of me, even though I was last in the class. Afterwards, she and I went out for tea and pastries at a certain marvelous pastry shop just around the corner, on the Place de la Madeleine—it was called Fauchon's —the one where I had waylaid the hapless Miss Parris. As we enjoyed our *patisseries* and a cup of tea, Mother let me know I had done just fine as far as she was concerned.

In June, we went to Hardelot where we rented a different house that year. Due to my appendicitis, Mother had been unable to go there in April to renew the rental of Le Green Cottage. At the last minute, in late May, she had been able to arrange a rental of the Villa Sombra. Despite considerable dinner-table debate that summer, we never figured out how this villa came by its name, which means something like "shade" or "shadow" in Spanish. The house was on the corner of a block of contiguous houses, and its two exposed outer surfaces faced south and west, respectively. Both sides therefore received copious sunlight after about nine o'clock in the morning. The house had several generous bay windows and could not be called a dark or shady house by any stretch of the imagination. Nor were its cream-colored stucco exterior or its maroon timbers and shutters any further clue as to the reason for its name.

Although it overlooked the *digue* (promenade), the beach and the sea, Villa La Sombra was not nearly as nice as Le Green Cottage of the previous summer. It was at the north end of the *digue* and some distance away from my beloved tennis court amphitheater, where everything of importance in Hardelot took place. The remoteness of the villa in relation to the rest of Hardelot was why Father eventually declared that he preferred Villa Sombra to Le Green Cottage. He loved solitary spots and had a well-developed aversion to crowds of any sort.

The villa's nicest feature was a rotunda-style terrace at its southwest corner. This circular terrace was large enough to accommodate the dining table so that we ate most of our meals while enjoying the view, the sounds of the sea, and some magnificent sunsets.

That summer's activities were much the same as those of the previous summer, except for one important addition. Mother suddenly decided it was time for me to learn to ride a bicycle. She rented a small bike for me, and for several days, she spent half-hour sessions holding onto the bike as I wobbled along beside her. She was afraid to let go of me for fear I'd fall and scrape myself on the rough asphalt. However, it became increasingly clear to me that I would never discover the wonder of bike riding until she released me, something she appeared reluctant to do.

One day when Mother was away playing golf, I asked Raimond if he would teach me to ride my bike. Since it was low tide, he proposed that we go out on the exposed sand bars for the lesson. He carried my bike down the seawall and, when we reached our beach cabin, removed his shoes and socks and neatly rolled up his trouser cuffs. This done, he carried the bike across the strip of dry, soft sand and out onto the smooth, hard expanse of wet sand. There, he held the bike while I mounted it. Then, still holding the bike, he ran as fast as he could and eventually "catapulted" me off by giving me one final, mighty push. As he did so he yelled, "Pedal! Pedal like mad and keep pedaling!"

His instructions had been essentially the same as Mother's, but she had never allowed me to move faster than a walk. The speed I now traveled made all the difference. Sure enough, pedaling like mad, I found myself flying along at what seemed like breakneck speed, but upright and completely stable. I was experiencing one of life's great moments! I kept on pedaling, and since I had the whole beach to myself, I soon discovered that I could turn without any danger of falling over. I started making wide circles around Raimond, who was clapping and encouraging me on with "Bravo Alain! Bravo!"

Finally, as I passed close by him, I yelled, "How do I stop?" The bike was fairly rudimentary and had no brakes, nor did it have free-wheeling, so the pedals had to turn if the wheels spun. We hadn't discussed the important detail of how to stop before my triumphant launching.

As I zoomed past him again, Raimond yelled out, "Just stop pedaling!"

"I can't do that—I'll fall down!" I yelled back on the next flyby. For indeed, my initial instructions had been clear: pedal or perish! I was convinced that if I stopped pedaling I would keel over in a disastrous crash and be annihilated. Not even the trusted Raimond could now talk me into stopping my pedaling. Would I be forced to keep on pedaling like this forever, and what would happen to me when the tide came up? On each successive pass, I repeated, "I can't stop pedaling! I mustn't stop pedaling, or I'll fall and be killed!"

Raimond was laughing and continuing his refrain to stop pedaling, but started what seemed like a deliberate walk along the beach as I continued to ride circles around him, all the while pedaling like mad and loudly demanding a resolution of my crisis each time I orbited close to him.

His plan became clearer when he stopped walking and stood beside a huge pile of seaweed. As I passed by him once more, he yelled, "Just ride into the pile of seaweed! That will stop you safely!"

Half-plausible instructions at last! I looped around once more, screwed up all my courage, and still pedaling furiously, I charged full speed into the seaweed. My wheels and pedals were immediately entangled in the kelp and the bike came to an abrupt halt. To my surprise, I was still upright, in one piece, and with my two feet resting on the mounds of seaweed on either side of the bike.

We spent some time untangling kelp from the bike as Raimond explained what I had found so hard to believe. I could pedal slower and slower and still remain stable, he said, and doing this, I would end up going so slowly that all I had to do was put one foot down on the ground and stop. It all seemed so absurdly simple! Why wasn't I told this before?

Within a day, I was riding with only one hand on the handlebars and within two days, no hands on the handlebars. Mother was terrified and stupefied at my prowess. Fortunately, Raimond was present, beaming with pride and pleasure, and reassuring her that I would be fine.

Being able to ride a bike gave me unlimited new freedom, or so it seemed at the time. I was allowed to ride one block in all directions from our house. And I could ride on the beach at low tide, as long as I stayed well away from the water's edge and went no farther along the beach than where the seawall extended (a distance of about one mile). What Mother didn't know was that, while she was away playing golf, I extended this boundary in a direction unspecified by her. I rode down the beach about a half mile until I was opposite Hardelot's main street and shopping area. There, I carried my bike back across the soft sand strip, up the seawall, and remounted it once I was on the *digue*. From there it was just a block or so to the town's *bazar* (general emporium), which had a large assortment of toys on display. I had neither money nor illusions that I could ever own any of the toys, but I enjoyed the thrill of these clandestine excursions and loved to ogle the toys in the shop window.

One day, I unstuck my face from the window pane of the *bazar* to discover Mother standing beside me. She asked me how I had reached this spot. Always candid when caught red-handed, I carefully described my circuitous route to her. "I'll let you do that, as long as you stay off the busy streets where a car might squash you. But you mustn't go in the shops. And it's all right for you to ride on the *digue* if you like, as long as you don't knock over anyone promenading there." My roaming rights had just been tripled, and I was ecstatic. That same day, Mother and I also visited the bike shop (conveniently found next door to the *bazar)* and upgraded my rental bike to one that had hand brakes and freewheeling. What a difference and what further ecstasy!

One of my favorite activities on the beach became riding my bike at full speed into or across the shallow tide pools. The resulting *panaches* of water fortified my fantasy that I was driving a speedboat or taking off in a seaplane. One day, a group of five bike riders, all about my age, stopped to watch my antics as I tore through, circled around and repeatedly raced and splashed across a tide pool with unabashed enthusiasm and reckless abandon. When I ended my performance, sopping wet and in a state of intoxication, I came to a stop near the edge of the tide pool to catch my breath. The wheels of my bike and my feet were still in the shallow water. My audience approached me, and one of them asked me how I could get away with such activities when *les parents* had forbidden them to ride through tide pools.

I replied that no one had ever told me not to, and, as long as I wore a bathing suit, what was wrong with riding a bike through tide pools, anyway?

"Aren't you worried that your bike will soon be completely rusted? One day, it will fall apart while you're riding it," one of my spectators warned portentously. Their bikes all looked far nicer than mine, and it turned out that they all owned their bikes. My rented bike already had its share of rust spots, but it ran well enough, perhaps because Raimond frequently scrubbed the chain and sprocket wheels, and other key parts, with an old toothbrush soaked in olive oil. I offered to let them take turns riding my bike through tide pools to their hearts' content while, in exchange, I did some "dry riding" on their more elegant steeds. It quickly dawned on me that I had the better bargain. The fact that a bike was newer and fancier did not seem to add any particular magic to its riding qualities, and I decided that having to stay out of tide pools was too big a price to pay for the vanity of an elegant bike.

The lending of my unfettered bike won me membership in the group, and before long, we formed *une escadrille*, a squadron (of fighter pilots in the French Air Force). Among my fellow flyers was a boy we all called by his last name, "Blériot." His grandfather was Louis Blériot, the first man to succeed in flying across the English Channel in 1909. By coincidence, the pioneer flyer died that year (1936). The Blériots owned the largest and most ostentatious villa in Hardelot. Villa Blériot had light gray stucco with sky blue trim which were, Mother whimsically commented, "the same colors as the sky he was flying through in 1909." However, she disapproved of the color scheme, describing it as too subdued and colorless for a seaside resort.

Many years later, Mother told me a story about Louis Blériot that I found quite surprising. She said that she had seen Blériot take off from the beach (at low tide) on one of his cross-Channel attempts. She said that soon after takeoff, the plane's single engine sputtered to a stop. Blériot was already flying over the water but managed to turn the plane around and make a forced landing in the water close to shore. The plane apparently floated. She said that Blériot climbed out of the plane's cockpit and sat on its rim so as to be higher out of the water. He lit a cigarette and puffed away nonchalantly as he waited for the beach guard's lifeboat to come and rescue him and his plane.

I asked Mother if she was in France when this happened. She replied that she had never been to France before she was twelve years old! I pursued the subject by saying, "So you must have been in Westende [in Belgium, where Grandpa had a seaside villa] when you saw Blériot's crash."

"Of course it was Westende! Where else would I be?"

I questioned her further, "Are you are sure it was Blériot you saw? And that he was making a cross-Channel attempt? How could you see the cigarette lighting business from so far away? I mean, were you close to where he crashed?"

"It was Blériot," she insisted. "I saw him making his plane take off from the beach with all the people running next to him until he was flying in the air. He had not yet flown across the Channel from Belgium, and his crash was told in all the newspapers, and so was the photo with him puffing a cigarette while he was sitting in the water on top of his plane. It was mostly wood with a little cloth, so he was floating quite well. They used a photo from somebody who was in the lifeboat which was going to rescue him. Myself, I didn't see the cigarette. I was on the beach not far away and saw the big splash of his plane when he crashed in the water and sat on it, floating while the lifeboat was going to pull the plane back to the shore by rowing."

Mother's description was finally clear. After Blériot's world famous 24-mile cross-Channel flight from France to England, he apparently attempted a longer flight (about seventy miles) from Westende to England. Whether he made another try from Belgium, Mother couldn't tell me.

It was during the summer of 1936 that I became interested in the matter of nationality and the importance people attached to it. I believe that Raimond may have had the most influence in the matter, though I don't think it was through a conscious effort on his part. Raimond was fiercely proud that he was French and couldn't resist any opportunity to celebrate France's achievements. Hardly a day went by that he didn't point out, as he read *Le Paris Soir* newspaper, that a French football team had beaten some European rival. He never missed a chance to demonstrate how the French were good at everything, and he seldom mentioned or lamented French defeats or losses.

Of special interest to Raimond and me were the biweekly races between the two competing transatlantic ocean liners, Cunard's Queen Mary and the French Line's Normandie. Each time either of them completed a crossing between Europe and New York, *Le Ruban Bleu* (the Blue Ribbon) was awarded to the ship whose port-to-port time had beaten the previous record, often by only a few minutes, over a trip that took five days. The results of this contest elicited much fanfare and attention in the newspapers. If Raimond seemed unusually subdued, it usually meant the Queen Mary had surpassed the Normandie in a recent crossing. He could then be seen reading the paper with deep and frowning attention, carefully scanning every phrase of the newspaper article for minute scraps of information that might explain this untenable state of affairs. When he found a possible reason, there would be a relieved "Aha!" followed by the reading aloud of the explanation: there had been unusual storms or headwinds (the steamers never crossed simultaneously), the Normandie had been forced to take a more circuitous route around icebergs, or heavy fog had forced the Normandie to reduce speed. For Raimond, there was not the slightest doubt that the French were superior in anything that mattered, but he conceded that the British ran a close second.

I had the vague feeling that I was British and that Father had settled the matter in some mysterious way. Nevertheless, I held Raimond's intelligence in high esteem and found his arguments in favor of being French quite convincing. I wasn't sure I had any choice in the matter, and if I did, I would have to decide who was supplying me with the more plausible observations and facts concerning matters of national superiority, Father or Raimond.

It may seem strange that I would consider Raimond's views more significant than Father's. But the difficulty was that Father never said much to me about anything, whereas Raimond daily referred to some new French triumph or national virtue. On the other hand, there were the occasional statements from Father for which Raimond did not have a good rebuttal. For instance, Father once said that he felt safer flying on Imperial Airways than he did on Air France. When I asked him why, his reply had been, "The British have better aeroplanes, and the French pilots fly as if they were still fighting aerial dogfights over the trenches."

When I repeated this comment to Raimond, his answer was in the form of a list of aircraft performance statistics obtained from a book on French aviation. His most recent data was for aircraft that were new in 1930. I wondered if the British had taken the lead in the intervening six years. Coincidentally, as a Christmas present, Uncle Bob in England had sent me a book showing all the very latest British aircraft. It provided performance data for each aeroplane shown, but had nothing on current French aircraft. Most notably, it showed the two previous years' winners of the Schneider Cup Seaplane races, and they were all British monoplanes designed by a man named Mitchel, whose seaplanes were apparently winning these races by huge margins.

Raimond pointed out that these single-passenger, one-of-a-kind, specialized planes did not count in the airliner contest under consideration. As to the flying style of Air France pilots, Raimond, who had never flown in a plane, explained that the only time French airline pilots did aerobatics was to avoid bumping into some of the heavier clouds, and that they did so very adroitly. It was difficult to argue with him as I, too, had never flown.

Another realm of contest between the two nations were the fast, steam-powered trains, which were setting world records in regular passenger service. England had the Flying Scotsman traveling between London and Edinburgh (at an average speed of something like 130 miles an hour), and France had La Flèche d'Or (the Golden Arrow), running between Paris and Marseille. Hardly a week went by that a new speed record wasn't reported in the *Le Paris Soir*, even when the improvement was only a few seconds over a journey that took almost a day. Father, who read the *Daily Mail* and the *London Times*, only occasionally mentioned new records achieved by the Flying Scotsman. The British generally seemed to rest on their laurels for some time before having another try. The French struck me as jumpy and high-strung, whereas the British were more easygoing and orderly in the way they went about doing things. I could see virtue in both characteristics: in one, I could see excitement, and in the other, a dignified wisdom and prudence.

Father could convert miles-an-hour to kilometers-an-hour and Raimond could not. Father even did it in his head! Surely this was a clue as to who knew the most! To this observation, Raimond's rejoinder had been, "Who cares about miles-an-hour? Who else in the world uses miles?" Raimond's world didn't extend much farther than continental Europe, or perhaps, French borders.

Why was Father living in France if he thought England the better country? He never said so outright but implied as much, as opposed to Raimond whose statements were far more explicit. Why did Father own two French cars and boast that the Peugeot was better than anything the British made, even better, mechanically, than the Rolls Royce? And why did he buy all his suits and golf clubs in England? And where did Belgium fit into this complicated picture? After all, Mother occasionally reminded me that I was half Belgian—that's how she interpreted the fact that she was originally Belgian and had acquired British nationality through marriage. Then, Raimond pointed out that I was actually French because I was born in France, and that French law was unequivocal on that score. There was really no argument about my nationality in his mind.

When I told Father about Raimond's assertion, his reply was short and to the point: he was British and I was his son, so I was automatically British. To add to this chauvinistic clamor and confuse me even more, Mother outdid herself extolling England and all things British, but then she raved about French fashions and made fun of the way British women dressed. She also thought French perfumes, books, films and plays were superior.

Looking back on it now, it's obvious that my parents were in the enviable position of being able to buy and own the best of everything that was available in whichever country those items were to be found. As to my own affinities at the time, I think that Mother's loyalty to Father set the strongest example, and that little by little, I became convinced that I was English, though I felt it possible that something could come along which might make me change my mind. After all, I had never really lived in England and the best I could do was hope I wouldn't be disappointed when I went there. In the meantime, I was tactful about mentioning my sentiments around Raimond. I loved him dearly and didn't want to hurt his feelings or offend him. When he got a little carried away with his chauvinism, I joined him in his good feelings about France. At school, no one seemed to think I was British, and the subject of nationality never came up.

I already knew that when I was ten I would be going off to boarding school in England. Based on this, it seemed inevitable I would end up in England on a bigger scale of life than just schooling. Everything I had ever heard about England sounded good, and I used to daydream about all the new and wonderful things I would discover when I finally went there. For now, I reveled in the French aspects of my life and savored the possibility that things might be even better in England. Perhaps I could even do what Father seemed to be doing—enjoying the best of both worlds.

Brenda, who neither asked about the subject, nor paid the slightest attention to any of these important considerations and arguments, never swerved from a lifelong fealty to England and maintained she couldn't wait for the day when she could marry an Englishman and live in England. Where she found such strong convictions puzzled me. I now realize that Raimond had no influence on her the way he did on me.

On my sixth birthday, I received from my Auntie Gladys, Uncle Bob's wife, a complete English schoolboy's uniform (minus any school crests, which usually adorned the blazer pocket and flannel cap). The gray flannel blazer, cap, and knee-length shorts were even accompanied by a matching gray flannel shirt and gray knee-high wool socks. I wore this all-gray outfit with pride on weekends when we had guests, and when Mother took Brenda and me shopping in the more elegant boutiques of nearby Le Touquet or the finer shops of Paris. It was made clear to me that to be elegant and properly dressed, I had to don my British attire. Auntie Gladys also brought me a Royal Ensign (on a short stick) as a gift when she came to visit us at Villa Sombra, and urged me to fly it on any sand castle I built. Although I didn't know it then, it's obvious that my indoctrination was already well in progress.

An incredible scene from that summer which I will never forget occurred on a somber, stormy day in early September. A seaside resort in rainy weather can be a dreary, depressing sight, especially after the summer's end when there are few souls about. In an effort to fend off the blues, Mother had a fire going in the fireplace. She sat by the hearth sewing contentedly, but I found myself restless and hoping for a clearing in the clouds so I could go out bike riding. I eventually peered through the rain-spattered window of the Villa Sombra and saw an unbelievable, almost terrifying sight. An army of darkly clad people was marching out of the sea onto the beach directly in front of our villa. It was nearly high tide, so they weren't that far away. I hurried to Mother to describe this unsettling scene. She refused to believe me. In a distracted, indifferent tone she just said, "Alain, what are you inventing now? You and your imagination!"

Undaunted by her put-down, I went back to the window and looked again. Near the water's edge, I could now make out numerous fishing boats with small sails, and several horse-drawn carts on the beach, some of them in the water up to their axles. On the beach were dozens of people, all scurrying around, occasionally stooping over, picking up large fish, and dumping them in huge baskets that dotted the wet sand. A hundred or more men were in the water up to their chests, fully dressed, and were marching together in a line, first in one direction, then back again, apparently pulling hard at something under the water. Once more, I described the scene to Mother in excited tones and finally roused her curiosity. As she came towards the window, I begged her to take me to the beach so we could have a closer look at what the people were doing. When she reached the window, she gasped with surprise and exclaimed, "Sacré bleu! Tu n'inventes pas!" (Good heavens! You're not inventing!)

It was still raining, so Mother and I donned raincoats, Wellingtons and sou'westers and walked briskly out to investigate. The rain was coming down in sheets, but the air was warm, and there was almost no wind, so we would have been quite comfortable in our swim togs. The sea was almost black, the sky was a dark and turbulent gray, and what light there was seemed to come from the expanse of ochre-colored wet sand at the sea's edge.

As we approached the mob of fishermen on the beach, the scene was a maelstrom. There must have been well over a hundred people, all of them engaged in a variety of urgent tasks. The most conspicuous were women in long black skirts which fell almost to their ankles, scurrying barefoot along the hundred-yard length of a narrow gill net spread out on the beach just above the water line. Dozens of fish, all of the same size and kind were entangled in the net, held there by their gills. The women ran from one fish to the next, stooping to tug violently at them, deftly releasing the fish from the net and then tossing them higher up onto the beach, well above the waterline. The freed fish were everywhere, thrashing and flapping on the glistening wet sand, their cruelly torn gills bleeding red and pulsing, as if in voiceless screams of pain and terror. Other women followed the first group, picking up the still-wriggling fish, which they carried to large baskets that dotted the beach.

Offshore, spaced about ten feet apart and up to their waists in the water, men were apparently holding onto a submerged net that must have been at least a hundred yards long. They seemed to know when it was time to haul the net to shore. At that point, they started heaving and pulling in unison at the net, dragging it through the small waves breaking at the water's edge, where a crew of fisher-women awaited them. As soon as the fish-laden net was on the beach, the men left it and waded back out to the waiting fishing smacks. The slope of the beach was so slight that even a hundred yards from the shore, the men were still in water only up to their waists. There, they uncoiled another net from a large bundle onboard the boat and deployed it parallel to the beach. The men were fully dressed in blue denim, but were barefoot, and they wore no gloves to handle the rough cordage of the nets.

The work continued for well over an hour and ended only when, finally, an empty net was brought ashore. The surviving fish of a large school of sea bass had abruptly ended their frenzied feeding on the little gray shrimp of the shallows, and had retreated to deeper water and safety. The women rounded up the last of the still-struggling fish on the beach, and helped each other heave the heavily loaded baskets onto the horse-drawn carts. The empty nets were dragged back into the water and eventually coiled back onto the waiting boats.

I watched, fascinated. Meanwhile, Mother dashed home to get her purse. When she returned, she bought a sea bass almost two feet long from one of the women for a couple of francs. Mother asked the fisher woman how they happened to be there at just the right time. The woman told her that near the autumnal equinox, during heavy rainstorms and at a certain stage of the tide cycle, large schools of sea bass came into the shallow water to feed on shrimp. It only happened about once in ten years, she said, because the weather was usually fine at that time of the year, and the fish only came in close to shore when the sky was heavily overcast. She said that when the conditions she described were present, the fishermen were confident the bass would be there, so they came to this spot from all the nearby fishing harbors, and even from as far away as Dieppe, about a hundred kilometers distant. They could make more money in a few hours on this beach than they could in a month fishing in the normal fashion. This extraordinary catch only happened in Hardelot, she said, adding that, according to local lore, these miraculous catches had been occurring since the time of Saint Augustine, who had passed through this region on his way to England around 600 AD.

When Mother went back to the house for her purse, she coaxed Brenda into coming out, and the three of us now stood on the beach watching the last stages of this ritual. Eight horse-drawn carts, each creaking under the load of six huge baskets brimming with fish, were laboriously hauled up the gentle slope of the seawall. It took about twenty men pushing on a cart and pulling on ropes, along with the efforts of the horse, to get it up this sloping obstacle.

With some difficulty of my own, I proudly transported our heavy, slippery prize back to the Villa Sombra. Françoise was waiting in her usual state of high-pitched excitement at the prospect of cooking something out of the ordinary. She poached our magnificent fish whole, sprinkled it with a mixture of olive oil, lemon juice and chopped parsley, then served it on a bed of spinach garlanded with slices of hard-boiled eggs.

Alain and Brenda fly the Royal Ensign at a sand house, Hardelot, 1936

Dan reading to Alain and Brenda, Villa la Sombra, Hardelot, 1936

CHAPTER 6

A Prison Term and a Saucy French Governess

In the autumn of 1936, Mother was casting about for my next school when she discovered that our new neighbors, the Poujet family, had two children almost the same ages as Brenda and I. A little later, she heard that Madame Poujet had also been looking for a private school and had found one. The gregarious Raimond, whose pastimes included comparing gardening methods and exchanging gossip with neighboring gardeners, was the purveyor of all this useful information.

Madame Poujet and Mother soon arranged that the four of us, Charlie and Monique Poujet, my sister, Brenda, and I would ride a school bus that passed in front of the Poujet's house. The two mothers would take turns bringing us home from school by car, a distance of about four miles. The only obstacle to this plan was an eight-foot-high stone wall separating our property from the Poujet garden.

To get to the Poujet's front gate, our future bus stop, Brenda and I had to walk down our street about a quarter mile, then up their street about the same distance. It was a hilly neighborhood, and the "up and down" were real hills. Françoise, who would have to escort us, wanted no part of the arrangement. "I already have to walk down to the village to get bread, milk and groceries every day," she complained, and because Françoise was someone with whom you didn't cross swords, something else had to be dreamed up.

I had just seen the film "Mowgli, the Elephant Boy," and was longing to swing from tree to tree on hanging vines. So I suggested to Raimond that he install a rope in the large linden tree next to the Poujet wall. "I could climb into the linden tree and from there swing on the rope to the top of the wall," I proposed. "Then, I could walk along the top of the wall to a place near a tree on their side of the wall and swing down to the Poujet garden on a second rope tied in one of their trees."

Raimond pondered my scheme, and my hopes mounted when I thought I detected a gleam in his eye. Finally, he announced that I had given him an idea. "We will use ladders on both sides of the wall. I think I can make it work, but I may break a few tiles doing so." He was referring to the terra cotta tiles that topped the wall. To me they looked like a little roof, and I asked Raimond why the wall needed a roof. Raimond had a good explanation for everything, and I had already discovered the pleasure of drawing him out on just about anything that crossed my mind. He enjoyed our exchanges as much as I did. "Most walls have shards of glass firmly anchored in the mound of mortar that caps the wall," he said, "but tiles look better and work just as well as the broken glass." I then asked him about the shards of glass.

"At the time of the Revolution, the landowners behind their high walls thought they were fairly safe from rabble mobs, but for good measure, they capped the walls with broken glass set in mortar. There are no longer revolutionaries, but if a burglar climbs the wall and holds onto a tile, it just breaks and he falls to the ground, discouraged and thwarted, so the result is the same as if broken glass is used, and there is no blood to clean up." The explanation for the glass shards seemed plausible enough. I was confused about the revolution, but I let the matter drop.

Raimond changed his mind about risking damage to the elegant barrier atop the communal wall. Instead, he built a wooden "saddle" that sat astride the wall and spanned the tiles, leaving them intact. The saddle incorporated a level platform and even a low handrail, so we children wouldn't slip as we clambered from one ladder to the other. The platform also gave Raimond a place to which he could firmly nail the two ladders. He built these himself because he wanted flat rungs, like steps, set close together for the small children who would be using them. For good measure, he moved a large pile of composting leaves to the area directly under the ladder and talked the Poujet's gardener, Auguste, into doing the same on their side of the wall. "That way if you fall . . . ." Raimond had a way of not finishing cautionary sentences.

The project was finished several days before the start of school and was acclaimed on both sides of the wall as one of the great engineering marvels of the world. Brenda and I quickly became fast friends with Monique and Charlie, who came over to our side as often as we went to theirs. Just climbing across the wall provided a distinct thrill for us, and many a flimsy pretext was found to use the overpass. I soon gave it the formal name of *"La Passerelle Raimondoise,"* the "Raimond-ish Overpass." By the age of six, I had already acquired the French tendency to assign formal and pompous-sounding names to things and thought it sounded grownup to do so. I often saw Raimond watching us as we used his *passerelle*, beaming with pride and vicarious pleasure.

Raimond usually found time to do all sorts of things to help us in our play, in spite of his numerous chores around the house, the garden, and the kitchen. He was very easy going when he was doing something for us, acting as though he had nothing else to do. Nevertheless, he was really a ball of nerves. He had a wiry build, was forever smoking a Gauloise Bleue, and his way of moving was jumpy and somewhat high-strung. He turned down Father's suggestion that he obtain a driver's license because he maintained that he was too nervous to pass a driving test.

Raimond's continual state of nerves may have been because he lived in quiet terror of Françoise. Perhaps due to a previous indiscretion on Raimond's part, she was constantly suspicious of him and all his activities. He could expect to be in hot water if he visited with a neighboring gardener for more than a half hour. When it came to his comings and goings, he was on a short leash and Françoise had a short fuse. I don't want to give the impression that Françoise was mean-spirited. When Raimond didn't arouse her suspicions, she was pleasant and good-natured with him. And in relation to Brenda and me, she never lost her temper and was just as kind and patient as was Raimond.

On the first day of school, Monique, Charlie, Brenda and I gathered outside the Poujets' front gate. The bus was running late, and as we stood around waiting, anxious as are most children going off to a new school for the first time, I started a little game. At the sight of every vehicle that rounded the bend and started up the hill towards us, I cried out, "Here it is! This is it!" Peals of laughter would ensue as various decrepit and scruffy vehicles drove on past us. What we found so funny was that most of these trucks and vans must have dated back to World War I and were quite comical as they struggled on their way up the hill, gears grinding noisily, engines faltering as they shifted, and looking as if they weren't going to make it. Naturally, we were expecting a vehicle worthy of our status in society—nothing less than a gleaming *char-a-banc* (bus) with plush velveteen seats!

An unbelievable vehicle then appeared, more dilapidated and grubbier-looking than any we had seen thus far. It listed heavily to one side, one headlight had become detached and hung by its electric wire, torn strips of canvas-like material dangled from its roof, and it sounded as though it were in a death rattle. Once more, I called out, "*Le voilà!*" and we all laughed heartily as we watched this incredible vehicle approach us. It might once have been an elegant bus, but its windows were so dirty and cracked that we could not see inside. It obviously hadn't been washed in a decade and looked as if it had just come through a dust storm. It couldn't possibly be the bus we were waiting for.

But, to our amazement and dismay, the noisy grinding of its engine suddenly ceased as it came to a stop right in front of us. The driver leaned out of the window and asked if we were the Poujet family. It was indeed our long-awaited bus! The driver struggled for some time trying to open a balky door, then hopped down so as to lift us, one-by-one, onto the high running board and into the bus. Inside the bus were wicker benches or what had once been wicker benches. They were so broken and punched through that we literally sat on one or another of the small wood slats that had once supported the wicker. Some of the bus windows were cracked and everything about it was heavily soiled and battered.

Continuing on its rounds for about an hour, the bus coughed, sputtered and backfired, covering about six miles as it picked up other children. When we reached a hill far steeper than any yet encountered, the driver stopped the bus and called out, *"Allez les garçons! Sortez et poussez le car!"* ("Come on boys! Hop out and push the bus!") About twelve small boys climbed down from the bus and we pushed with all our might. We were among strangers, but our situation was so absurd that we couldn't help giggling together as we pushed; one boy even remarked on the stupidity of our struggle to attain a destination none of us really wanted to reach. The hill was steep, but we didn't have to push far before the street leveled off on the brow of a small hill. The old bus, even with our help, had barely made it, and just as it seemed to be rolling by itself, we felt it faltering. It came to a stop in front of a gate set in a high wall that bordered the street. The girls, who had remained on board, now dismounted, carrying their book satchels and those of the boys. The superannuated bus was apparently past repairing, for we pushed it like this every day, often in heavy rain or falling snow.

The entrance gate was imposing in its size and detail and was set in an equally impressive archway. The ironwork arch incorporated a sheet-metal scroll with an undulated outline meant to look like a large piece of ribbon fluttering in the breeze. The words *"Ecole Sugerre de Vaucresson"* were proudly emblazoned in gold lettering across its dull black finish. On either side of this archway were shields and crossed arrows tipped with gold points. The tips of the gate's iron bars were likewise painted gold. Surely, this property had to be an annex to the Palace of Versailles, only five miles distant. The two dozen children now stood before the gate in disbelief and wonder at the contrast between our dilapidated conveyance and the ornate splendor of our destination.

The bus driver, whom I now scrutinized for the first time, was wearing a grimy, gray bus driver's smock and an official-looking cap with gold-colored ornamentation. He opened the massive gate and, in a gruff, impatient voice, ordered the young children to follow him. Brenda and Charlie, who were both experiencing their first trip to school, were petrified by the bus driver's threatening tone and refused to budge. Charlie was whimpering, and Monique, who thus far had remained blasé throughout our expedition, now snapped angrily at Charlie, only making matters worse. The bus driver was already leading the group of children up the drive, apparently unaware of, or perhaps indifferent to, the little crisis he was leaving behind. I asked Monique to take my satchel and go on ahead. She did so gladly, looking relieved that she didn't have to be associated any further with her younger brother. She was a year older than I was and had already attended another school, so she was accustomed to being treated angrily by adults. I put one arm around Brenda's shoulders and gathered Charlie up under my other arm, and talked to them as reassuringly as I could, doing what Marcel had done for me on my first day of school. The two of them calmed down, and we began walking just as the bus driver shouted at us to hurry up.

Brenda, Charlie and I, now hand in hand, followed the other children along a wide gravel drive that zigzagged its way up a broad, grassy hill. We passed several well-kept flowerbeds, numerous ornamental trees and bushes, the latter well suited to concealing players in a game of hide-and-seek. Now reassured and excited by the sight of such a congenial garden, I pointed out the better hiding places to Brenda and Charlie as I led them up the sloping path.

At the top of this drive was a level, circular zone of gravel where, in times past, tired horses still harnessed to their carriages would have waited patiently while their owners sat on a nearby terrace, sipping tea. From this turnaround area, we proceeded up an elegant flight of granite steps to the aforementioned terrace and on to the entrance of the palace.

So far, everything about the place had indeed seemed palatial, but we were now abruptly brought down to earth by the building itself. It was really just a very large, ugly house, finished in that orange-colored *Meulière* stone masonry so popular in that part of France at the turn of the century. The building had numerous small pointed turrets, and all sorts of ornate wooden decorations protruding here, there, and everywhere, or dangling from the eaves. It was the French version of Victorian gingerbread architecture.

Once inside, we stood in the dimly lit hallway while a teacher issued us the usual black school smocks. Another teacher appeared and assigned a numbered coat hook in the front hall to each of the arriving students. We were read the rules that applied during recess. We were to place our book satchels on the tiled floor beneath our own numbered hook and we were not to remove our black smocks during recess.

My classroom, with its single, small window set well above eye-level, a black slate-tiled floor and drab, gray walls, lacked any warmth or intimacy. For sheer grimness, it reminded me of the first school I had attended, and while that classroom had been little more than a shed, this one was nothing less than a dungeon. My second school, with its wide studio windows overlooking the Paris skyline, had permanently spoiled me. Here, there were no communist riots on the Place de la Concorde to watch, no mating pigeons doing their mysterious dance on the roof next door—absolutely nothing to distract me from my daily drudgery. All I could see out of that narrow, north-facing window was a scrap of sky, often dreary and overcast. I felt trapped.

I was looking forward to recess, happily anticipating playing games on that huge entrance lawn, but here, too, bitter disappointment awaited me. The convivial lawn was off limits to students. Instead, all of the hundred or so children in the school were confined to that carriage turn-around, a mere fifty feet in diameter. It was so crowded that making one's way across it was like walking across a crowded jail yard.

On rainy days, recess arrangements were scarcely better. The teachers herded us into a coal cellar lit by a single bare bulb hanging from the ceiling. Although this vast cellar was mostly empty, there was one huge pile of coal roughly at its center. We were ordered to form a circle around the coal pile, holding hands. Just as in the first school I had attended, we skipped along sideways and danced up and down while singing songs. No attempt had been made to remove the vestiges of coal that remained in the corners and along the walls of this cavernous room. A fine black dust clung to the bricks and to the cobwebs that festooned them. If we touched anything, our hands became smudged with grime. I must now confess that I indulged a furtive pleasure on these occasions.

At the time, I was mesmerized by the coal merchant who delivered coal to our house. He carried large sacks of coal on his shoulders and wore a special leather hood to keep the coal dust out of his hair. Beneath the hood saturated with coal dust, the only parts of his face that weren't pitch black were his eyeballs and his teeth, which shone a brilliant white in contrast. His total blackness fascinated me, and for some dark reason, I envied him. When someone asked me what I wanted to be when I grew up, I invariably answered, "*charbonnier!*" ("coal delivery man!"), to the considerable consternation of Mother. When I discovered a little later that my face could get just as black if I were a locomotive driver, I immediately switched my allegiance from coal delivery to locomotive driving. Driving a locomotive had to be a lot more fun than hauling sacks of coal.

For this reason, the subterranean recess periods held a certain fascination for me. When I became filthy, no one caterwauled and scolded me. In a coal cellar, one could expect to become grimy. Those black smocks absorbed and concealed most of the black dust. The teacher always made a concerted effort to get the odd "piglets," such as myself, cleaned up before sending us home. When she scrubbed my face and hands muttering, "What a dirty little boy! Oh you filthy little boy!" she was merely stating an interesting and accurate fact. It didn't bother me in the least; her words were music to my ears. If I'd been a cat, I'd have been purring. Of course, I never told Mother of such delights, as she might have found a way to put a stop to them.

Our book satchels traveled with us wherever we went in the school, except during recess. They not only contained our various workbooks but also an elongated wooden box with a sliding lid. The wooden box was for our ink (dip) pens. We also carried a ruler for neatly underlining, in ink of course, at the bottom of any column of numbers that we were totaling. A long multiplication required two underlinings.

There were other important items in our book satchels: a blotter and *un essuie-plume,* a pen-wiper, which consisted of a stack of small, square pieces of cloth stitched together at their center. Without these invaluable tools, no student could hope to lead a clean and blameless life in this world of dip pens and indelible black ink. I have already hinted that I was not overly obsessed with cleanliness, but I don't want to give the impression that I was a total and continual mess. My attitude in this matter was quite clear, at least to me: I arrived clean and left clean, and that seemed to me to be about fair. I felt that what happened in between these two events was strictly my business.

Scholastically, my classmates marched doggedly forward, with me, as usual, bringing up the rear guard. Arithmetic continued to be my best subject, though even here I was by no means in the vanguard. At the age of six, we were multiplying five-digit numbers by five digit-numbers, doing long divisions, and using the "proof-by-nine" to verify the answers in both processes.

We were expected to use our rulers wherever a line should appear in these problems. I found this infernally difficult because the ink flowed under the ruler and smudged when I moved the ruler off the paper. In such cases, I was supposed to try again on a new sheet of paper—provided this was the first underlining of the multiplication problem. Often, I found myself working on my fourth sheet of paper before I even started the actual multiplying. So much for the vanguard! If I got past that first underlining in a multiplication problem, it would be clear sailing until I reached the second underlining. At this stage of the proceedings, there was no trying again; my unremitting creation of ink smudges haunted my life. The proof-by-nine showed I had the right answers, but the smudges branded me as a failure and earned me zeros.

We were introduced to French history and geography. I remember an engraving of Louis the XIV in my history book. He was wearing full-length white stockings that went all the way up to some bouffant knickers. On his long white legs, I inked in some men's argyle socks, supported at the calf by modern V-shaped men's garters like the ones Father wore. When the teacher saw my artwork, she scolded me severely for lacking respect. I tried explaining that I was concerned about King Louis getting cold feet and that I meant no disrespect. She didn't buy that, and I had to spend two whole recess periods writing out a hundred times over, "I will not lack respect for *Les Grands Personnages Historiques.*"

We ate lunch at the school, and the food was as dreary as was almost everything else about that place. Over all, the memories of my days there are not happy, though I did enjoy the camaraderie of my fellow students, who were friendly and quick to make humorous comments about our teachers and the various silly routines to which we were subjected.

Charlie Poujet was almost two years younger than I was, so we were not in the same class, but he dogged me like my shadow during recess. He was a pale and timid little boy who continually needed reassurance. I liked being a big brother to him, and, because I played that role well, I soon became the leader of a group of the younger boys.

As such, my duties were to decide what game we would play and to make assignments as to who would do what. We might be a band of cowboys fighting our way westward or a squadron of airmen dogfighting over the trenches. For these games to work well, it required planning and coordination of the participants as we "flew," arms outstretched, around the small play yard making loud airplane noises. And there were tactics and maneuvers involved if other groups of kids joined in. It was all good-natured play and devoid of any rough stuff. We used our hands and arms to represent pistols and rifles, and the cry was *"Piff! Paff! Tu es mort!"* the French version of "Bang! Bang! You're dead!"

One rainy, gloomy day, in the spring of 1937, I found myself in math class making my third try at underlining in a large multiplication problem. Failing once more to accomplish a smudge-free line and filled with despair and exasperation, I think I quietly went crazy. I remember becoming fascinated with the amount of ink that already besmirched my thumb and index finger. With a little wiping and smearing, the ink soon spread to my entire right hand and, with a couple of discreet dips in the inkwell, to my left hand as well. From there it was an easy leap of daring to wipe some ink onto my face. I had no mirror, of course, but I was sure I was achieving something quite special.

The teacher was reading a book instead of keeping her usual vigilance over the class, thus allowing me enough time to achieve my goal, which was now fully clear to me: a totally black face, for indeed, the ink was jet black. Just when I felt certain I had completed the job, there was a piercing shriek from the teacher, who, for a moment, looked as if she had seen the devil incarnate.

What followed amazed me. The teacher left the classroom in great haste, slamming the door behind her as if she feared the apparition would follow her. At first, my fellow-students sat in stunned silence, pondering what might have caused this strange occurrence. Since my seat was in the back of the class, they had no way of knowing. But someone eventually turned around, and his exclamatory gasp caused the other children to turn and stare in disbelief. Soon, their gaping wonder turned into smiles and then to a murmuring awe. For one brief moment, I felt as if I were basking in a sort of collective admiration. It was a short-lived thrill. The door opened and a large group of adults—Madame Jaumont (the principal), my teacher and several others, and even the janitor, the gardener, and the school cook—streamed in to stare at me. At first, I think they didn't know who I was. Perhaps a total stranger had wandered in. Surely, no student of the Ecole Sugerre would be capable of such a dastardly act!

Unfortunately, my teacher and the principal knew all too well who I was, and in short order, I was led out of the class by Madame Jaumont, who guided me by holding onto my ear, quite possibly the only part of me still unstained. Held at arm's length and being removed from the company of my peers, I felt as though I had become contagious.

Our procession—Madame Jaumont and I in the lead, and all the other adults bringing up the rear—marched right past my anticipated destination, the principal's office, and headed on down a side corridor that was out of bounds to students. Our little cavalcade stopped at a door labeled *remise* (storeroom). Madame Jaumont unlocked the door and unceremoniously discarded me inside the *remise* by brusquely releasing my ear as soon as she had dragged me across the threshold. She ordered me to stay there, pulled a string that turned off the ceiling light and slammed the door shut. I heard the key turn in the lock, and, among the words spoken outside the door, I heard someone say, *"Il peut rester là, en prison."* ("He can stay there, in prison.")

In the overpowering darkness of that closet, the possibility that I had been truly naughty began to sink in. Until that moment I had floated, entranced and above it all, savoring the amusement and admiration of my peers and intoxicated by the shock and outrage of the adults. But now I began to wonder how serious my misdeed might be and how much trouble I was in. Had I caused anyone any harm? No, but on the other hand, hadn't I heard talk of prison? I knew very little about prisons. Mother had once pointed out a prison as we drove through an unfamiliar part of Paris; she had said it was where they put really bad people. Had I been really bad?

There was in my history book a chapter about a prison called La Bastille, where the peasants had put the nobles, who were also supposedly really bad. Would I be moved from this closet to La Bastille in a tumbrel, as shown in my history book illustration? And after prison came the guillotine. Wasn't that the eventual fate of people they put in La Bastille? A second picture in the history book came back to me in all its gory clarity, of the guillotine with a headless man kneeling and bent over at its base, blood pouring out of his severed neck like water from a jug, his head lying in a basket beneath him. But now, in my mind's eye, the face on that head was completely smudged with black ink.

As these images coursed through my imagination, I began to panic. I wailed and pounded on the door with my fists, but no one came. Eventually, I calmed down and resigned myself to the idea that this closet was indeed a prison.

A little light entered through the crack under the door, and my eyes must have grown accustomed to the near-darkness. I could just make out some brooms, mops, and pails. I turned over a pail and sat down on it to ponder my fate. The smell of cleaning products and moldy wet-mops was overpowering. The place was cold and dank, for the weather outdoors was wintry, and the closet had no heating. It felt as though darkness itself formed the prison walls around me. If I could only turn on the light! I arose and, standing on tiptoes, waved my arms over my head hoping to find the pull-string for the light, but it was out of my reach.

My misadventure had occurred during the first period of the day, so if I weren't taken to La Bastille or the guillotine first, I had a long wait until Mother came to fetch me in the late afternoon. Or perhaps there were rules that said I would have to stay a certain period of time in prison, in which case Mother would have no say in the matter. She would be forced to leave me here, and I would have to stay in this dreadful little room after everyone else went home.

I heard the mid-morning recess bell and the distant, boisterous voices of my schoolmates as they went out to play. None of them knew where I was, I supposed. Would they care, or miss my game planning? I realized for the first time how much I enjoyed the recess periods. I wondered if I were now forever banished from association with *mes camarades*—I felt desperately lonely. The bell for the end of recess rang, and I banged some more on the door, hoping someone passing by might hear me. However, only the janitor ever came by this door, so my pounding and cries were in vain. I now pinned my hopes on the lunch bell. Surely, they would let me out then, if only to eat. That event, too, came and went with the rest of the world seemingly indifferent to my plight.

Sitting on the upturned pail, I pulled my smock over my bare knees, for I was becoming cold and had started to shiver. In an effort to keep warm while sitting on the pail, I wrapped my arms around my knees, tucked my hands under my armpits and put my head on my knees so that I formed a tight ball.

Sometime later, I awoke with a start as the door opened. It was Madame Jaumont who ordered me to follow her to the school office. There, I saw Mother and ran into her open arms, crying and begging her not to let them keep me in prison.

After a moment, Mother released me and, sizing me up at arm's length, exclaimed, "*Mon Dieu!* What have you done to yourself—and why?"

I had completely forgotten that dirty little detail, as well as the various excuses and explanations I had conjured up and rehearsed in my mind during my imprisonment in the broom closet. My best explanation was that I had stooped over to tie my shoelace and, while doing so, had accidentally bumped the desk quite hard. The bumping had caused the ink to jump out of the ink well like a fountain, and it had hit me square in the face. I had also contemplated a second scenario: the sleeve of my smock had snagged on the hinged lid of the inkwell, so that the sleeve had become soaked in ink. When I had raised my hand to ask the teacher for help, the ink-soaked sleeve had dribbled all over my face, and since it stung my eyes, I had tried to wipe it off. I had debated the relative merits of both fibs but had not been able to decide which one sounded more plausible.

Now, under the cold stare of Madame Jaumont, neither of these stories seemed credible to me. Besides, she was already speaking, even before I had a chance to answer Mother's question.

"This child is obsessed with becoming a filthy mess. We simply can't have him setting such a bad example for the other students. We have been watching him for some time, and he appears incorrigible. We want nothing more to do with him. We therefore consider him expelled and ask you to leave now and to take him with you, before classes are over."

Mother got out her old saw about being well rid of a situation in which I was under the influence of humorless teachers. Somehow, her words didn't ring as true this time as they had when she had first used this speech at the Ecole de la rue Pradier and, judging by her grim expression, she must have been a little short of humor herself at that moment.

My book satchel had been placed beneath my hook in the front hall, and I gathered it on the way out. Mother and I walked down the long, winding driveway without saying a word. Then she and I sat silently in the car, waiting for Brenda and the two Poujet kids to be let out at the normal time, which wasn't far off.

After a while, Mother asked, "What on earth was going through your head when you committed this *bêtise* (stupidity)?"

"I was getting angrier and angrier because I couldn't underline without making ink smudges. Then I just gave up. I was fed up. After that, I don't know what happened. I think I went crazy. There was ink on my fingers, and I started painting more ink all over my hands, just to sort of even things out. Then, it just seemed like fun to go on, so I painted my face as well."

That seemed to satisfy Mother. She put her arm around me and gave me a reassuring squeeze. "You know Alain, you're going to be seven years old in two weeks, and that's *l'age de la raison* (the age of reason). Once you reach that age you can't go on doing *un*reasonable things such as painting your face black. So it's just as well you got it out of your system. And now you've also learned that such *bêtises*, though fun at the time, aren't worth all the trouble they cause you later—are they?"

I couldn't have agreed with her more. Nevertheless, did Madame Jaumont know that I wasn't even seven years old and hadn't yet reached "the age of reason"? Surely, this was a logical explanation for my *bêtise*. Under those circumstances, wasn't it unfair to put me in prison the way she had? That prison business was still preying on my mind. I very much wanted Mother's clarification of the matter and framed the question for her, adding, "Was I really, *really* bad? Would I have been forced to stay in prison longer if I were seven instead of six years old?"

Mother was puzzled by this question and asked me what I meant. I gave her a full account of my eventful day. Suddenly, she was furious at the school and the way they had treated me. "They left you in a dark, cold broom closet all that time, without even letting you out for lunch? That's criminal— you wait here in the car!" She got out and walked back up the hill. Not long after, she returned with Brenda in tow. She had apparently given Madame Jaumont an earful, and had decided that Brenda, too, should not remain a student in that humorless and ruthless school.

A little later, Monique and Charlie joined us in the car, and we drove home. The two of them sat in the back seat of the car, one on each side of me, but keeping their distance as much as possible, staring straight ahead, and not daring to look at me or say a word. My face was still as black as the ace of spades.

The pain of that day wasn't over yet. The ink still had to be removed from my hands and face. Mother scrubbed me with a washcloth soaked in lemon juice, intermittently rinsing me off and applying olive oil to sooth my raw skin. Several times the lemon juice got into my eyes, causing me to shriek with pain. Thank God, I would soon be seven, and there would no longer be any danger of my being tempted into another *bêtise* like this one!

Two weeks later, I received a fountain pen for my seventh birthday. Having now reached "the age of reason," I believed that I was automatically protected from committing any *bêtises,* as one is protected from becoming wet when under an umbrella. The possibilities for *bêtises* might be all around me, but I would never be tempted again. I was fascinated by the idea of a magical age at which such a change would abruptly take place. I pressed Mother for more details, which prompted her to name two more magical "ages" I would attain. At fourteen, I would reach *l'age de la sagesse* (the age of wisdom), and at twenty-one, *l'age de la majorité.* Thus, I assumed, until I was fourteen, I would be reasonable but not necessarily wise. At fourteen, I would be mysteriously imbued with wisdom, and that would make the going easier, but I would still lack "majority," whatever that was. Like reason and wisdom, it was bound to be something helpful in dealing with life. At twenty-one I would emerge like a butterfly from my chrysalis, both reasonable and wise—a shining, splendid, and complete adult possessing full and glorious "majority." It all sounded so exciting and reassuring, and I earnestly looked forward to these momentous events in my life. At the age of seven, I took these words as the gospel truth because they gave me milestones on which I could depend. Father and Mother were leading what seemed to me an idyllic life, and I was now convinced that before I could lead a full and exciting adult life such as theirs, I was still faced with a long and arduous struggle before I reached "majority," the boundary between childhood and adulthood.

After the inking incident, the Poujets would no longer talk to me, or even to Brenda. Monique had been in my class and probably had not painted too rosy a picture of the incident to her mother. She was a prissy little girl, overly neat and fastidious, not the type who would have the slightest sympathy for the likes of me. I suppose I was viewed by Madame Poujet as unreliable and possibly a bad influence on her children. The *Passerelle Raimondoise* remained in place, but when I climbed over the wall and tried to talk to Charlie, he did not reply and ran indoors as if he had seen an apparition. Auguste, their gardener, came out and, from a safe distance, ordered me to climb back over the wall. When I told Mother what had transpired, her comment was, "It's outrageous. They're treating you like a rabid dog."

Monique and Charlie had been our only friends, and I sorely missed playing with them. I kept on going over the wall about once a week, but each time I was rebuffed the same way.

Although the garden at Ville-d'Avray was a pleasant and spacious one, it was also a solitary enclosure for Brenda and me. Our house bore the name of "La Closerie", and not without good reason. The word "*closerie*" means "small estate," but its phonetic proximity to the adjective *clos* suggests something closed in, which the property certainly was.

The only access to La Closerie from the street was by a two-hundred-foot-long alley bordered by high walls. Large trees on both sides of this alley obscured the sky and gave the entrance to the property an air of dark mystery. The turnaround at our end of the alley was open to the sky, its sunny brightness contrasting with the deep shade of the approach, and I recall thinking, as we entered from the street, that this driveway resembled a tunnel leading to an enchanted place. Upon reaching the turnaround, I could see our lush and verdant garden through the bars of the front gate.

Our flower-filled garden was surrounded by an elegant stone wall and by other neighboring properties so that it had no frontage onto any street. In the center of the garden was a house that, with its symmetry and blue slate mansard roof, resembled a miniature chateau in the classical French style. It had been built by one of

Louis XIV's courtiers, over 200 years before. The garden surrounding the house covered about two acres and comprised abundant flower beds, a sweeping front lawn, several majestic trees of great height, an orchard with numerous varieties of fruit trees, a generous vegetable garden and a huge greenhouse. A wide gravel path curved its way to the front door and on around the house. The rest of the garden was criss-crossed with smaller gravel paths, many bordered by low boxwood hedges. Lilac bushes and other shrubs arranged in clusters on the spacious lawn provided ideal hiding places and little "nesting places" that were ideal for Brenda and me when we played house or hide-and-seek.

My favorite garden path was bordered on both sides by a row of closely planted chestnut trees, giving the appearance of a covered gallery as it paralleled the east and north walls of the property and made a sweeping curve where the two walls met. As I ambled down this lane in its deliciously cool shade on a warm spring day, I had the impression of being in a cloister. The chestnut trees formed the columns of the cloister, and the sun-dappled lawn and bright flower beds visible between the trees were the cloister's courtyard. This shadowed lane created a pleasant balance of light and shade in the overall aspect of the garden, and the chestnut trees hid the surrounding walls, making the garden seem larger than it was.

The high walls around the garden blocked all contact with our neighbors, but did not stop the sound of children playing beyond them. Of the two neighboring properties on our south side, one was a large and handsome edifice similar in architectural style to our own house. This once luxurious mansion had been turned into an orphanage. From a third-story window of the children's home, the kids watched me playing my solitary games. They often called out to me, but I never answered because Mother didn't want me to associate with them and had ordered me to ignore them. She maintained that the orphans were *mal élevés* (rude or uncouth). I obeyed her injunction and the price for this was an occasional catcall from the orphans. When I heard the happy sounds of their playing in the next-door playground, I sometimes wondered if it might not be more fun to be an orphan.

The other neighbor along the south wall was a White Russian called "Romanov." For reasons unknown to me, he didn't warrant the title of *Monsieur* Romanov, perhaps because he and his family were dirt poor. Mother explained that their poverty was because Romanov had far too many children. They lived in a one-story tarpaper shack on a small plot of ground, originally part of the estate that was now the orphanage. We once had a closer look at the Romanov family when Mother took Brenda and me around to deliver some old clothes as a Christmas gift. About twelve children, some very young, came tumbling merrily out of their tiny hovel when we arrived. They were dressed in rags and were conspicuously filthy but didn't look underfed. We were invited to come into their abode, but Mother declined because, as she later explained, she was afraid we might get fleas or lice. It wasn't much safer outside. Their dog was friendly and severely mangy. The mutt took an immediate liking to me and kept trying to lick my face. It was all I could do to fend of his advances.

The shack they lived in was so small that it was difficult to imagine that it could contain even two rooms. Mother later commented that, judging by its shape and style of construction, it must once have been a chicken coop on the larger estate and she wondered whether they had running water and electricity. She also postulated that the children had to have been spaced less than a year apart in age.

The Romanov brood used to sit on the ridge of their shack's peaked roof, looking like a flock of bedraggled crows. From this roost they could see over the wall and watch me play when I was at that end of our garden. I wasn't supposed to talk to them either, but they were much nearer than the orphans, and I often spoke to them if Raimond or Mother were not around. I always found the Romanov children friendly and engaging. I was dying to know what *mal élevé* was really all about, and I was even somewhat disappointed to discover that they were not rude at all. I very much wanted to discuss my discovery with Mother, but fearing I would be scolded for having talked to the Romanovs, I never did.

The father of this large brood later made a name for himself by inventing a silent aircraft engine. It was before the days of radar, and approaching enemy planes were successfully detected long before they were within earshot by means of gigantic "ear trumpets." I saw his plane, *Le Silencieux Romanov,* at the Paris Air Show of 1938. And indeed, the plane maneuvered over us without making a sound. People mistook it for a glider, but we could clearly see the plane was maintaining altitude through the use of its propeller which, according to Father, had to turn very slowly for the plane to remain silent. Romanov was a freelance inventor, which provided an additional and more interesting explanation for his abject poverty than Mother's version. The extensive publicity over his invention produced no noticeable change in the Romanov lifestyle.

The garden at La Closerie was Raimond's pride and joy. He worked out there a good part of each day, often in the rain. Through his efforts, *le jardin potager* (the vegetable garden) produced a generous supply of vegetables all year round. It consisted of four square growing-beds, each one thirty feet across. Each bed was fully bordered with low, boxwood hedges, which Raimond maintained were impassable to snails, thus avoiding the need for snail poison.

The *escargots* gathered in profusion on a nearby section of the wall that never saw the sun, and where Raimond enticed them by placing vegetable scraps at the base of the wall. He made sure his snails felt at home by hosing their snail-breeding grounds during dry spells. Occasionally, he chose the plumpest ones and he and Françoise regaled themselves with a plate of *escargots à l'ail* (snails done in garlic butter). Both Mother and Father disapproved of this dish because the whole house, and Raimond himself, reeked of garlic for two days following this repast, so that this *dégustation* (devouring with gusto) only happened when my parents were away. I don't remember being bothered by the garlic smell, but I do remember watching the *dégustation* of snails and feeling a bit queasy.

When my parents were away, Brenda and I ate in the kitchen with Raimond and Françoise. I enjoyed these meals because Raimond never failed to be entertaining. In truth, he was a lot more entertaining than our parents were at table.

Raimond and Françoise always mopped their plates clean with *mie de pain* (the non-crust part of bread), then turned the plates over and used the bottom side of the plate for dessert. I admired the practice as an eminently sensible one, but I got nowhere when I advocated its use to my parents during Sunday dinner in the presence of guests. No one present even thought the idea worthy of comment, and a prolonged hush prevailed until Mother brought up another subject. When I glanced at Raimond, I thought I detected a restrained smile and, when he saw that I was looking at him, he gave me the hint of a wink.

I heard more on the matter from Mother in private. "If you think that following the example of people less well brought up than you is a good idea, we might have you eat in the dining room when I am not home, with Raimond serving you there." Thankfully, Mother never followed up on her threat, but I became cautious about revealing to her much of what Raimond said or did when she wasn't around.

Perhaps because Mother wanted more time to herself and felt she couldn't burden Raimond and Françoise with watching over us, the hunt for a governess resumed and before too long, she stumbled on the person who would be our fourth and last governess.

Minette Danglosse was a young woman who lived right there in Ville-d'Avray. She must have been in her late twenties and belonged to a class of women now nearly extinct. She had no education beyond high school, had received no training for anything, had no special skills, no income, no job, and lived with her mother, a widow of only modest means. Minette's stated goal in life was to get married. By her own admission, she was too busy roaming the landscape in search of a husband to become involved in any kind of a full-time job, even if she had possessed the necessary skills.

155

The arrangement was that Minette would continue living in her own home and would come to our house only when Mother wanted to be away for any length of time. It was understood that Minette's services would only be required two to three times a week at most, occasionally overnight, and that she would always get at least a full day's advance notice when she was needed. This arrangement provided Minette with a little pocket money, while allowing her the flexibility to continue her search for a husband, something she joked about freely and frequently.

"Minette" is the diminutive of "Minou," a term of endearment and a name often given to a kitten. However, there was nothing diminutive about the buxom Minette, who was quite statuesque and just this side of plump.

I was especially struck by the beauty of her wavy mane of golden blonde hair. It must have been an especially warm and sunny spring, for Minette generally arrived at our house attired in extremely brief shorts and an even briefer halter, straight from having played tennis. In Ville-d'Avray, a staid, old-fashioned, dressed-in-black Catholic village that had never seen bare thighs and midriffs in broad daylight, the brevity of Minette's attire and her deportment generated no small amount of talk. Mother paid no heed to such gossip and eventually became fast friends with Minette, whom she found lively, entertaining, and a bit vulgar in her speech. Vulgarity is a characteristic that doesn't easily offend or shock most Belgians, even those who, like Mother, did not normally indulge in it. My own recollection of Minette is that she was heavily tanned and usually glistened with sweat or a sweet-smelling sun-tanning oil, I can't remember which—perhaps it was both. She was a bouncy, cheerful woman whose presence lit up a room. She laughed a lot and easily.

Minette was a *laissez faire* governess, so she and I soon came to terms and enjoyed an easygoing time when we were together, usually on Wednesday and Saturday afternoons, when we only had school in the mornings. When I had homework to do, she was not strict or hard driving, and possibly some of my poor performance at school could have been laid at her door. But who was I to complain? Her attitude in watching over Brenda and me at play was equally lax, so I did a lot of exploring and experimenting with things that Mother or Pia would never have tolerated. I made up for what I wasn't learning in school by what I was discovering in these games. I'm referring to such activities as climbing very tall trees, building "sand" castles in the dark, rich soil of the vegetable garden, and playing with the garden hose to create rivers, dams and lakes, until I was soaking wet and a muddy mess. Minette helped me clean up and change my wet clothes without criticism or complaint. All cleaning up took place before Mother returned, which prevented discovery of what (in Mother's eyes) might have been unreasonable misdeeds. While I conducted my mischief outdoors, "Tante Minette" ("Aunt Minette", as she liked to be called) lounged indoors, reading romantic novels, occasionally glancing out the window, and waving and smiling at me.

Minette would sometimes take Brenda and me to her house and leave us in the care of her elderly mother while she went off on what she called "errands." Mother eventually heard that these were really *des petits rendezvous clandestins et inattendus* (brief, clandestine, and unplanned meetings), as she delicately described them to me, decades later. Having to stay at Madame Danglosse's house always made Brenda and me uneasy because she was a mystic and clairvoyant who talked of little else besides her experiences with the supernatural. Ghosts and poltergeists, she maintained, frequently visited the Danglosse household. Her house was unusually dark and gloomy, a spooky kind of place. Her black clothing, her tattered and disheveled look, suggested a witch down on her luck, and the only thing that kept this image of her from being totally convincing was her adiposity. I always thought of witches as being skinny and shriveled up. Once Minette had left the premises, Madame Danglosse shuffled her Tarot cards and did her best to amuse us by telling us our fortunes. Brenda and I sat there saucer-eyed, expecting a ghost to appear at any moment, but none ever did.

It was Minette who talked Mother into taking riding lessons. The two of them went off to *L'Académie d'Equitation Petipas,* a riding academy in nearby Versailles, leaving Brenda and me with

Raimond and Françoise. After several weeks of lessons, the riding proficiency of the Petipas students improved to the point where their instructor organized an equestrian gymkhana. Family and friends were invited.

On the day of the show, Brenda must have stayed at home, perhaps because of a cold, for I remember going to this event without her. Mother showed me where to sit in the bleachers and told me to stay there until she came back to get me. It was the first time I found myself alone in the midst of total strangers, and I remember it well.

Capitaine Petipas, a retired and bewhiskered cavalry captain, excessively bow-legged from decades of riding, or perhaps from rickets, was the academy's owner and sole instructor. He started the performance that day by having the students make their horses do a strange in-place trotting which he called "*faire le petit pas,*" a performance that was apparently his trademark.

After doing an assortment of similar exercises, the group of about two dozen riders started to trot in close formation. They were going around a large, oval indoor paddock that had once been part of a special training facility for the French Army Cavalry. A fair-sized crowd of spectators was seated on bleachers within this spacious, enclosed building.

By coincidence, I believe, Mother was among the lead riders of the group and seemed to be doing fine. After the riders had trotted around the oval several times, the horses cantered around the arena displaying fine form. Then Capitaine Petipas blew his whistle sharply, and all the horses simultaneously broke into a gallop. Almost as suddenly, Mother seemed to be sliding to the back of her horse, and there, without anything to hold onto, she fell off. There was an audible gasp from the spectators, and my immediate thought was of Mother being trampled to death by the twenty horses that had been following her. I watched in horror as the horses kept on galloping, passing over Mother as if she weren't there.

All the spectators stood up, and I could no longer see what was happening. I pushed my way forward through the crowd, wailing in alarm and anguish. During my struggle to reach the front row I heard the people start to cheer and applaud. When I broke clear of the crowd, I was stunned to discover the cause of the cheering. Mother was standing up where she had fallen. All the horses had come to a stop some distance beyond her. I couldn't understand or believe what I was seeing. Had she perhaps performed a deliberate stunt?

Capitaine Petipas was now running towards Mother, who was looking dazed and disoriented. When he reached her, he held her by the shoulders and shook her, as if trying to coax from her an answer to some question he was asking. Finally, he announced boldly, "Madame Holmes is all right! She has a bruised shoulder, but she will remount and continue with the show!"

The crowd clapped and cheered once more as Mother whispered some discreet words to Capitaine Petipas. Then she left the arena, apparently having indicated to the good captain that she had no intention of remounting and continuing. She had dislocated her shoulder and needed medical attention.

Forty years later, reminiscing (in English) about this incident, Mother told me her side of the story.

"I was trotting along very well when all of a sudden my horse shooted out underneath me—I don't know why—and was leaving me to fall off behind him, which I did by falling on my shoulder and on my back. Suddenly I was seeing all these brown shining stomachs flying over me and thinking one of them is going to land in my face. But no! The hoofs were flying fast by my head, so close one *froled* [coined word, meaning grazed] me, landing on my hairs and pulling them when it pushed them into the soft floor of the *areen* [coined word, intended to mean arena]. They all were being careful in not putting their horseshoes on me. I thought they were going on forever, and I thought I am probably going to die before they all have passed over me. They were old horses already retired from the French cavalry so they were all well intrained and were used to people falling down from on top of them. Capitaine Petipas told this to me later. Finally they had all gone by me and I realize that I am still alive, so I should now stand up before they come around the areen one more time to ride over me, and everybody started clapping as if I had done a marvelous thing, which I had not. What is so marvelous about falling off a horse? It was all the horses that had done the marvelous thing in not galloping their hoofs on me—don't you think?"

"Maybe they were clapping for the horses," I teased.

"Of course! You are right! I had not thought of that!" Mother said, laughing heartily.

That was the last time she went riding, but not on account of the mishap (which she said instilled in her a high degree of respect for French cavalry horses), but because of a strange episode which happened not long after the riding accident.

Minette's mother held a dinner party and a séance. After dinner, the guests sat around Madame Danglosse's large, oak dining table that had been cleared but was still draped with the tablecloth. Around the table were seated my parents, two other guests, Minette, her brother, Xavier, and Minette's mother. (Madame Danglosse was a widow, so it's quite possible her deceased husband was present as a ghost). They all placed their hands palm down on the top of the table while Madame Danglosse went into a trance intended to invoke the spirits that haunted her house. Here was Mother's version of the séance, as told to me in English many years later:

"We sat there for fifteen minutes in silence total, wondering what is happening, except that Madame Danglosse was talking sometimes to her *revenants* (ghosts) in a *lugubre* voice. Then this large, round, heavy table was suddenly lifting itself a little bit from the floor, floating with all of our hands just lying on it. Then Madame Danglosse said, 'I have reached them, is there something you want to ask them?' She was talking to all of us in the room now, with her habitual voice, of course.

"Dan always likes to joke people who are believing in *revenants*, and he said to Madame Danglosse, 'Should Jenny ever ride a horse again?' After many minutes of silence, the table started floating in a horizontal way, turning first on the left and then towards the right and back on the left again. Madame Danglosse announced that this means very strongly 'No.'

"I was quite angry with Dan," Mother said. "He was asking a question which was my right to ask and not his, though I never would be asking such a silly question. So I asked immediately to Madame Danglosse, 'Can an answer be believed which is about me and which I did not myself ask and is a silly question which I would never be asking?'

"And right away the table shakes in a horizontal way again, left and right like before, which she already said to us means 'No!'

"So I told Dan, 'You tried to joke the *revenants* and now they are joking you!' and everyone laughed, and Madame Danglosse said, 'Shhh! *Revenants* don't like laughing. They might leave us!'

"But Dan just said to me, still in laughing, 'If it's *your* right to ask a question, why don't *you* ask the *revenant* the *same* question?'

"So I did ask. This time the table shakes in a horizontal way again meaning I must not ride, which was an answer I did not at all like, and I made a face which Dan could see.

"Now Dan was saying it's his turn again to be asking questions and he said to the table—I mean to the *revenant*—'Is the answer to Jenny's question a correct answer and one which she must believe?'

"This time the table moves up and down strongly. Madame Danglosse now says to me, 'Because Dan is asking the question that way, it means definitely 'yes', and you must believe the answer, because if you do not, you will have a terrible accident!' This answer was clear to me, and I decided then and right there not to be riding again, although I was very angry because I did not believe there would be any danger for me at all if Dan had not first asked the silly question and forced me to ask it again, and the *revenant* would never know that I am riding again with no danger."

Mother continued her tale. "When the *revenants* have gone and the table again is on the floor and the séance is finished, Dan lifted a corner of the tablecloth, and he said he was seeing there only the four legs. I reply to him in laughing, 'What do you expect to find there? Some *revenants*?'

"He bended down and looked under the table once more. Then he shaked his head, and he said, 'This table is too heavy to be lifting with just a few knees—I just don't understand how she is doing this.' Dan was refusing to believe they were real *revenants*. Which I did."

And so it was that Mother ended her riding. But Minette kept on with her lessons; most of her fellow riding students were eligible young men. "I'm not going to miss a chance like that!" she explained.

Shortly after the séance, Mother told Brenda and me about her experience with the spirit world. Upon learning that ghosts had been able to lift a heavy oak table at Madame Danglosse's house, I resolved I would never set foot in the place again. The next time Minette took us to her mother's home for safekeeping, I dug in my heels and vehemently refused to cross the threshold. After a futile struggle with me, Minette tried to coax Brenda into entering, also to no avail. Tante Minette was furious, but eventually capitulated and parked the two of us a short distance away at the house of Madame Saïce [rhymes with "mice"].

Madame Saïce, whom Brenda and I already knew, was only a slight improvement over Madame Danglosse, but at least her house wasn't haunted. Madame Saïce was a graying woman whose usual attire was a dark gray, pinstriped, somewhat soiled and tattered tailored suit that no longer quite fit because she had gained weight over the many years she had owned it. She was an elderly spinster who was guardian and surrogate mother to her niece, Simone. The latter was the love child of Philippe Narnier, Ville-d'Avray's only doctor. A month after the baby was born, her mother left Simone with Madame Saïce on the pretext that she had errands to run, and had then disappeared, never to be seen again. Docteur Narnier, Simone's alleged father and a bachelor, had turned to Madame Saïce for help. The child had been in her care ever since.

At the time, I didn't know that Simone's parents were not married; I knew only that she had no mother, that Docteur Narnier was her father and that Madame Saïce was her aunt. I assumed that the doctor came home to the Saïce household in the evening, which in fact, he didn't. Not only did he not live there, he apparently never came to visit his young daughter.

Docteur Narnier was a youngish, dark-skinned and very handsome Tahitian native. Mother said he looked like one of the figures in a Gauguin painting. Simone was a frail, white-skinned little girl who bore absolutely no resemblance to her strong, swarthy father. I was too young to appreciate such details at the time, but now wonder if Narnier, rather than being the scoundrel his peers took him for, had done a noble deed by falsely owning up to being Simone's father to spare the child the stigma of illegitimacy. At the time, illegitimacy was still an extremely burdensome cross to bear.

I also heard (much later) that Minette had an affair with Docteur Narnier. "But it got her nowhere," said Mother. "It was a pity for Minette—he was such a handsome and wealthy man. It was also sad for poor Simone. She would be enjoying living with her father and a better mother than Madame Saïce was being for her. I think Minette was not thinking at all on that side of it when the *affaire* was going on and would be changing her mind about marrying him when she realizes that she is suddenly becoming Simone's mother."

Simone was a pale, anemic, and sickly child about my age. Continually nagged and over-pampered by the overwrought Madame Saïce, Simone must have led a miserable life. This situation was hardly conducive to enjoyable visits to their household.

Madame Saïce had no garden, and there was precious little to do indoors. Simone was so cowed, timid and nervous that she found it impossible to play the game of *crapette,* a card game simple enough for young children to enjoy. Mother had brought a deck of cards on our second visit, for it was clear that Madame Saïce didn't own anything as frivolous or potentially enjoyable as playing cards.

When we arrived at Madame Saïce's house, it always seemed to be time for Simone to take a spoonful of cod liver oil. It was as though something about our arrival made Madame Saïce think of cod liver oil as a way to fortify Simone against whatever germs we had brought in with us. Worse yet, Madame Saïce's idea of hospitality included the notion that she was obliged to give Brenda and me a spoonful of the foul tasting oil, which made us gag. "It's absolutely the best thing for you, and you can't go wrong taking a little dose," Madame Saïce explained as she went to the kitchen for extra spoons.

Mother stood there, more amused than alarmed, as I refused Madame Saïce's offering and clenched my teeth when she tried to push the spoon into my mouth. Madame Saïce had experienced such resistance before and knew the appropriate countermeasures. Her tactic was to pinch my nose and jam the spoon into my mouth as soon as I let out a yelp of protest. Much of the stuff spilled on my clothes and onto the floor. Nevertheless, that didn't stop Madame Saïce from repeating the performance on our next visit. Each time, Mother appeared bemused and indifferent to our plight. I think she agreed with Madame Saïce that the cod liver oil couldn't harm us and might even do us some good. I remember once asking Mother, "If the stuff's so good for children, why is Simone such a sickly little girl?"

"We just don't know how much more sickly Simone might be if she didn't get her cod liver oil," was Mother's reply, to which my rejoinder was, "Or how much *less* sickly she might be, for that matter."

When the proffering of cod liver oil was over, Madame Saïce usually turned her attention to the peeling of a tangerine, something else she was apparently convinced would ward off a possible invasion of germs. Brenda and I detested those tangerine wedges almost as much as the cod liver oil. It wasn't that we didn't like tangerines, but the whole house already had a strong medicinal smell which seemed to emanate from Madame Saïce's hands. They reeked so much of disinfectant that just being near them overpowered the pleasant, pungent smell of the tangerine wedges.

The Saïce household was also overheated, dark, and profoundly gloomy. Madame Saïce left her faded olive-green velvet curtains permanently closed, saying she believed that sunlight bleached the upholstery and carpet. She had apparently never opened her curtains, for if she had, she might have noticed that all her windows faced north and therefore never admitted the sun's rays.

Mother's overt sympathy and concern for Simone prompted me to ask her how Simone could survive under such conditions. "The poor child! She is so used to it, and she has never known anything else," Mother replied. It's quite possible that Simone had never left Madame Saïce's household since the time of her arrival there as a tiny infant, and that she had no idea that an outside world even existed. I once proposed to Mother that we invite Simone to our house, so she could play with us in the garden. I feel obliged to admit that this seemingly charitable proposal was motivated by a desire to deflect our next visit to the Saïce household. When mother acted on my proposal, Madame Saïce surprised us by accepting the invitation.

On the appointed day, Madame Saïce appeared at our door without Simone, explaining that the weather was much too cold for Simone to leave their house and that she had left her with the woman who came to do the housecleaning. It was, in fact, a warm, pleasant spring day. Brenda and I had been outdoors all morning, wearing only light clothing. Simone was not ill, Madame Saïce insisted—she just didn't want to take chances on a chilly day like this one. Simone might catch something—it was just too risky. Madame Saïce, it seemed, was quite willing to brave the frigid outdoors herself and was happy to partake of an especially fine afternoon tea that Mother had asked Françoise to lay on for the occasion. After Madame Saïce's departure, Mother opened the windows to get rid of the lingering smell of disinfectant that had trailed Madame Saïce into the house, and as soon as the offending party was out of earshot, she vented not only the dining room but her anger as well. "That stupid old bat! She'd rather leave the child indoors, breathing in clouds of dust stirred up by that inept servant of hers."

Except for our cousins in Belgium—and the next-door Poujets when they were not ostracizing us—Simone was the only other child with whom we associated. The only compensation we had for the lack of playmates were Françoise and Raimond. He took a real interest in Brenda and me, and sometimes participated in our play. And when it rained and I couldn't be outdoors, I spent many happy hours in the kitchen watching Françoise as she prepared meals, asking her a thousand questions about what she was doing. She was always happy to answer me and to elaborate on the whys and wherefores of cooking. Sometimes she even let me perform some of the easier, safer kitchen chores. Everything she did to prepare our elaborate meals fascinated me, and the cooking knowledge I learned at her side serves me to this day.

Alain attains the Age of Reason (7th birthday), Ville-d'Avray, 1937

Brenda, Jenny, Jock, Lottie, and Alain, Hardelot, 1937

CHAPTER 7

An Airplane Crash and Some Bloodletting

When I was about seven years old, Father started taking more of an interest in me. Years later, when I asked why he had been so aloof during my early years, his explanation was, "Babies and infants are quite unapproachable to the average man and are best left to the care and company of women, who generally seem to understand them better."

Over breakfast one Saturday morning, Father announced that he wanted to see if I could catch a ball. I wondered why he thought I might be able to achieve this since no one had ever thrown me one. I did own a ball, a large blue thing about the size of my head, an ancient and unused Christmas present from Auntie Gladys, who lived in England. I had, in fact, once taken a careful look into what possible use this ball might have, and noted that it rolled and bounced. I found this mildly amusing, couldn't see much fun in it, and didn't enjoy having to chase after it when I threw or kicked the beastly thing. When it rolled into the flower beds where it wreaked havoc, Raimond joined me in my dislike for it. As a result, the ball resided, abandoned and disgraced, in a corner of the garage.

In defense of my shortcomings in this regard, I should add that none of the children on the playgrounds of schools I had attended ever owned or played with any kind of ball. I can only conclude that young French children of the time didn't make a habit of playing with balls, as most English boys apparently did.

The reason for Father's sudden interest in me, I later learned from him, was not some innate parental instinct awakening in him, but that Auntie Gladys (Uncle Bob's wife) had put a bee in his bonnet. Gladys had expressed concern about my ability to throw and catch a ball, "Something they don't do much in France," she had said in a cautionary way to Father. "The ability to throw or catch a ball is essential to even rudimentary popularity, if not survival, in an English boarding school," she had added. Since my birth, Gladys had never missed a chance to needle Father about bringing me to England for what she called "a proper education and upbringing."

I greeted Father's interest in my ability to catch a ball with no small apprehension. After all, he had never participated in any athletic activity with me, except once. That was when he carried me, protesting and squealing in terror, into the cold ocean in Hardelot. I had been enjoying a ride on his shoulders as he walked along the beach when he unexpectedly turned and waded out to deep water and dropped me in. The purpose of this deed was "to see if the boy could swim," he explained to Mother. He did, of course, rescue me when he found out I couldn't, but the episode had left me nervous about any athletic activity in his presence.

After breakfast, I discovered to my dismay that Father was serious when he took the ball out of the garage and ordered me to join him on the front lawn. Standing about twenty feet from me, he lobbed the ball so that it headed for my knees. I managed to deflect it with my hands but not catch it.

"You're supposed to catch it, Sonny, not just fend it off sideways!" he said with a touch of sarcasm. I ran after the ball, carried it back to him, and backed off the required twenty feet. "Next time, I'd like you to throw it to me, instead of carrying it to me," he now said, barely concealing his impatience.

Once again, he threw the ball at me. It was heading right for me, somewhat faster than I considered safe, so I turned and ducked to avoid its hitting me in the face. This time I ran after it and attempted to throw it back to him. I was off the mark by a wide margin, and it rolled on down a slight hill, forcing Father to go after it. When he returned to his position, he paused before another throw and said, "The point of this is for you to catch it, not duck when it comes at you! Do try to make *some* effort to put your hands where the ball is going to be, or you'll never catch it, Sonny!"

This time, the ball came at me, but with an upward arching trajectory. I put my two hands out where I thought it would be, but it fell short. We continued in this fashion two more times, with the ball once falling behind me and completely out of reach as it flew over me, and the other time with the ball once again falling short of where I was. On the fourth try, the ball's trajectory actually coincided with the space occupied by my hands. At least his throwing was improving! But I was so startled by the coincidence that the ball slipped through my hands as I failed to grasp it.

"It's no use, butterfingers! You're absolutely hopeless!" Father said, sounding displeased and exasperated. He walked away, leaving me grateful that this humiliating episode was over, and that he didn't have his heart in this project any more than I did. I went to the garage, put the ball back in its place of disgrace, wheeled out my bike and pedaled around the periphery of the garden ten times at breakneck speed. I was very good at bike riding. And tree climbing, too. Who needed to catch a ball, and why would anyone want to?

There were few things Father didn't do well, but teaching a young child something completely new happened to be one of those things. Even though I remember it vividly, I never attached any importance to this incident; I adored Father, and he could do nothing very wrong in my eyes. He occasionally did things I didn't like, but I believed he knew best. I always thought of him in terms of the good things he did for us, such as providing us with a nice house and garden to play in, employing Raimond and Françoise, and reading to us every night if he arrived home before Brenda and I went to bed.

Father was a superb reader of children's stories. After our bath and supper, Brenda and I went to the living room in our pajamas, where, having just returned from the office, he usually sat enjoying a glass of sherry. Sitting on the arms of his Father's huge armchair, on either side of him, we listened attentively as he read to us from *Winnie the Pooh*, *The Wind in the Willows*, *Babar the*

Elephant, or from one of the many Beatrix Potter books. His voice was gentle and beautifully modulated, neither sentimental nor syrupy, and his innate kindness, his respect and love of things simple and true came across in the reading. His marvelous sense of humor made the funny parts of a book seem even funnier than when someone else read them.

Brenda and I saw very little of our father. On Saturdays, he often played golf all day, so that left Sunday dinner and Sunday afternoon as the only times we were with him. On these occasions, the dictum "children should be seen and not heard" generally prevailed, though I was allowed to speak if I first raised my hand and was recognized.

I was expected to show up on time for dinner with my hands and face clean and my hair combed. On one occasion, I had dilly-dallied too long in the garden and, pressed for time, I thought I could get away without washing my hands if I just wiped them on my pants. I certainly couldn't show up late for dinner; that, too, was a mortal sin in our household. The fact that my hands had not recently seen soap and water was instantly apparent to Father, who dragged me by the collar to the cloakroom. There, holding me bent over the toilet, he swung a long-handled hairbrush at my posterior with high velocity. The burning sting of that one spanking stayed with me all afternoon. Before returning to the dining room, he scrubbed my hands vigorously with a nail brush until they were red and sore. That was the only time he ever spanked me, and I made sure it never happened again.

After dinner on Sundays, my parents had coffee in the garden if it were sunny and warm, or in the drawing room if it were cold or rainy. As Mother and Father each submerged into the silence of their books, the quiet hiss of a smoldering log in the fireplace and an occasional sigh of contentment from Jock, lying on the carpet, was all there was to be heard. When we didn't have guests, reading after lunch on Sunday afternoons was a lifelong ritual for my parents. Later in the afternoon, if it weren't raining, Father usually went out to do some gardening. He lavished his attention on two rock gardens that grew luxuriously and contained mostly wild flowers he had carefully brought home from distant places, including some plants from Africa. The rock gardens were off limits to Raimond, except that he was expected to weed and water them in a very specific manner, something he did conscientiously.

Because Mother felt that Father saw so little of Brenda and me, we were expected to stay in the living room with them on Sunday afternoons. Since they were both engrossed in their reading, I was allowed a small toy with which I could play. Making highly authentic-sounding engine noises was an essential accompaniment to the pushing of a toy car along the carpet, but my doing this apparently drove Father crazy. Mother, who dedicated her life to the cause of family harmony, solved the problem by providing me with what she called *"ton jouet du Dimanche aprés-midi"* ("your Sunday afternoon toy"). It was still a push-along toy, but one that required no noisy renditions to provide me with gratification. It had been a Christmas gift from Minette to Mother, an elegant and unique belt, which Mother had decided to banish from her wardrobe.

The reason this belt held such attraction for me was because it was a superbly executed, though stylized, representation of a snake. Its exquisite rendering of a serpent's appearance was both its virtue and its curse. Mother couldn't stand the sight of snakes and wanted nothing to do with it. It was made of hundreds of small metal pieces that interlocked and overlapped, forming the scales of the skin. Its clever design endowed it with graceful flexibility and gave it credible solidity. Resting on the floor, it would have felt like a real snake if you stepped on it. The bright green eyes were fake emeralds, and its two fearsome fangs somehow latched into the tapered tail to close the belt. Noiselessly, I made the snake slide around chair legs and under sofas, causing Jock to eye it nervously and to move to another spot on the carpet whenever the snake slithered within a few feet of him. I adored my Sunday afternoon toy and could play with it contentedly for hours, sometimes pretending it was a sleek and super-silent high-speed train.

Long drives in the surrounding countryside were another occasional Sunday afternoon diversion. Again, Mother saw the drives as an opportunity for Father to get to know Brenda and me, despite the fact that all we did was sit in the back seat without saying much. Here too, I indulged in that same pastime—or bad habit, depending on your point of view—of imitating car engines. Actually, I wasn't imitating a car. Rather, I thought of myself *as a car* when I made these noises. Although I knew Father didn't like my sounds, I was sure I could get away with my renditions whenever the real car's engine was running loudly enough to blend with the quieter purring of my own engine. I was so good at controlling these sounds that I successfully indulged in my motoring ritual on numerous outings until one day when, in the middle of nowhere, Father suddenly slowed and brought the car to a stop. My own engine slowed down commensurate with the deceleration of Father's car, and I shrewdly switched off my own engine and coasted silently before the real car's engine reached an idle. After stopping the car, Father got out and looked under the hood, then climbed back into the car saying, "That's very odd, I could swear I heard a strange engine noise—it was quite distinct—and the pitch increased whenever I speeded up and decreased when I slowed. But when I opened the bonnet, the noise had completely disappeared!" Father was easily upset, if not obsessed, by strange or unwanted noises and went out of his way to pursue them to extinction.

Mother, who was well acquainted with my automotive behavior and preferences, surveyed the back seat, saw me doing my best to look innocent and said, "It's Alain again, pretending he's a Citroën."

Father turned and looked me straight in the eye and said quietly, "Alan, I happen to be driving a very comfortable and quiet-running Peugeot, the sound of whose smooth engine I profoundly enjoy—not one of those noisy Citroëns. Would you be kind enough to park your car and join me in the Peugeot as a silent passenger?" I quietly heaved a sigh of relief and complied with his request.

On another Sunday afternoon, Father had gone out to do some gardening, and Mother had stayed indoors to work on a difficult picture puzzle whose pieces were spread out on a card table placed in front of the living room window. Every now and then, I arose from playing with my snake on the floor, stood beside her a minute or two, picked up a piece, popped it into its rightful place, and returned to my snake. It was while inserting a piece that I glanced out of the window and noticed Father traveling across the lawn in great haste, carrying a watering can in each hand. I didn't give the matter much thought.

Mother's puzzle, which represented the Coronation of King George VI in Westminster Abbey, was nearing completion. I was fascinated by the details of the King's regalia and the various surrounding personages in their elaborate finery as portrayed in reduced size on the puzzle's box cover. I was anxious to see the full-size completed picture, so I eventually abandoned the snake and devoted my entire attention to helping Mother put the last few pieces into place. As I worked at this task, I once more saw Father dash by the window with his watering cans. Mother was sitting with the window to her side and must have seen him out of the corner of her eye.

"Who was that going by the window just now?" she asked, deep in thought over some piece she was holding.

"That was Father," I replied. "He's been going by every five minutes like that."

"That couldn't have been Father. It had to be Raimond. Whoever it was went by very fast, and you know Father never runs," she said, still in a distracted voice and paying more attention to the puzzle than on what could be seen through the window.

"Raimond and Françoise went to Paris to see a film," I reminded her. "I'm sure it was Father," I added casually.

"I refuse to believe it. Your father has never run in his life. He does not know *how* to run—why would he start running today, of all days?" she insisted. Then absent-mindedly, for she was still focusing on the puzzle, she said, "I'd have to see it again to believe it."

We both waited, looking out of the window, and saw Father saunter by in the opposite direction, carrying two watering cans that seemed to be empty. "There—you see!" said Mother, "He is walking in his usual slow and sedate way. I don't know who it was I saw running before, but it wasn't your father."

I told her to keep watching out the window and popped another piece into place on the puzzle, quietly certain we would see him race by once more.

Sure enough, a couple of minutes later, he passed the window doing the hundred-yard dash, carrying two large and unmistakably full watering cans. This time, I noticed the reason for his haste. The lower seams on both metal watering cans were leaking badly and were squirting small jets of water in all directions around him as he ran.

Mother burst into laughter, and the more she laughed, the harder she laughed—peals of laughter, until the tears streamed from her eyes. When Father whizzed by five minutes later, she was still laughing uncontrollably. I began to worry about her, so I opened the window and, when Father walked by with his empty cans, I told him Mother was acting strangely and that he had better come in and see.

When he entered the drawing room, he asked Mother why she was laughing so hard. "Because I've never, ever seen you run before—I didn't think you could!" she said, slurring her words as she struggled to speak between bursts of laughing.

"Of course I can run," said Father indignantly. "When I have to—those watering cans were leaking badly, and there would be no water left in them if I walked," he added defensively. This only brought forth even more laughter from Mother, who had by now completely lost control of herself and sounded more as if she were crying than laughing. Father led her to her bed and called Docteur Narnier who immediately came over and decided that she needed a sedative. At dinner that evening, she was better, but would occasionally have an isolated and unprovoked fit of laughing. Fifty years later, I could still start her laughing hard enough to bring tears to her eyes, just by mentioning Father and his leaky watering cans. I too, had never seen Father run, nor had I ever seen him in a hurry, except on that one occasion. It was completely out of character for him to run or hurry. He would rather have missed a train than run to catch it. I once heard him say, "I haven't run since I was a boy. It's just not dignified for a grown man to run, unless the house is burning down."

One of Father's friends was an aviator who went by the name of Mormilly. In those days, aviators were usually people who were independently wealthy and could afford to dabble in aviation, or they were men who had flown in World War I, and had so distinguished themselves in aerial combat that they were sought after as test pilots or stunt flyers. Mormilly came under both headings. One of Mormilly's favorite stories was how the French trained and graduated their fighter pilots during World War I. According to him, on the day of their first solo flight, the student pilots were provided with a plane that was identical to the one in which they had trained. As they sat in the cockpit ready for takeoff, they were told that the controls (rudder pedals, joy stick and throttle lever) had all been reversed in their mode of operation. "That way, we ended up with pilots who really had their wits about them," Mormilly boasted. He never told us what happened to the ones they didn't end up with.

In the autumn of 1936, Mormilly was involved in the development and prototype construction of the first French warplane to have a retractable landing gear system, and he invited Father to witness its maiden flight. The event took place on a Saturday afternoon, and the whole family was invited to attend this momentous occasion. Mother knew of Raimond's passion for aviation and convinced Father that we should bring him along.

We arrived at Orly aerodrome (in those days, just a grass field with a few corrugated steel sheds), proceeded to one of the hangars, and found Mormilly, who was wearing a huge, leather flying coat. He was on a stepladder tinkering with the plane's engine. Standing nearby were not only a handful of his work associates (some in uniform) but also a coterie of Mormilly's civilian drinking cronies.

The plane was a single engine monoplane of medium stature, too boxy to be a fighter plane and too light to be a bomber, and ugly as a warthog, as were all France's warplanes of the period. Mormilly remained on his ladder for well over an hour, during which time his audience waited patiently, talking and joking among themselves. Although the plane was in a hangar, its tail poked out through the large, open door. It was a bleak November day with a light overcast. There was a chilly breeze and, even in the hangar, out of the wind, it was cold. Mother, Brenda and I retired to the warmth of our Peugeot which was parked just outside the hangar. We waited there until Raimond came out to tell us that Mormilly was ready.

We returned to the hangar just as Mormilly descended from his perch on the ladder, saying in a disgusted tone, "I don't like it, but it will have to do." He then announced that he would demonstrate the retraction of the landing wheels while the plane was on the ground. As we wondered how this could be done, he summoned two workmen to get *des gros chevalets,* which turned out to be two very stout sawhorses. These were placed under the wings, just outboard of the landing wheels, along with some other bits of heavy lumber to fill the space between the wings and the *chevalets.* Mormilly then impatiently insisted he wanted *des morçeaux de tapis.* A man ran off and disappeared for some time, and returned with a colorful assortment of carpet scraps, which he put between the wing undersurfaces and the wood supports.

Things now seemed to be to Mormilly's liking, and a mechanic relocated the ladder so he could climb into the plane's open cockpit. Men scurried to find some triangular blocks to place in front of the plane's wheels.

"The plane has no brakes," Raimond explained quietly to me. "Without those blocks, the plane would just fly away as soon as the engine starts." I really appreciated Raimond's comment, for I was watching every move and wondered as to each one's purpose.

Mormilly shouted the word *"contact,"* and a mechanic standing on a low platform spun the plane's propeller a few times before the engine came to life with much sputtering and smoke. After a few minutes of coughing and backfiring, the engine settled down to a noisy idle. Mormilly gave the thumbs up from his open cockpit and appeared to reach for a lever and pull it. The wheels slowly rose into the wings and came to a stop almost completely tucked into the wings, but still protruding slightly from the lower surfaces. The plane had descended an inch or two where it rested with its wings bearing on the two *chevalets*. Under his breath, Raimond said, "It's the best that can be done, short of having the wheels protrude through the top of the wings. They're bigger across than the thickness of the wing, so they have to protrude somewhere. They may as well protrude from the bottom of the wing, where they might do some good in a crash landing."

Mormilly shut the engine off, and in the sudden silence that followed, announced that he would now demonstrate how he could lower the wheels, even if there were no power from the engine. We saw him lean forward in the cockpit and appear to pump something. Sure enough, the wheels slowly descended, but it took about five minutes for them to do so, after which Mormilly was out of breath and considerably disheveled. I asked Raimond who would be driving the plane as it flew while this wheel-lowering business took place. It had obviously taken all of Mormilly's effort and attention to lower the wheels.

"Planes pretty much fly themselves, unlike cars which wander off the road if you don't continually steer them. There are no roads in the sky, so they can't wander off," Raimond replied in all seriousness.

Mormilly was now ready for his flight. He stood up in the cockpit, buttoned his great flying coat, donned a leather flying helmet and goggles, and snuggled himself back into the cramped cockpit. Three men gathered around the tail and, lifting it, turned the plane around so that it faced the open door of the hangar and once more spun the prop to restart the engine. The wheel chocks, which had been relocated when the plane was turned, were now removed, and the plane started a slow roll out of the shed and down to the far end of the grass aerodrome. We had all followed the plane out of the hangar, and now heard the engine roar and watched the plane become airborne after a short takeoff run. Still low over the field, Mormilly put the plane into a sharp and prolonged banking turn until his flight path passed right in front of us. At this point we saw the wheels rise into the wings. There was loud cheering and clapping from the assembled crowd as the plane headed for some distant low hills and soon disappeared from sight.

We returned to the shelter of the open hangar and waited, stamping our feet to keep warm. In the echoing silence of the empty hangar, Raimond said quite loudly, "He won't be long coming back. After all, he's only demonstrating the landing gear. Frankly, I expected him to land right away, after one circle around the field!"

Ten minutes passed—then, half an hour. We all moved out of the hangar, thinking we would be better positioned to hear the sound of the returning plane. The wind had died down, and it no longer felt so cold. A few minutes later, the mechanic foreman broke the silence that now reigned over the anxious crowd, and announced that Mormilly must have made a forced landing since he had only enough fuel for a very short flight. Raimond said to me in a reverential whisper, "The amount of fuel on board was kept small so he wouldn't die in a fireball if his plane were to crash."

There were over a dozen cars scattered around the outside of the hangar, and someone decided they should all go out in different directions to search the surrounding countryside for the downed plane. The foreman had a Michelin road map, and he assigned search zones to each able-bodied driver, Father included. The drivers then scurried to their cars, for dusk was coming on. I was very excited at the thought of participating in this important search, but my hopes were soon dashed. With darkness coming on, they would be out searching "who knows for how long," said Mother. It might also turn out to be a gory spectacle, too horrible for my young eyes to witness. A thousand objections seemed to counter my supplications.

Raimond asked if he could go with Father on the search. "That way, if Monsieur becomes stuck in the mud somewhere, there will be someone to push him out of it!" Raimond said eagerly, seeming to relish the prospect—not of the mud, but of the search for the downed plane.

A man who seemed to know Mother, and who had been conspicuously silent when the call for search volunteers was first issued, proposed to take Brenda, Mother and me home. He was Thiérry de Tapleine, a close friend of both Mormilly and Father, a charming and diminutive man, who was wearing an elegant pin stripe suit and a light gray Homburg. He was somewhat of a dandy, and his extremely long eyelashes accentuated his effeminacy, a detail even I noticed. Later, I asked Mother if it weren't unusual for a man to have such long eyelashes. "It is," she replied, "and they're real! The longest I have ever seen on either a man or a woman. Aren't they absolutely beautiful?"

We drove home in Thiérry's Delahaye, France's equivalent of a Rolls Royce at the time. It was an immaculately kept and graceful car, very quiet, and Thiérry's chauffeur completed the feel of elegance. "Much as I love Mormilly," said Thiérry as we drove to our house, "I couldn't see myself bogging down on some muddy country road in this car."

Mother invited Thiérry in for a drink and dinner. Françoise was extremely anxious about the absence of Raimond and wanted assurances from Mother that he was with Father. She was also severely derailed by the idea of serving dinner without Raimond to act as the butler. She eventually put a good face on it, donning a black smock, a white apron and a maid's cap for the occasion. She, like Mother, seemed to have a soft spot for Thiérry, though probably more for the generosity of his tips than for his eyelashes. When we rose after the meal, Thiérry asked if he could go to the kitchen to compliment Françoise on the dinner, something no guest had ever done. In the kitchen, Françoise apologized for serving *pâté Parmentier* (shepherd's pie), but excused herself on the grounds that she had no advance notice of his visit, and that she would have prepared something much fancier if she had known he was coming to dinner. I interjected indignantly, asking her why she was apologizing. After all, shepherd's pie was *my* favorite dish. Thiérry, a consummate diplomat, immediately said, "What a coincidence! It's mine, too!" Françoise was thrilled, and I felt honored to have tastes in common with a man who owned a Delahaye.

Just as this little ceremony was ending, Father and Raimond returned. They were the ones who had found Mormilly. They were driving in near darkness when Raimond thought he spotted a small light waving about in a darkened field. They stopped the car, turned off the engine, and called out. Raimond thought he heard a faint reply. A little farther up the road, they found a break in the hedge that allowed Father to drive into the field. They could still see the faint light waving back and forth and proceeded towards it, driving the car up a slight hill through deep grass. The form of the crashed plane eventually loomed in the car's headlight beams.

Mormilly was still in the cockpit and was waving a lighted cigarette lighter. He was pinned in by the crumpled plane and moaned that he thought he had broken both legs, probably in several places. Lest the reader ponder the wisdom of waving a lighted cigarette lighter in a crashed plane, Mormilly explained that he had run out of fuel after only fifteen minutes of flying. As Raimond and Father started the work of extricating him from the crashed plane, he described his mishap.

"When I took off, I headed for the nearby village of Longjumeau, where I have *une petite amie* (a lady friend) over whose house I did a few *manœuvres* (aerobatics). It took barely five minutes of flying to get there, and the plane was flying so well that I felt a bit intoxicated! I ran out of fuel on the way back. As the engine sputtered, I immediately set about lowering the wheels by hand and consequently wasn't able to devote my attention to finding a suitable field for some semblance of a proper landing. I must really do something about that! That pump is too far down in the cockpit and should be placed higher up. When I had finished lowering the wheels, I found myself heading for this hill at a rather steep angle and, with my engine no longer running, there was little I could do. I'm lucky to be alive! And I'm very glad I had my lighter for signaling, or I would have spent a cold night out here waiting to be found and rescued!"

Raimond and Father worked for half an hour by the light of the car headlights to pry Mormilly loose from the wreckage, a process that required the use of the car's jack to push apart some bent struts that were pinning him in. As they carried him to the car and then drove to the aerodrome, Father could see that Mormilly was in a lot of pain, although he was trying to conceal it with an uninterrupted stream of wisecracks. At the aerodrome, they applied crude splints to each of his legs, and gave him a generous slug of brandy before putting him in an ambulance, which someone had thought of calling. Mormilly's diagnosis of his injuries proved to be correct.

Considering the informality of the test flight procedure, I rather doubt this was a government project. Mormilly and de Tapleine were independently wealthy and I would guess this was a private venture done in the hopes of selling the plane or the landing wheel technology to the French Air Ministry. I distinctly remember Mormilly boasting that this would be France's first military plane to have retractable landing wheels. However, Mormilly was by no means an original inventor. Retracting wheels were in use on the Douglas DC-2 airliner, which had been in use by Holland's KLM airlines for about three years, so the concept was hardly new.

All this activity concerning aeroplanes, as they were then called, started me wondering about how I could bring a little aeronautics into my own life. Before long, it dawned on me that Raimond could perform one more transformation of that old perambulator, which had already metamorphosed first into a gondola, then into a locomotive. I decided it would now become an aeroplane, and I started soliciting Raimond's views on the possibility of such a project. One aspect of my existing locomotive was that it could not accommodate Brenda as a passenger. It seemed to me that removal of the flat, circular wood disk at the back of the old barrel, the locomotive's boiler, would allow Brenda to crawl into the barrel and sit inside it, assuming suitable cushions could be found. Raimond maintained that removal of this disk would cause the barrel staves to cave in. But I kept insisting that there had to be a way to do it, and my persistence drove Raimond to a solution. "I will build a *fuselage*," he said, "and the *fuselage*—instead of the disk—will hold the barrel staves in place."

Raimond had never flown in his life, to his immense chagrin, but he was an armchair flying enthusiast who read all he could about aeroplanes and knew many important aeronautical words. The fuselage was made out of lumber from old orange crates he obtained at the greengrocer. It was tricky work, but Raimond was a master craftsman. A rudder and tailfins were added to the new fuselage, which had no floor so I could stand on the ground while in the cockpit. I propelled the plane by walking and pushing on the cockpit's dashboard. After the complexity of the fuselage, the addition of two stubby wings to the barrel was straightforward and easy, as was the addition of a propeller at its front end. The latter turned freely on a nail, so I could spin it before every takeoff, as all pilots had to do in those days. The wingspan was carefully specified in order to clear the chestnut trees that lined both sides of my takeoff runway. A new paint job included portrayal of details such as the exhaust manifolds, wing flaps, ailerons, and windows.

The railroad emblem P.L.M. was replaced by the name "Air France." I would have preferred "Imperial Airways," which Father always maintained was a better airline, but Raimond did this part of the artwork during one of the family's Sunday afternoon drives. It was just as well I wasn't there to argue over the issue. I think Raimond would have balked at the words "Imperial Airways" painted onto his aeronautical masterpiece. Raimond even made me a boarding ladder because the cockpit sides (part of the fuselage) came to my chin, making it difficult for me to climb aboard. Once in the cockpit, I pulled the ladder in behind me with a stout string, stowing it inside the empty tail assembly, so it would be available for exit wherever I "landed." Brenda also boarded the airliner by this means and then squeezed into the cramped quarters of the barrel, an accurate portrayal of air travel to come. However, Brenda soon declared that she didn't care for travel in such cramped conditions. Her decision suited me just fine, as the plane was a heavy push even when she wasn't aboard. Fortunately, her dolls continued to travel frequently as unaccompanied children, now in uncramped comfort. I was grateful to have at least these paying passengers. I flew regular flights to various destinations in the garden, wearing flyer's goggles made from a discarded pair of sunglasses (with one lens missing) and making highly authentic engine noises during the flights. My renditions of the engine starting, complete with sputtering and backfiring, were particularly accurate and provoked much laughter from all who were privileged to hear them.

Raimond was marvelous in the way he managed to accommodate my various requests. Just after this loco-to-airliner transformation, he built me a large platform in the playroom for my electric trains. He did this because someone had eventually stepped on my track layout, which until the mishap, had been placed on the floor. The damaged track was beyond repair, even by the versatile Raimond.

The previous Christmas, I had received the first eight "starter" pieces of rail, which formed a circular track for my electric train. Mother had decreed that my model railroad empire would only grow in small increments at each Christmas or on my birthday. She had found the eight pieces of track and a little electric locomotive (missing its coal tender) at the Paris Flea Market. She had purchased my entire rolling stock—just one pathetic little freight wagon, at a proper toy store. Mother's rationale for such a minimalist train layout was part of her determination that I should not grow up a spoiled child. By her standards, Charlie Poujet next door was spoilt rotten. The previous Christmas, Charlie had, in one fell swoop, acquired at least ten meters of track, numerous switches, track crossings and a huge fleet of freight wagons that were pulled by a large and powerful loco, complete with coal tender. I was green with envy and spent most free rainy afternoons playing at his house and enjoying his more lavish setup.

Brenda usually accompanied me on these visits, as she and Monique Poujet shared a mutual enthusiasm for dolls. Although Monique was older, it was Brenda who had the lead in dolls, for she had a peeing doll that required frequent diaper changes, while none of Monique's dolls peed at all. Monique was always glad to have to change the diapers on the doll that Brenda dutifully brought with her. Brenda gently cradled the doll in one arm as she clambered over Raimond's *passerelle* on the way to the Poujets.

She was usually nervous about heights, but with the doll in one arm, she lost all fear. These happy afternoons, usually Saturdays, came to an abrupt stop after I was ostracized for painting my face with ink at school.

About a month before the inking business, Brenda and I were at the Poujet house for Charlie's birthday party. It was winter and already dark by the time we had to go home. We couldn't use the ladder overpass for the return trip because it was in an unlighted part of the garden. Mother walked the street route to come and fetch us, and stayed a while to chat with Madame Poujet as we kids continued playing upstairs.

As we set out for home, we had taken a few steps in their darkened garden when there was a piercing shriek from Brenda, accompanied by the angry snarl and snapping of a large animal. The Poujet's oversized German shepherd had attacked and bitten Brenda. Auguste, the Poujet's gardener, unaware that we were still on the premises, had unleashed the dog, who was supposed to roam the garden on his rounds as a guard dog. Mother struggled to pull the dog away and, with the help of Madame Poujet, who had come running at the sound of the ruckus, they were eventually able to control the beast. Brenda, it turned out, had been bitten in the posterior and was bleeding badly. Madame Poujet drove us straight to Docteur Narnier who gave Brenda a tetanus shot and used four stitches to close the wound.

Following this incident, Brenda had nightmares every night, but the bad dreams miraculously ceased when Madame Poujet gave her a consolation gift of another peeing doll, the twin of the first. I secretly nursed the hope that their dog would take just a small bite out of my behind and that Madame Poujet would then have to buy me a whole room full of electric trains to dispel my nightmares.

After my expulsion from L'Ecole Sugerre, little time was lost in finding me a new school. For the first time in this process, Father had something to do with it. As far back as I could remember there had been talk of sending me off to an English boarding school when I reached the age of ten. This would be to prepare me for attending an English "public school" when I was fourteen years old. Mother now wisely urged that I be placed in an English-speaking school in France before going off to England, so that I could adapt to the language change while still close to home. The Dennis School in nearby Sèvres was an English school for boys, and I began attending it in the spring quarter of 1937.

The staff, including the Headmaster, Mr. Dennis, consisted of only seven people, and they were all English. The school had an enrollment of about eighty boys and was situated in what had once been a luxurious private estate. The property had been abandoned as a residence when an obnoxious factory was built next door. The building had gone to ruin and was still in a state of extreme neglect and disrepair when I attended the school. The house once had a dozen or more decent-sized bedrooms and these now served as classrooms for small groups of students. We sat on an assortment of broken-down chairs and benches, and old tables of all sizes served as desks. This furniture had evidently been bought in junk stores, as no chair or table was identical to any other, and everything was in a dilapidated condition.

Though I didn't know it at the time, the Dennis School was exactly what I needed. It was casual and informal in the extreme. The masters and headmaster wandered in and out of these "classrooms," instructing each one of us briefly, sometimes collectively, as to our various assignments. Then they moved on to the next room, leaving the class of about eight students to fend for themselves. We were told to help each other as best we could and to leave the things we could not do until the reappearance of the next visiting master. That master then helped us with any difficulties we were having, reviewed our individual written work, and set new tasks before disappearing from the scene.

On the whole, the students were well disciplined, doing what they had been told to do, or making earnest efforts in that direction. There was a lot of talking and a fair amount of laughter and merriment, which was tacitly tolerated.

Our masters were well liked, and all of them had a sense of humor. I don't remember any raised voices or scolding. Their jurisdictions overlapped, and they seemed to be interchangeable in their jobs and assignments. They usually knew where the previous visiting master had left off and if they didn't, a few simple questions would quickly put them in step.

We had both French and English textbooks and moved back and forth between the two languages constantly, almost oblivious to the fact that the change was happening. The masters spoke both languages equally well, as did most of the students, many of whom were French. The students were from families who were either English or Anglophile, or anticipated the need for their offspring to be conversant in English as well as in French, as did my own family.

By the age of seven, I spoke both languages quite fluently, since Father always talked to me in English. I spoke French better because that's what Mother, Raimond, and Françoise spoke to me, and I saw a lot more of them than I did Father. Mother spoke English well enough to teach me to write in English during my sojourns at the three previous French schools.

I was the youngest pupil at the Dennis School. For reasons unknown, they had made an exception when admitting me; student ages ranged from eight to fourteen years, and I had just turned seven. There were no grades, no official classes, or "forms," as they call them in England, and each temporary group of students usually consisted of boys of varying ages. Each day we found ourselves with new and different classmates, and we remained in that classroom with the same students for a whole day. A new list was posted each morning, showing each student where to report that day. There were about ten groups, and the masters kept track of their visits as they moved from room to room throughout the day by referring to the group's room number. As to a method for the daily selection of students, we sometimes discussed among ourselves the possibility of a pattern, but conceded that we couldn't figure it out. I was already intrigued by the order and organization of everything around me and pondered this question on my own. However, I didn't daydream or waste much time over the issue as there was always something we were supposed to be doing and little opportunity for wasting time.

We read our designated texts or scribbled away at our respective assignments and problems, which, even within each group, differed from student to student depending on his age and level of ability. However, for a whole period, the subject under study was the same for all students in that classroom. We were urged to compare notes, to help each other, and older students often acted as coaches for the younger ones.

I remember one occasion when my group was composed of considerably older boys, and the subject was math. The boys in the class with me had never heard of the "proof-by-nine," which was taught and used in French schools, and were quite impressed by my use of it. In fact, I remember standing before the blackboard, showing the whole class how it was done, and then having to give a second performance when the master showed up. He, too, was impressed.

If we completed our assignments before the arrival of the next visiting master, we chatted amicably until he appeared. The resulting free-for-all discussions were wide-ranging and often became animated, but good natured debates. The subjects might be about such things as the *Tour de France* bicycle race, whether or why the Maginot line was truly impregnable, the latest model Citroën, or a trip someone had taken with his family over the weekend. On one occasion, it was about whether the authorities should have stopped *L'Homme Volant* who, with much fanfare, and with wings strapped to his back, had jumped off the Eiffel tower and promptly plummeted to his death. We all chimed in with our two centimes' worth. I remember how pleased I was that older boys would let me join in freely, even listened to me and asked me questions about what I said. Upon arrival in the classroom, the visiting master listened attentively to our comments and chitchat. If he thought the subject worthwhile, he would allow the discussion to continue for a short time and even participate in it.

There were three periods in a day, each one roughly an hour and forty-five minutes long. The break between the two morning periods was the high spot of the day for me, because the local baker brought over and sold us *petits pains,* exquisite little loaves of brioche bread still warm from the oven. His bakery was conveniently next door to the school. Mother dutifully armed me every day with a fifty-centimes piece for my purchase of *un petit pain*. Both the little coin and the small loaf it bought were almost sacred to me, and the coin afforded me my first experience with money and buying.

No ink wells and no black smocks! We were actually told *not* to bring pens to the school, and I remember being vexed that I wasn't going to be using my new fountain pen. We used pencils and carried a supply of them in special wooden pencil boxes. It was one of Raimond's daily tasks to sharpen my stash of pencils with a kitchen knife, and I left for school provisioned with enough sharp pencils to last me all day. The other boys carried penknives and sharpened their own pencils in class. Everyone wore a scout's belt with two special rings built into it. Each boy's penknife was attached to one of these rings by means of a snap-hook. From the second ring on each belt dangled a three-note whistle that we used during recess to summon friends or for tactics during our games. These items were *de rigueur,* along with short navy blue scout pants made of a coarse, heavy flannel.

Mother reluctantly agreed to the flannel pants, which she viewed as ugly, cumbersome, and even worse, they were cut in the French, rather than the English style—way too short. The snap-hook belt and the whistle she accepted, but she strongly objected to the penknife as being unsafe for a seven year old. But without a penknife, I felt wholly inadequate and unworthy. It was Raimond who understood my anguish and who bestowed on me an official scout's penknife. Although he carefully instructed me in its safe use, I soon confirmed Mother's foresight when I sharpened a finger instead of the pencil I was holding. Poor Raimond! That was the only scolding he ever received from Mother, and he earned it for an act of kindness towards me. As for me, I lost my right to carry a penknife.

Mother was a born problem-solver and soon found a way to stop me from pestering her daily for the return of my penknife. With a remarkable degree of trust, she allowed me to wear the penknife on my belt, on condition that I would never actually use it, or even open it to admire the blade. The solution suited me fine. The knife would dangle from my belt, a symbol of true boyhood, and this, as far as I was concerned, was all that mattered. In addition, I got Mother to agree that on my eighth birthday, I could start actually using the knife. In the meantime, I was allowed to use my penknife's corkscrew. In a wine drinking country, no penknife comes without a corkscrew!

Thereafter, I made a special point of being in the kitchen just before meals so I could officiate at the opening of the wine bottle. The ever patient Raimond reluctantly allowed me to turn my corkscrew into the cork, as long as it was only a *vin de table* and not a *grand cru*, which is what was usually served at Sunday dinner. Raimond did the actual pulling of the cork. He, too, was displaying a great deal of trust in me; it's so easy to mangle a cork by inserting the corkscrew crookedly.

At the Dennis School, class work ended at three o'clock, and after that, roughly two hours were spent at "games." This was a novelty for me because the French, unlike the English and Americans, saw no need for sports in school. The choice of a sport at the Dennis School was either soccer or "rounders" (the latter being a primitive form of baseball), or we could choose free play in the school's vast garden. We played all games in our street clothes, without special shoes or boots. The school had no showers, no changing room or even a locker room.

The playing field was in the far reaches of the four-acre garden and well separated from the school's main building by a grove of large trees. These great oaks, chestnuts, beeches, and lindens were spaced far enough apart so that, after years of neglect, a thick undergrowth of brambles, nettles, various small bushes, and tall grass flourished beneath them. This jungle was crisscrossed with a labyrinth of small, winding paths, ideal for all sorts of games. I have fond memories of heart-pounding excitement as we played "prisoner's base," "hide-and-seek," "capture the flag," and other games in this small wilderness.

On rainy days when we couldn't go out for games, we gathered in the ornately stuccoed drawing room of the old mansion, and the older boys took turns reading to the rest of us as we sat or lounged on the floor. It was here that I first encountered *Treasure Island* and Kipling's stories. Once a book was started, I prayed for rain every day because I was so impatient to hear the rest of the tale.

The soccer and rounders playing field, which had once been a vegetable garden, was surrounded on three sides by high masonry walls and, on the fourth side by the "wilderness" just described. Soccer balls never cleared those high walls or made much headway into the jungle. It would have been an ideal spot for a playing field, except for the fact that it was dominated by a tall, brick smokestack, which looked as if it were leaning towards our field and about to fall on us. It usually belched thick black smoke, and on some days, the smoke and soot drifted towards where we played our games. The factory also emitted a continuous and unpleasant whining noise.

"Tu es noir comme l'ace de pique!" ("You're black as the ace of spades!") was how Mother greeted me when I returned from that school. The soot from the smoke stack fell on us like snow and accumulated everywhere on the grounds, so that we became dirty even when the wind favored us. Needless to say, there were now no teachers cleaning me up before sending me home. Mother was baffled as to how I became so grimy. She didn't know about the smokestack which wasn't visible from the school building.

I couldn't understand why Mother was so upset. Even before I attended the Dennis School, Brenda and I always had a communal bath at the end of the day, come rain or shine, whether we needed one or not. So why all the fuss about a little extra dirt? Why not make the bath really worth taking? Besides, getting dirty was one of the great pleasures of life, or so I thought at the time. Perhaps it was those black rings which daily graced the bathtub that upset Mother. In any case, I was not about to enlighten her as to the origin of the dirt, for I really liked this school, and one could never tell what she might do if she knew the truth of the matter.

Pierre, my best friend at the Dennis School, had no such problem with *his* mother, whom I heard greeting him cheerfully at the school door with, *"Je vois que tu t'es bien amusé à te salir!"* ("I see you've had all sorts of fun getting yourself dirty!"). She, like Mother, probably didn't know the real source of the grime and that her son hadn't deliberately made himself dirty, but she, at least, understood what makes young boys thrive. It wasn't so much the process of acquiring griminess that mattered, but the fact that being grimy at day's end usually meant the day had yielded a fair share of unfettered fun.

At about this time, it must have become clear to Mother that Raimond and Françoise were excellent babysitters for Brenda and me, and that the couple's work and routine seemed unimpaired by the extra responsibility. Mother queried Raimond and Françoise about their feelings on the subject. They replied that they greatly missed their son, so they were more than happy to have children to watch over, even if it interfered a little with their work.

The frequency of Minette's being asked to baby-sit Brenda and me gradually decreased so that she was tactfully eased out of her job. Minette remained a good friend of Mother's despite the fact that one of Minette's traits greatly irritated Father, who described it as "a surfeit of gall." It was during the Minette phasing-out period that she amply demonstrated what Father meant by this term.

Mother and Father were having a formal gala dinner for some of his business friends and their wives. There were to be eight guests in all. Because Raimond and Françoise were so busy with preparations, as was Mother, Minette was engaged to see that Brenda and I had our supper, and that we were put to bed before the guests arrived. When Minette arrived to assume her duties, she was carrying a suitcase which she managed to smuggle in without anyone noticing. After she had seen to our supper and tucked us in, she pulled out the suitcase and, in the unused guest room, changed into an evening dress and made herself up for an elegant *soirée*. Then, she waited patiently for the right moment to come sweeping majestically down the spiral staircase in the front hall at the very moment the guests were arriving. Her timing was apparently chosen so that Mother could hardly remonstrate with her over the fact that she had not been invited to the party.

Raimond, who was in the entrance hall taking guests' coats, immediately realized there was a problem. He went out to the kitchen to alert Françoise to set another place at the table. He had a further problem to solve. At the last minute, an out-of-town business colleague of Father's, and his wife, had unexpectedly arrived in Paris. Father had found it awkward not to invite them, too. Although the invitations had gone out for eight guests, Françoise had prudently special-ordered twelve partridges, so that Father's additional last-minute guests created no problem. Now, here was Minette, a thirteenth person at the dinner table. Where would they find an extra partridge at this late hour?

Raimond rose to the occasion with brilliance, demonstrating how adept and ingenious he could be. He saved the day by slicing one partridge neatly in half and resting each piece on a potato. The two potatoes used for this delicate operation were carefully chosen for size so that the "semi-partridges" rested at the same height on the plate as their unhalved counterparts. For this to work, all the partridges had to be served lying on their sides, instead of on their backs, as is the usual fashion. By careful arrangement of parsley and other victuals around the supporting potato on each of the two diminished plates, Raimond succeeded in making each half partridge look like a whole bird. He then served these half-birds to Mother and to Minette, respectively, taking care to forewarn Mother of his legerdemain. Minette was left to discover the shortfall on her own, and was, so to speak, hoist with her own petard. The next day, when Father heard about Raimond's sleight of hand, he guffawed and was all praise for his feat.

Minette got herself into even deeper water during dinner by telling off-color jokes of the crudest variety. By the end of the evening, she had consumed too much wine and, in slurred speech, complained that there were no single men at the party. She culminated her performance by making indecent proposals to two of the men in front of their wives.

For quite some time after that we didn't see Minette. A few months later, Minette restored her friendship with Mother by apologizing for her behavior.

In the middle of that happy spring term, Mother decided I needed to have my tonsils out. A year had passed since my appendix operation, and I remained undersized and underweight for my age. Docteur Narnier told Mother that it was because I had inflamed tonsils, which prevented me from getting all the air I needed for normal growth and weight gain. The tonsils absolutely had to come out, he insisted. Docteur Moronguet, the surgeon who had removed my appendix, claimed it was a minor operation that could be done at home. I still marvel at the fact that Father and Mother went along with this harebrained proposal.

It was all supposed to be very simple, but with the day of the surgery approaching, preparations became more and more elaborate. A room was designated as the operating room, which then had to be given an extra thorough cleaning. It had to have a washbasin so the surgeon could do a good scrub-up before starting. Father's bathroom had just been remodeled and repainted and was the logical choice. The place shone brighter than did any other room in the house. Father was going to be away that week, so after the operation I could be carried to his huge double bed, not ten feet from the proposed operating room.

Raimond built an elaborate operating table, actually a kitchen chair supported by a framework of lumber. He tilted the chair back to meet the surgeon's requirements and to place me at the right height for the surgeon's maximum convenience. In the days preceding the surgery, I was asked to mount this contraption numerous times, like a prisoner mounting the guillotine platform several times before an execution. This allowed Raimond to rehearse various arm and hand motions near my mouth, studying the advantages of this or that height and various tilt angles for the chair and its crude, homemade headrest. Coincidentally, Docteur Moronguet was about the same height as Raimond.

When he had achieved *la position optimum*, Raimond painted what Mother referred to as *"l'assemblage"* with white enamel. "So the germs won't be able to hide on it," he explained confidently, but the real reason was probably to hide the scruffy appearance of the old chair and the scraps of lumber he had garnered from dubious places. For good measure, he also painted white an old side table on which the surgeon would place his surgical instruments.

The ceiling light fixture was altered to accommodate more light bulbs. A series of oversize, slightly erotic photographs of Rodin statues (among them, Rodin's "The Kiss") were removed from the bathroom walls, presumably to avoid distracting the surgeon or perhaps to keep them from becoming blood-spattered.

On the big day itself, Raimond draped a white sheet across the end of the bathroom where the toilet was. "Microbes can fly out of toilets like gnats," he explained. Then Raimond donned a white surgeon's gown, which Mother had bought him for the occasion. He would be standing by to carry me to Father's bed. I viewed all these arrangements with apprehension, though everyone, including Mother, was trying to make it look like the preparation for a musical comedy.

At the last minute, Docteur Narnier called to announce that he was tied up on an emergency and wouldn't be able to attend. Narnier was supposed to administer the anesthetic, but Docteur Moronguet declared there was no reason why Raimond couldn't do this simple task. *"C'est bête comme chou!"* ("simple as pie!") he said. All Raimond had to do was to hold a folded tea towel snugly against my face and trickle the chloroform slowly over the towel until the small measuring bottle was empty. Docteur Moronguet and Raimond discussed the details of this procedure in front of me and rehearsed it (without chloroform) as I listened and watched with growing dismay. Mother was holding my hand, and saying things like "everything will be all right," and "there will be no pain." By now she must have been wondering how she ever got herself into this situation and was probably even more nervous than I.

With the rehearsals completed, Docteur Moronguet went over to the washbasin, rolled up his sleeves and, revealing arms as hairy as an ape's, set about a very thorough scrub. When he was done, he ordered Raimond to do likewise. Raimond did as painstaking a job as the surgeon had done and presented his hands to Moronguet for inspection. Moronguet told him to scrub once more. The trouble was that the skin of Raimond's hands was rough and stained from years of gardening and numerous other dirty jobs he did daily. The many cracks and nicks of his hands were deeply encrusted with soil and still looked black against his now-clean skin. After the second scrub, the surgeon looked at Raimond's hands once more and said impatiently, "I don't think your hands will ever get any cleaner, which isn't good. They must be clean because you may have to pass me implements or just hold things for me. However, it will have to do."

The surgeon now set about unpacking from a little black case an extraordinary assortment of fearsome-looking scalpels, tongs and clamps, which he set out neatly on the white table at my side. Then, out came the little bottle of chloroform. And two more bottles of it, "In case he wakes up too soon," Moronguet explained. At that point, I decided that was all I could take and leapt from the assemblage, bolting for the door. I didn't get far before Raimond, Mother, and the surgeon jointly grabbed me and forcibly lifted me, kicking and screaming, back onto the assemblage. I continued shrieking at the top of my lungs.

"I can't operate on a child in this condition," said Moronguet in an irritated tone. "You must calm him down before I do anything more." Then he went into Father's bedroom, saying he needed a smoke.

Mother held my hand and said soothingly, "You are now seven. You have reached the age of reason, and you must be reasonable." But I continued my loud wailing knowing that if I stopped I was doomed; I was prepared to keep it up forever if need be.

Then Raimond pronounced the magic words, "If you're good and let us do what we need to do, I have a nice surprise for you!"

"What is it?" I asked, bridling my wails to an abrupt halt.

"If I tell you, it won't be a surprise anymore, but I promise you it will be something extraordinary and that you won't be disappointed," said Raimond. He had never let me down or disappointed me, so I weighed his proposal carefully for a few seconds.

"All right," I agreed grudgingly. However, before the deal was sealed, Raimond extracted one more condition from me. I had to allow him to tie me loosely to the assemblage with a bandage so I wouldn't "accidentally fall out of the chair while asleep." I could see through that one, but I already knew I was outnumbered and it was useless to resist or bargain further. Indeed, I was now seven and discovering that "being reasonable" was really quite easy and might even yield unexpected rewards. So I let Raimond loosely tie my legs, my arms, and even my waist to the assemblage with various pieces cut from a bandage roll.

The doctor returned from his smoke and, without washing his hands a second time, told Raimond he was ready to begin the surgery. It was time to administer the chloroform. Both he and Raimond donned the surgical masks that already hung from their necks, and Raimond dutifully placed the folded tea towel over my nose and mouth. I watched him slowly trickle the contents of the little bottle as he moved it in a circle above me, and I felt the cold fluid on my face as it seeped through the tea towel. The smell was intense, and the room started spiraling around me as I slurred the words, *"Une belle surprise, n'est ce pas?"* ("A nice surprise, all right?").

When I awoke, I found that a ball of burning pain had replaced my throat. Mother was beside me, her eyes red from weeping. I remained in great pain and in a drugged stupor for several days, and all I remember is hearing a lot of hammering and sawing and dreaming that Raimond was building a high tower from which I could launch a glider. In my dream, I owned a glider big enough for me to climb into and fly. For some reason, I never got around to flying it, though I climbed into it.

When I finally woke up properly, my throat was still painful, and I felt even weaker than I was after the appendicitis operation.

I had apparently lost a huge amount of blood. It seems the operation was not very far along when I started hemorrhaging badly, and Docteur Moronguet had struggled long and furiously to bring the bleeding under control. He had not been able to remove the tonsils because he could not see them in the cascade of blood.

Mother told me many years later that, at one point, Moronguet seemed to be in a panic and out of control. He had yelled angrily at Raimond to apply pressure on my neck. Raimond had stayed calm, followed instructions adeptly and even made some remark which seemed to calm the agitated surgeon. Once the bleeding was under control, the doctor announced to Mother, who had been holding my hand the whole time, that I might have lost too much blood to survive the next few hours. Although blood transfusions were known, they were rarely tried, and the use of intravenous solutions was still unknown at the time; furthermore, I wasn't at a hospital, even if something along those lines had been available. Once the surgeon had done all he could, Raimond lifted my limp body out of the assemblage and carried me to the bed in Father's room, where he and Mother stood vigil over me for three hours until I awoke.

It was back to drinking raw beef blood, and when I was back on my feet, two weeks later, I weighed considerably less than before the operation. I was a walking skeleton. Worse yet, I still had my wretched tonsils.

Oh, yes—the surprise! After five days in Father's bed, Raimond carried me to my bedroom, which was also our playroom. There, it took me a moment to notice my electric train setup. I have mentioned the foot-high platform on which a simple circular train track was assembled. When I scrutinized the platform, I saw that the track now had a branch which forked off the platform. Supported on a series of realistic-looking piers, this branch of the track descended in a spiral to the level of the floor. The track then disappeared into a tunnel under the platform and re-emerged on the other side. From there, it spiraled back up onto the platform and rejoined the original loop at another switch point. And parked on the track was a new locomotive connected to a brand new passenger carriage.

The loop under the platform had been entirely Raimond's inspiration, and the idea had only come to him after considerable thought and debate with Mother as to how he could provide me a surprise worthy of his promise. Mother told me that the day after the operation, he had taken the bus into Paris to buy the extra pieces of track with his own money and that he had worked late into the night to put it all together before I was transferred back to my own bedroom. When he finished his construction work, he discovered to his dismay that my little flea market locomotive could not pull my one little wagon up the spiraling slope of the track without spinning its wheels. Raimond had been about to dash back into Paris to buy me a more powerful and heavier locomotive when Mother stepped in, went herself, and actually bought me a new locomotive and a passenger car.

Mother had literally been derailed in her goal to keep me from being spoiled, and my railroad empire had undergone a major expansion without my having to suffer a bite in my *derrière* from that nasty Poujet dog.

CHAPTER 8

The Great Rabbit Race and a Horse Named Lili

In the spring of 1937, Father bought Villa "Les Buissons" ("The Bushes") in Condette, a sleepy farming hamlet about six kilometers inland from Hardelot. The first thing he did was to give the house a new name because he considered "Les Buissons" too mundane. Raimond was asked to paint a new sign declaring its name to be "Villa Champs de Mai" ("Villa Fields of May"). Mother's birthday was in May, and Father bought the house that month, announcing that it was a birthday present. Years later, Mother confided to me that she would have much preferred to continue renting a villa in Hardelot, a lively, bustling seaside resort, a place she loved as much as I did. Condette was quiet and peaceful, but too quiet and too peaceful for everyone in the family except Father. He abhorred the Sunday crowds on the beach, and since he was only there on weekends when the crowding reached a crescendo, Hardelot was far from ideal for him. Father longed to spend his leisure hours in a more serene and rustic setting. His goal was achieved in spades when he bought the villa in Condette.

I hadn't been in Condette more than a day before it sunk in that Villa Sombra was to be the last villa we would rent in Hardelot, and I was thrown into a deep gloom over my new surroundings. I could see Mother was not her usual cheerful self either, but she was a good sport and not inclined to protest or resist Father, so she promptly threw her considerable energies into making the new house a success.

Father immediately started transforming Villa Champs de Mai into his dream house. This involved remodeling four bedrooms downstairs and adding four new bedrooms upstairs in what had been a huge attic. In each of the eight new bedrooms, he installed electric lighting and wash basins with hot and cold running water. The original house had been a hunting lodge entirely devoid of these amenities. A single hand pump in the kitchen had taken care of all the household's water needs.

Father imported from England a special brand of stove, the famous Aga cooker, probably the best in the world at the time. In France, it's hard to imagine a household item that plays a more important role in daily life than the stove, yet the French had nothing that compared with this magnificent British invention. The Aga was far too elaborate for Françoise, whose short temper was further shortened by the fact that she couldn't read the English instruction manual. However, with Mother's assistance in translating, and with technical help from Raimond, she gradually mastered this Rolls Royce of stoves, and by the end of the summer she liked it so much that she wanted one for the kitchen in Ville-d'Avray.

Though lacking other amenities, one thing the house did have was a spacious and well-built larder. Three huge meat hooks attached to its rafters hinted at the whole carcasses of wild boar or stags that may have hung there in times past. In spite of this excellent larder that stayed at 55 degrees Fahrenheit no matter what the outdoor temperature, Father insisted that he wanted an electric refrigerator, something rarely found in French households in those days. It was such an exotic item that the only model he could find was an American-made Frigidaire. During a visit to the United States, Father had developed a taste for dry martinis and had become addicted to having ice in his drinks.

We had always managed nicely without a refrigerator, and Françoise couldn't see why things shouldn't continue that way. She refused to turn on the refrigerator, protesting that she didn't like its quiet humming. However, the refrigerator wasn't a total loss. Françoise unplugged it and found it a convenient place to store bits of string, reusable scraps of paper, and other miscellaneous odds and ends that didn't quite seem to fit in anywhere else and that she wanted out of sight. Nevertheless, ice was now needed for Father, and Mother, who knew that having a harmonious household depended on humoring both Françoise and Father, made a point of buying a very large block of ice from the wine merchant in Étaples before Father's weekend return from Paris. In the larder, covered in old cartons to delay its thawing, it lasted us through the weekend.

The block was large enough so that it also provided crushed ice for a hand-cranked ice cream maker, which made ice cream far superior to anything a refrigerator could produce or that we could buy in any shop. Françoise's most famous dessert was melon ice cream. It was Raimond who deserved the real credit for the making of this exquisite confection. After Françoise rounded up the heavy cream, crushed melon pulp, sugar, a pinch of salt, and some ground vanilla, it was Raimond who did the hard work of cranking the ice cream maker's handle for at least twenty minutes. As this masterpiece neared completion, I made it a point to be present for the removal of the paddles that churned the ingredients. Someone had to undertake the messy chore of licking off the delicious gobs of ice cream that clung thereto, and I gallantly volunteered for the task.

Before completion of the new construction, the house appeared old, run down, and had a fusty smell. The place was depressing in the extreme, and I sorely missed the welcoming and festive appearance of the villas we had rented in Hardelot. I longed for the beach. I missed the sea. Instead, the house in Condette fronted on the village's communal pasture, a vast meadow, at least a mile across. Almost every farmer in Condette owned one or more cows, and some fifty animals grazed in this marshy pasture right in front of our house. I didn't have anything against cows, but I found their lowing at first dawn a poor substitute for the steady rumbling of the ocean's breakers, loud when the tide was up, faint at low tide, but always present in the background. I missed Hardelot's animated passing scene and the sound and promise of children playing on the beach. No shrimping, no sand castles, canals or dams, no sand sculpture contests, no sand yacht watching, and no high speed bicycling into tide pools—in short, where was fun?

Upon hearing of our new house in Condette, I had anticipated with great pleasure riding my beloved pale yellow trolley to Hardelot every day. The little streetcar passed within a quarter mile of Villa Les Buissons when we had summered in Condette three years before. The daily ride to Hardelot could well have been a pleasant and exciting way to retain our ties with that seaside paradise. However, the very year we bought the house, the trolley service was discontinued. Most of the residents of Hardelot now owned cars. The women shrimpers alone couldn't make it pay.

The garden at the Villa Champs de Mai was all deep grass and weeds, with no paths on which to ride a bike. Beyond our front gate was a rough grassy track a quarter mile long, bordering the communal pasture and connecting our house to the nearest paved road. The track was partly coarse gravel and partly rough, tussocky grass, making for a bumpy, unpleasant ride on a bike.

Indoors, the situation was even less promising because the workmens' activities made much of the house off limits to me. Adding to the pervasive gloom, Raimond was miserable because Françoise was still out of sorts over the Aga cooker. For him, life was tense enough when Françoise was "in sorts."

The house was quite unlike any I have ever seen. It was about a hundred feet long by sixty feet wide, with a central corridor running its full hundred-foot length. The four existing bedrooms on the main floor had French doors that opened onto a wide, covered terrace, as did the drawing room. The terrace bordered the entire length of the south and west sides of the house.

I was intrigued by the construction work in progress, but my curiosity was largely thwarted by the fact that I was ordered to give the workmen a wide berth. Raimond also took an interest in what was being done or about to be done.

While standing at the top of a contractor's ladder propped on the lip of a ceiling hatch, Raimond had surveyed the attic where the new construction was about to begin. Later, while serving us lunch, he reported that there was so much old furniture, bric-a-brac, and discarded junk in the attic that it was *impassable*. He explained that since there was no floor to the attic, this mountain of junk was placed across the exposed joists that supported the ceiling below. He wondered how the builders would get all that stuff through the small hatch that led out of the attic. One false step while moving the junk out and they would come crashing through the ceiling, Raimond predicted portentously.

One day, I noticed an electrician's ladder leading into the attic hatch. Since the workman was not around, and since Mother was away playing golf, I decided it was an ideal time to conduct an exploration of my own. Cautiously, tentatively, I climbed the wobbly ladder, determined to discover what this "impassable junk" was all about. The rungs were spaced far apart, and each step up was a huge stretch for an undersized seven year old. I was acutely aware that each one represented a successively greater danger as the floor below me receded. The fear of falling, the intoxication of height, and the thrill of adventure were a heady brew. When I finally reached enough altitude to put my head inside the attic, I found it was too dark to see anything.

As I stood there resting after my perilous climb and wondering what I should do next, my vision became acclimated to the low level of light that eventually proved not only adequate but surprisingly abundant. Light from outdoors suffused through a myriad of horizontal slits between the ill-fitting tiles. The steep-pitched roof was antique, and the hand-made tiles didn't fit together neatly and snugly as they rested on the widely spaced lath that spanned the roof beams.

A tabletop missing its four legs had been placed beside the hatch opening as a landing platform. I climbed a few more rungs of the ladder, stepped cautiously onto the tabletop, which seemed sturdy enough, and surveyed the vast, unexplored territory that surrounded me. There were mountains of stuff, mostly old broken-down furniture: headboards, chairs, small tables, outdoor wicker furniture, as well as chamber pots and slop buckets, wooden boxes full of old kitchen utensils, mattresses, some saddles and other horsy stuff, such as riding boots, britches, and crops. The list went on: broken fishing rods, tennis rackets with strings missing, canoe paddles, battered oars, moth-eaten carpet rolls, and mounds of what might have been curtains, blankets, bedding and piles of old clothes. These things extended in all directions, sometimes piled, sometimes carelessly thrown one on top of another. It looked as if a string of owners had successively dumped all their unwanted or worn-out belongings up there and as if nothing had ever been retrieved.

Dust-laden cobwebs draped everything like a single large drop cloth. The dust was not the usual pale gray, fluffy house dust, but a fine, gritty powder, dark gray, almost black. When Raimond had first told us of his foray into the attic, he had mentioned the excessive amount of gritty dust, explaining that it was an accumulation of the local topsoil, which streamed through the slits between the tiles when the wind blew.

There seemed to be one direction in which the piled-up junk was the lightest, hinting at an ancient track through this overgrown jungle, so I sallied forth that way. By lifting and moving some of the lighter objects as I advanced, I was able to open up and leave some hint of a clear track behind me. I pushed on, taking care to place my feet on the joists, and making sure that all the things I relocated rested on the joists.

At some point in my journey, I encountered a pith helmet that I thought might look well on me; it would complete the picture I had of myself as an intrepid explorer. It had been discarded topside down, and when I turned it over while putting it on my head, a cascade of black dust and dirt fell over my face, hair, and clothing. Undaunted, I forged on fearlessly.

When I reached the outermost end of the attic and was about to embark upon my return journey, something caught my eye. It was a heavy cast-iron box about three feet wide and two feet high. Several small cast-iron doors set in the side that faced me had swivel latches on them and looked like the oven doors on Françoise's old cooking stove in Ville-d'Avray. If this were a stove, it would be a tiny one, since it was only two feet high. With growing curiosity, I removed a mound of curtains from the top of the iron box, revealing two sets of cast-iron stove rings. The top surface also had a sooty hole near the back edge, suggesting a place where a stovepipe had been attached. Everything about this play stove was authentic, but on a miniature scale.

I tried to lift the stove for a better look and, while struggling in this futile effort, I put both feet on the lath and plaster. I heard a loud cracking sound and felt the plaster surface give way under my feet. To my surprise, I only dropped a couple of inches before my abrupt descent came to an unexpected stop. The plaster ceiling was holding me, as if deliberating whether to let me go on through. I remained motionless, not daring to move, lest I unleash the disaster Raimond had predicted. Fearing that even the quick movement of my eyes would trigger my swift descent into the quicksand, I turned my gaze slowly downward. There, I could barely discern some light shining through several cracks radiating from around my feet. The stove seemed steady enough, sitting as it did across two joists. If I hung on to the stove, I reasoned, it might save my life, and I wouldn't go on through the plaster. Gingerly, I moved my hands to a place on the stovetop where I found purchase, then I cautiously shifted my upper body weight onto the stove and eventually felt it was safe to move my feet back onto the joists. The plaster seemed to rise as I lifted my feet from it, and the cracks vanished.

At the moment of my misstep, I had been too alarmed to notice that the loud cracking noise of the ceiling had disturbed the sleep of several bats, which were now screeching and flying around me in a state of alarm. With my heart thumping so loudly that I could hear it, I retreated across the joists as fast as I could. But when I reached the attic opening, my only exit from this hellhole, I discovered to my horror that the ladder was gone! I called out for help; no one answered. I listened for footsteps; the house was utterly silent. The bats had stopped their screeching, but still fluttered silently around me. One bat looked as if it were trying to attack me, repeatedly flying straight towards me and, only at the last moment, veering away. The creature may, like me, have been trying to leave the attic through the open hatch. Whatever its intentions, I found its constant swooping towards me unnerving. I knelt down on the tabletop, leaned over and lowered my head through the hatch, hoping my calling would carry farther from this vantage point. *"Aux secours . . . Aux Secours!"* ("Help . . . Help!") I called and yelled, ever louder and more desperately.

After a minute or two, I heard footsteps echoing through the deserted house, and to my immense relief, Raimond appeared. He chuckled good-naturedly when he saw my predicament. He told me the electrician had left with his ladder and that there was no other ladder in the house. He rubbed his chin and pondered the situation for a minute. Then he said, "Wait!" and disappeared in the direction of the kitchen. When he returned, he was dragging a heavy butcher table, and on a second trip, he was carrying a chair which he used as a step to climb onto the table.

I passed my legs over the rim of the hatch as instructed by Raimond. He then reached up and, putting his arms around my upper legs, eased me down.

Once we were both back on terra firma, Raimond observed that I looked like a coal merchant after a long day's work and advised me to take a bath before Mother returned from her golfing. "And when you're done, I'd better scrub the tub right away and destroy the evidence," he added wryly. I implored him not to tell Mother about my misadventure, and Raimond promised me that he wouldn't.

As soon as Raimond went back to his chores in the kitchen, I conducted a careful survey of all the ceiling areas downstairs and, to my great relief, could see no cracks anywhere. I decided to remain silent about my mishap.

Raimond was curious about what I had found during my exploration. After extracting a promise he would not tell Mother that I was the one who had found it, I told him about the miniature stove and how anxious I was to play with it. Raimond was as intrigued by the stove as I was and proposed a solution. "I'll just say that the electrician asked me to go up there to pull on a wire he was installing. Then I discovered this remarkable little stove and decided it would make a beautiful toy for you and Brenda."

The next day, with the help of the electrician, he lowered the stove down from the attic, along with a complete battery of miniature cooking utensils that he found in a box not far from the stove. He soon had all these items clean and ready for play, leaving Brenda and me in a state of utter delight that lasted for days. I vastly augmented my chef's repertoire of dishes that could be prepared by using a variety of garden weeds, soil and pebbles to represent an assortment of exotic foods. Brenda's dolls and teddy bear seemed to have an insatiable appetite as they devoured these dishes with relish all day long.

This game soon lost its luster, and it gradually dawned on me that we should light an actual fire in the stove and cook real food on it. Once again, Raimond was ready and waiting. He had found the original piece of stovepipe, uncovered when the workmen systematically emptied the attic, and he had put it aside for just this purpose. He set up the stove in the lean-to woodshed at the back of the house where, out of the wind, we could light it with its stovepipe poking out of the open side of the shed.

It took a long time to get the chimney pipe hot and drawing well, but eventually, with a lot of help from Raimond, we had a good fire going in the stove. That done, I set about preparing some *pommes poêlées* (pan-fried sliced potatoes) in the miniature frying pan, and some *carottes Vichy*. At one point, the carrots caught fire when I added the required sugar, but Raimond quickly had it under control, without even spoiling my deliciously caramelized carrots. Then, Françoise brought out a tiny piece of steak, which I browned nicely on both sides and served rare, the way Brenda and I liked it. With the cooking successfully completed, Brenda and I sat down at a play table and ate what we both considered the best meal we had ever eaten. With the help of Raimond we had everything cleaned up before Mother's return from an afternoon of golf. Raimond swore us to secrecy, fearing that the thought of our playing around a lighted stove might upset Mother.

On the occasion of France's national holiday on July 14th (Bastille Day), Condette was the site of a fair that consisted of a small merry-go-round and some game stalls assembled in one of the village's pastures. Raimond and Françoise had the afternoon off for the holiday, and it was Raimond's first chance to try out the fishing at a small lake at the far end of the communal pasture. Françoise felt at loose ends and offered to take Brenda and me to the fair.

When the three of us reached the fairgrounds in midafternoon we were amazed to see the large crowd that had already gathered. All of Condette's farmers as well as the populations of several neighboring villages seemed to be in attendance. The scene was a lively one, with bright orange canvas awnings at each of the stalls, an ornate merry-go-round, a bandstand decorated with the traditional blue, white, and red bunting, and everywhere a profusion of French flags attached to poles and fence posts, singly or in clusters like flower bouquets.

Despite the hot summer day and the animation of the occasion, most men and women were wearing their Sunday best: the men in dark suits, and the older women in black skirts, black shawls and fancy, wide-brimmed black hats. But the younger men were in freshly laundered workaday clothes consisting of pale blue denim trousers and tunics. Young women and girls wore skirts almost to their ankles, embroidered peasant blouses, and colorful kerchiefs on their heads. Françoise, in her finest Sunday attire, could have passed for a farmer's wife. Brenda and I stood out as *estivants* (summer vacationers) in our bright orange terry cloth shorts and shirts purchased at a fashionable Paris boutique.

After a few rides on the merry-go-round, I asked Françoise to let me try my luck at one of the games of chance. Mother had given Françoise twenty francs for such ventures. After carefully surveying all the stalls, most of which involved activities I didn't understand, I opted for the one that offered what, to me, were the most attractive prizes. I was convinced that I was bound to win whatever contest I entered.

The stall I chose was at the far end of the fair, well away from the noisy merry-go-round. There, a hand-lettered sign beside an unused grassy patch proclaimed the area to be a *Hippodrome pour Lapins* (Racecourse for Rabbits). A Gypsy stood at a nearby stall taking bets on competing rabbits, as well as bets on the fates of some forty carrots neatly spaced out on a patch of grass so as to form a large circle, towards which the rabbits would presumably race.

Six large, docile-looking rabbits lounged lazily in hutches inside the Gypsy's stall. Numerous wire mesh cages close to the rabbit hutches contained an assortment of small barnyard creatures. A sign above the cages proclaimed that these animals were the prizes to be won. This is what had attracted me to this contest. I had my heart set on winning one of those creatures. Meanwhile, the Gypsy was touting the event through a homemade, cardboard megaphone, *"Allez! Tout le monde! Je vous invite à voir la Grande Course aux Lapins! Il faut voir l'événement le plus palpitant de la foire—la Grande Course aux Lapins!"* ("Come one! Come all! I invite you to see the Great Rabbit Race! You must see the most thrilling event at the fair—the Great Rabbit Race!").

The Gypsy stood beside a chalkboard with numbers on it. Each of the numbers on the board corresponded to one of the numbered carrots. I could bet five francs on one of these, and if my carrot were the one chosen by the winning rabbit, I would win fifty francs *and* my choice of one of the small farm animals in the cages beside the main rabbit cage.

The contest had a double punch, at least for the Gypsy, because bettors could also bet on the rabbits. Unlike racehorses, however, the rabbits wore no racing colors. Their names easily identified them, since they were named for their distinctive characteristics, such as fur color or other distinguishing features. For bets on the rabbits, a second chalkboard listed the six rabbits by name, and underneath each one were added the names of people who had placed five-franc bets on that rabbit. Françoise explained to me that the people listed under the winning rabbit would divide the entire money bet on all of the rabbits, but only *after* the gypsy took half of that money for himself. The rabbit bets confused me, especially that business of the Gypsy taking half the money—that sounded fishy to me—so I decided to bet my money on one of the carrots. Besides, my goal was to win one of the small animals, and I could only do that by betting on a carrot.

I placed my five-franc bet on carrot number seven. The Gypsy wrote "Alain" beside the number seven on the chalkboard. I walked over to the carrot marked seven and decided that it looked like a plump and tempting carrot and that I had made a sound choice. At my urging, and after a careful scrutiny of the carrots, Brenda and Françoise also placed bets, Brenda on carrot 22 and Françoise on carrot 13.

The race wasn't until five o'clock, and in the meantime, taking numerous rides on the merry-go-round did little to calm my anxious excitement. Brenda, who rode the merry-go-round with me, seemed quite ho-hum about it all but was perhaps too young to appreciate the high stakes involved.

By half past four, a large crowd had gathered around the rabbit hippodrome, and all the numbered carrots were spoken for. The Gypsy was anxious to get more bets placed on the individual rabbits, so he touted each one by name as he held it up by its ears. He reached into the cage, grabbed the ears of a gray one and holding it high for all to see, chanted, *"Et alors! Voilà Grisette, la plus vive, la plus rapace. Elle est superbe, n'est ce pas?"* ("And now! This is Grisette, the liveliest, the most rapacious. She's a beauty, isn't she?") An assistant posted the last minute bettors on the board as the spectators called out their names, and the five-franc pieces found their way into the Gypsy's pocket.

When he couldn't coax anymore bets from the audience, the Gypsy, still using his megaphone, explained the rules of the race. *"Le premier lapin qui grignote sérieusement une carotte sera le gagnant."* ("The first rabbit to seriously nibble on a carrot will be the winner.") Just sniffing a carrot did not constitute a win. None of the rabbits had eaten a thing in two days. They were famished, the Gypsy assured us. He went on to explain that he wanted complete silence during the race. *"Il ne faut qu'un rire pour faire sauter la course."* ("It only takes one laugh to blow the race.") And naturally, there was to be no cheering until the race was over! Anyone causing even a minor distraction would be

211

disqualified from winning any prize money if his rabbit or carrot turned out to be a winner. If this happened, the second carrot to be nibbled would be declared the winning carrot.

The Gypsy then adopted a grave and dramatic voice: "It's the obligatory silence which gives this race its heart-pounding suspense! During the fateful silence of this event, fortunes are made or broken!" The audience listened in silent awe.

A few minutes before the start, a small chicken-wire enclosure with neither top nor bottom was placed in the center of the carrot circle, and six very nervous-looking rabbits were carried in by their ears and placed in this small, round holding pen. At last, the big moment was upon us! The Gypsy was handed a long pole that he then used to lift the chicken-wire enclosure gently up and out of the carrot circle, all the while keeping his distance from the rabbits. The merry-go-round's calliope fell silent. A reverential hush descended over the crowd that had been chatting excitedly until now.

When the starting enclosure was lifted, the rabbits just sat there appearing bemused, staring at the spectators and looking as though they didn't know what they were supposed to do. I realize now that the rabbits probably could not see the carrots lying in the grass some ten feet away and that for the rabbits, the new "enclosure" formed by a solid wall of spectators standing only five feet beyond the circle of carrots must have been a daunting sight.

We stood in rapt attention and total silence for what seemed like several minutes. The rabbits took a few unconvincing rabbit hops leading nowhere and seemed content to remain near the starting zone. Then, one of the rabbits hopped around to Grisette, looked her over, and mounted her. It was a rabbit called "Grand Bonhomme" ("Big Guy"). There was a round of muted tittering. I became alarmed because the people standing next to me had been the loudest with their tittering, and I feared I might be lumped in with them and disqualified. Furthermore, I had no idea what Grand Bonhomme was up to and couldn't see what was so funny. Fortunately, the entire circle of spectators had tittered, and it didn't seem to have disturbed any of the rabbits. They just pricked their ears and stood their ground.

Grisette shook off Grand Bonhomme and scampered about four feet out of the starting zone, where she came to a stop and turned around to face Grand Bonhomme as if to keep an eye on him. He decided to have another try and nonchalantly took a few lopes towards Grisette. When he was within a foot of her, he apparently thought the better of it, made an about face and put on an air of indifference and innocence. More titters from the crowd and quiet shushing from the Gypsy ensued.

In the meantime, some of the rabbits made a few haphazard lopes toward the carrot circle. "Ti-Noir" ("Little Blackie", who was actually bigger than Big Guy) seemed to be making the most progress and was now only three feet from a carrot—unfortunately, not mine. Then Ti-noir sat up on his hind haunches and, from this vantage point spotted something that caused him to make a headlong dash across the center of the circle. At the last minute he slammed on the brakes and came to a stop beside carrot number eight, right next to mine. Ti-Noir's sudden movement had ignited the other rabbits into action, for they were now scurrying left and right, each eventually coming to a stop near the circle of carrots.

It seems that rabbits, at least French rabbits, have to stop and contemplate any carrot they are about to eat. Every one of the rabbits was now beside a carrot, and remained motionless, eyeing the closest one. Grisette even sniffed a carrot without actually eating it. Ti-Noir seemed distracted by all the commotion he had caused, lost interest in carrot number eight and turned his gaze to carrot number seven. Then he nonchalantly loped two feet towards my carrot and, as all the other rabbits had done, initiated the required period of cogitation.

Famished indeed! Every rabbit was now contemplating a carrot, and for at least a minute, none of them moved so much as a whisker. The suspense was intense as the crowd held its collective breath. The moment of truth was upon us! No one dared budge for fear of disqualification. Then, Ti-Noir took a tentative nibble at my carrot and, finding it to his taste, finally started some serious munching on it.

The crowd went wild, unleashing a tidal wave of pent-up excitement. Françoise, beside me, was ecstatic. She clapped vigorously and rubbed her hands together in a prayer-like gesture.

I collected my fifty francs, handed them to Françoise, and walked over to the cages to receive my farmyard creature. I now had to choose from an assortment of chickens, ducks, and rabbits of different breeds and colors, but I already knew exactly which one I wanted. From the start, my eye had been on a mallard duck. The iridescent deep green color of his head plumage was the most entrancing color I had ever laid eyes on. It didn't seem possible I would be the owner of such a fantastically beautiful bird. I would call him "Ploof" after the celebrated mallard, Plouf, in the *Albums du Père Castor* (a superbly illustrated series of children's books).

The Gypsy lifted Ploof out of the cage and tied a string to the duck's leg, the free end of which he told me to tie to my belt. This done, he handed me the duck which seemed quite content to rest against my hip with my arm around him. I left the fair strutting proudly with my prize under my arm and Brenda and Françoise in tow.

Upon our arrival home, I saw that Mother had returned from her game of golf and was resting in a *chaise longue* on the lawn, reading a book. As I approached her, I called out proudly, "Mummy! Look at the beautiful duck I won at the fair! His name is Ploof, and I'm going to train him to do all sorts of tricks and to follow me wherever I go!"

Before Mother could comment, Françoise, right behind me, interjected, "For our dinner Madame, would you like it served *à l'orange* or just plain roasted *chasseur?*"

Without even waiting for Mother's answer, I started to run, holding tightly onto my duck. I had no clear plan for dealing with this crisis, but I headed for a small wood in the back of the garden where, hiding, I might have a little time to work things out. On my way, I passed the open garage door and saw Raimond inside, tidying up his fishing tackle. Raimond had always been a dependable ally, so I stopped and, out of breath, told him how I had won Ploof at the fair and that Françoise was planning to serve my beautiful duck for dinner. Raimond was appalled, and immediately went to the kitchen where I could hear him remonstrating with Françoise.

It was the only time I ever heard him telling her off. Somewhat to my amazement, Raimond soon emerged unscathed from the kitchen. He immediately set about looking for materials to build a cage. In the meantime, I tied Ploof's string to a sapling and went off to the compost pile where I knew Raimond was breeding a slither of snails for gastronomic purposes. I gathered a handful of the biggest ones I could find and returned to the garage. Raimond had shaped a piece of wire netting into a circle about a yard in diameter and about the same height. It was open at the top, and Raimond was lowering Ploof into this rudimentary cage as I returned. I offered the snails to Ploof, who tore into them voraciously, shell and all. "*Alors!* Monsieur Alain! Just like that you offer my precious snails, *my* dinner, to the duck!" Raimond said, teasing me.

There was still plenty of time before dinner, so I went for more snails. When Ploof had devoured his second helping, I took him out of his cage so I could admire him more closely as I held onto his short string. I spent an hour or so drinking in his exquisite beauty, petting him and talking lovingly to him. He was even more beautiful than I realized. I hadn't noticed the little white ring where the lustrous green ended on his neck. Nor had I seen the panels of snow-white feathers on his sides and a small, upright curl of black feathers centered on his back. And when he stretched himself by opening and flapping his wings, I was amazed to discover two more large swatches of an iridescent teal blue color on his sides. In elegant contrast with his feathers were a bright yellow bill and his two yellow feet. I happened to notice that the web was missing from between two of his "toes," the only blemish on this otherwise perfect creature.

Ploof seemed unafraid and quite friendly, and kept uttering discreet little "kwuck" sounds which I took to be the equivalent of a cat's purring, probably thanking me for all those snails. They must be like ice cream cones to a duck, I told myself.

When I heard Mother calling me for dinner, I reluctantly put Ploof back into his cage, confident that I had made some headway in befriending him. That night at dinner, I regaled my parents and the guests with a description of the Great Rabbit Race. Each successive detail created a great deal of laughter, except the business of Grand Bonhomme and Grisette which, mysteriously, only produced an awkward silence.

The next morning I awoke to the crowing of a rooster at the neighbor's farm. It was a sound that occurred daily and, as a rule, didn't awaken me. But on this day, the realization that I owned a magnificent duck galvanized me into action. I slipped into my clothes and tiptoed through the silent house and out into the dew-laden garden. The sun was not up yet, and a low-lying mist lingered, adding to the tranquility of the scene.

When I reached Ploof's enclosure, I was horrified to discover he was gone! Alarmed, I initiated a search through the little wood, then through the rest of the garden, all to no avail. I opened the front gate and marched up the grass track along the communal pasture, keeping a sharp eye out for places in the hedge to my left where Ploof might be hiding. My shoes were sopping wet from the heavy dew on the grass, and I was so intent on my search that I soon grew inured to the chill air, even though I was lightly dressed.

Some distance from our house, the grassy track that I was on made a sharp left turn away from the meadow. At this corner, there was a gate into the meadow where all the cattle in the pasture had congregated. The cows stood absolutely still and the only sign of movement among them were the puffs of vapor from their breathing. An occasional plaintive lowing conveyed their collective impatience as they awaited their various owners, who would soon take them to their respective home barns for milking. I walked past the cows and on around the bend. Before me lay a hundred-yard stretch of grass track bordered on both sides by thick bramble hedges that ended at a paved road. Looking down this stretch, I saw no sign of Ploof and realized the futility of continuing my search. Thoroughly disheartened, I turned back towards our house.

Halfway back, I passed the entrance to the Baichant farm, our immediate neighbors to the north. As I went by, Madame Baichant came clattering out of her farmhouse in her wooden *sabots*. She opened the gate onto the grassy track and greeted me cheerily, "You're up very early, Monsieur Alain!"

I told her my sad tale and asked her if, by chance, she had seen an unfamiliar duck wandering around her farm. She replied that she hadn't seen any ducks, and that she was hurrying to bring Mémé in for milking. She would have a look around as soon as she was done. "Mémé can't wait," she said. "But would you like to join me in fetching her? You can tell me more about this duck on the way."

Madame Baichant was a cheerful and friendly woman, so I gladly accepted her invitation. We walked up the track and when we reached the gate where the cows were gathered, she called out in a shrill voice, *"Viens Mémé! Viens Mémé! Viens!"* until one of the cows started to move slowly through the closely gathered herd towards the gate. Every cow in the meadow was called "Mémé," but each cow knew its owner's voice and could be depended upon to come forward obediently upon being called, as the others stood by looking envious. Madame Baichant opened the gate, and *her* Mémé ambled through. With her massive udder swinging gently from side to side, and without any guidance or coaxing from Madame Baichant, Mémé resolutely led us along the grassy track, through the open farmyard gate, and thence to her milking stall.

Once inside the cowshed, I stared in amazement at the vigor and speed with which Madame Baichant milked Mémé. It didn't take her much more than five minutes, during which time I continued my account of how I had acquired Ploof and of his disappearance.

"Tell me, were his wing-tip feathers clipped?" Madame Baichant asked, working smoothly and rhythmically at two of the teats.

"What do you mean?"

"Did the feathers look as though they had been cut with scissors? Were the tips of the feathers straight, or were they rounded?" she elaborated.

"Rounded," I replied with certainty, for I had admired their shape from close up.

"Ah! There's your problem! That Gypsy didn't trim the wing feathers, hoping the duck would fly back to him if it is left in a place open to the sky, like this one," she said, waving towards the walled-in farmyard outside the stall. "That way, they can use the duck again and again. Ducks are like homing pigeons; they will fly back to where they came from, especially if they are part of a family of ducks that have grown up together."

"But I gave that duck some fat snails, and he really liked them. He must have realized I was going to be a good friend. It doesn't seem possible he would return to that nasty old Gypsy who probably never brought him a single snail. For an hour last night, I petted Ploof and talked to him in a friendly way. How could he betray me like this?" The tears came welling up as I spoke. I continued, "When he belonged to the Gypsy, he had to live in a tiny hutch all day long. How can he prefer that to . . . ."

There, I stopped, realizing I hadn't provided Ploof with any kind of shelter, and perhaps he feared a fox might come while he was asleep in Raimond's open-topped cage. Also, I hadn't tied his string to the cage when I put him in it after I had finished admiring him, believing that he couldn't fly straight up to escape.

Madame Baichant had filled the pail, relieving Mémé of her great load of milk, and asked me if I'd like a drink of fresh milk. I accepted her offer and followed her across the farmyard to her house as she carried the heavy pail.

On entering her front door, I found myself in a spacious kitchen that also served as general workroom, dining room, and living room. What struck me first was a smell that was a mixture of many pleasant things. There was the smell one finds in a seed and grain store, chiefly that of bran in bulk, combined with the smell of a hearty meat stew cooked with aromatic herbs.

Two small windows pierced the house's thick stone walls and cast dramatic side lighting on a small part of the room, leaving the rest in dim light. The only other light was a warm glow from the other side of the room, where a fire was burning in a large fireplace. The room was further darkened by a black earthen floor, uneven, but packed hard and polished to a high glaze in places of heavy use. The crooked timbers of the low ceiling were rough-hewn, and their wood was old and riddled with tiny woodworm holes. The room's darkness was not oppressive; rather, it created a strong sense of shelter and coziness. It felt solid and permanent and made me feel at ease and safe.

I was enthralled by Madame Baichant and the way she led her life and was so taken by her farmhouse kitchen that I completely forgot about Ploof.

Madame Baichant invited me to sit at the table, unhooked an enameled ladle from a wall hook, took an earthenware mug from a shelf, and ladled milk from the pail into the mug.

"Couldn't be fresher," she said, handing me the mug, "and still warm from the cow."

As I sipped Mémé's creamy milk, Madame Baichant intimated that Ploof was a lost cause. "You had better forget about him. If you like ducks, you can come over here any time you want and feed ours. We have a dozen or so. Some of them are mallards, and there are even a few ducklings," she volunteered. The offer sounded genuine and was, for me, a solution to a problem that had been nagging me all morning: if I did find Ploof, how would I keep Françoise from snatching and cooking him?

"I'd like that very much, Madame Baichant," I replied. Without a thought of what Mother might think of this scheme, I followed up with, "May I come again later today?"

At that moment, a door opened, and through it came a sleepy-looking young girl wearing a flannel nightshirt so large that she held big bunches of the shirt in both hands to keep from tripping over it. I had seen her numerous times as we drove up the grass track on our way in or out of Villa Champs de Mai and I knew she was Madame Baichant's daughter. Until that morning, I had never known her name. It was Michelle. She was about the same age as I and the same height, but, unlike me, she was a sturdy, tough-looking child.

She was a towhead whose home-styled, gamine haircut with its straight bangs accentuated the sharp features of her face and imparted to her a rather feral look. A few minutes of listening to Michelle talking with her mother soon dispelled this unfavorable first impression and made it clear that she was a happy, easy-going young girl.

Madame Baichant gave her a large bowl of milk and a massive slab of bread. As Michelle dunked large chunks of the bread into her milk and spooned them up with much slurping and gusto, she and her mother went over a list of chores that awaited Michelle after she finished her bread and milk. Michelle asked her mother about the carrots she wanted her to gather. From which of the planting beds should she take them? How many did she want? Madame Baichant also reminded her that she needed four dozen eggs collected, and that the mare had to be brought out of her stall and taken to the barn for hitching to the cart. Finally, as she opened the door to leave, Madame Baichant announced, "I'm taking Mémé back to the pasture." It all seemed part of a daily routine and only the specifics of this particular morning were under discussion.

We already knew Madame Baichant from our two years of summering in Hardelot. She ran a "general" farm, which supplied eggs, milk, poultry, fresh fruit, and vegetables six days a week to the summer residents staying at the seaside resort six kilometers away. When we rented a villa in Hardelot, Françoise relied heavily on Madame Baichant's horse-drawn cart loaded with its colorful assortment of homegrown, freshly picked vegetables—so much fresher than anything from the greengrocer. From her cart, Madame Baichant also sold eggs individually from a basket lined with straw, and milk she ladled from a huge milk can straight into her customer's pitcher. On the morning of my hunt for the missing Ploof, Madame Baichant was winding up her preparations for a round of deliveries.

After Michelle finished breakfast, she invited me to join her in the collecting of carrots and eggs, and told me to wait while she went to her room to dress. Without delay, she disappeared through the door she had entered. As I waited, I noticed that sunlight was finally streaming through the small windows and I could now discern other details of the kitchen. A large galvanized tub on sawhorses served as kitchen sink where it sat beneath the spout of a hand pump. Numerous shelves along the walls held plates, porcelain platters, cooking pots, kitchen utensils, and tools of all kinds. A cauldron and a large cast-iron kettle hung from racks inside the fireplace, directly over the fire. Neatly braided bunches of onions and garlic hung from the ceiling beams, as did several oil lamps. The room was devoid of any decoration, except a wall crucifix, and was simply furnished with a massive kitchen table, a large chest of drawers, and a dozen or so straight-backed chairs, most of them pushed against the wall. Coveralls, rain gear and various farming implements hung from large wooden pegs along the wall closest to the entrance. The room served every conceivable purpose except sleeping.

Michelle soon reappeared wearing a plain, dark gray smock and small wooden *sabots* without socks.

"*Viens*," she said, taking my hand and dragging me out through the back door that led into a large vegetable garden. To my surprise and delight, she was already acting as though we were lifelong friends, and in contrast to her mother, she was using the familiar *"tu"* instead of the formal *"vous."*

With Michelle pulling five carrots for every one I pulled, we soon had the required sixty, their greens still attached, all piled neatly into a wooden hand basket. Egg gathering proved more challenging. We found most of them in chicken hutches located under a roof overhang of the barn. Michelle counted them twice, coming up with thirty-one the first time, and on the second try, forty-five. She was hopeless at counting. As she counted aloud, I had noted her numerous errors, but she was rattling the numbers off with such determination and speed that I couldn't find a spot to jump in and correct her. Compounding her problem, the eggs were at least three-layers-deep in the basket. I proposed we go into the barn, where we could count the eggs as we removed them from the basket and set them on a bed of straw. Michelle conceded that would be a better idea.

In the barn, she still insisted on being the one who did the counting, but when she skipped "sixteen," this time, I was able to stop and correct her. She steadfastly maintained that seventeen came after fifteen. A brief argument ensued, but she eventually capitulated and let me do the counting. Then she had the audacity to quarrel with *my* order of counting. Madame Baichant was within earshot, and I heard her call out to Michelle that she wanted Alain to do the counting, and that Michelle was to stop interrupting me. My tally revealed that we still needed nine eggs. We had emptied every hutch, and I wondered where we would find more.

"This way!" Michelle exclaimed, leading me by the hand to the vegetable garden and along a thick bramble hedge that bordered the entire west edge of the garden. As we walked, she suddenly stopped, stooped over and reached into the brambles, bringing out an egg as if by magic. Michelle seemed to know the telltale marks of a secret chicken nest. A few hens apparently preferred the peace and quiet of a country hedge to the busy city life of the hutches near the barn. In some places, a disgruntled chicken fluttered out, squawking raucously after Michelle nudged her off the nest to get at the egg.

After retrieving the required number of eggs, we headed back to the stable to get "Lili," a gigantic Boulonais mare. Here too, Michelle proved adept and sure of herself as she climbed easily onto a diagonal beam in the horse's stall in order to pass a halter over Lili's head. She then led the huge horse out of the stall and to the barn.

Madame Baichant was in the barn sorting and arranging the baskets containing her produce. The barn served as a garage for the cart, whose shafts were suspended by ropes tied to the rafters. This arrangement allowed Madame Baichant to guide the horse backwards between the two shafts, and then to put the massive collar on the patient mare. Michelle helped her mother with the numerous straps that went over, around, and under Lili, with Michelle doing the work needed at the lower levels and Madame Baichant working at the straps that were out of Michelle's reach.

The two-wheeled cart was little more than a rectangular box about eight feet long by five feet wide, surmounted by four upright steel hoops supporting a pale green canvas roof. A padded bench at the front of the box had side handles to keep the passengers from sliding off when the cart went around a bend. Beneath the bench at the front of the cart was a footrest with an elegantly curved front panel to protect the driver's feet from road splash. A roll-up canvas flap at the back of the cart protected the produce from road dust, rain, and sun. The body of the cart was painted dark green, and the spokes and hubs of the wheels were fire engine red. The two huge wheels placed the body of the cart at my eye level. A single step at the end of a gracefully curved iron shaft dangled from the cart and was probably of some help to any long-legged—and supple—adult attempting to mount the vehicle.

Michelle and I now formed a bucket brigade to hand vegetable baskets up to her mother, who was in the cart placing them according to what seemed to be some preordained plan. In short order, they were ready to go. Madame Baichant reached down and, holding onto Michelle by one hand, gave a mighty upward heave to place her daughter where she could set one foot onto the step. From there, a second heave lifted Michelle aboard, where she sat down beside her mother. They said goodbye and thanked me for my help. Madame Baichant handed the buggy whip to Michelle, who gave the horse's croup a light tap. Lili clopped slowly out of the barn. As they emerged from the barn, the horse and cart were suddenly outlined crisply, shining brightly in the early morning sun. Upon reaching the gate, Lili made a sharp left turn onto the grassy track and broke into a trot. I closed the barnyard gate as I had been instructed and watched the cart disappear around the bend.

Reflecting on my enchanted morning all the way home, I reached our front gate and remembered my unsuccessful search for Ploof. The strong impression Madame Baichant and Michelle had made on me, and her kind offer to let me feed the ducks had assuaged my earlier despair and disappointment over Ploof's disappearance.

Through the kitchen window I saw Raimond and Françoise at breakfast. I walked in on them feeling as if I'd just returned from a long and adventurous trip. Raimond sensed my mood right away, saying, "Well, Monsieur Alain, you look very pleased with yourself. It's so early. What have you been up to?" I looked at the wall clock, which said a quarter to seven. There was still a whole hour before the time of my usual morning appearance downstairs.

"Ploof has disappeared. I went all over looking for him," I declared, "and I didn't find him." There was a gasp as Françoise put a hand over her mouth in a gesture of horror and uttered the words, "*Mon Dieu!*"

Raimond looked at me, then at Françoise. It wasn't quite a guilty look, but there was something in his expression that suggested he already knew the bad news. It was Françoise who broke the tense silence. "You deliberately set free Monsieur Alain's duck!" she said contentiously to Raimond. "You did it because you didn't want me to cook that bird!" She walked briskly to a counter where she had some pans. Raimond beat a hasty retreat through the door. A skillet flew across the room and hit the door as it closed behind him, landing noisily on the tiled floor.

"No, Françoise! That's not what happened," I said, trying to sound calm. "I just talked to Madame Baichant, who told me we should have clipped Ploof's wings if we didn't want him to fly away. She said all ducks fly away from a new home if not clipped, and she knows that Gypsies never clip the wings of ducks they give as prizes, because they know the ducks will fly back to them the next day." I was stretching the truth somewhat in a trial use of a white lie.

"Raimond knows about ducks and about Gypsies and should have done as Madame Baichant said," replied Françoise, still fulminating. *"Je vais encore l'attraper, celui là!"* ("I'll catch him yet, that one!") Her remark prompted me to realize that there was still more in need of doing if Raimond were to be spared being hit by a frying pan or some other flying object upon his return to the kitchen.

I went to Mother's room and woke her out of a sound sleep. She wasn't pleased, but when she had somewhat recovered, I explained the crisis and its background. I had to repeat the story twice for her, as she was still groggy and a bit overwhelmed by my avalanche of details. "We absolutely have to save Raimond—he's in grave danger!" I said, winding up my recital.

"All right," she replied, "but stay here and tell me more about this early morning visit to the Baichant farm. Françoise will be here any minute with my coffee, and we'll see what I can do to intervene on Raimond's behalf." I went over Madame Baichant's explanation of Ploof's escape. As I started in on the events in the kitchen, Françoise knocked at the door and, without waiting, barged in with the coffee tray.

"*Bonjour Madame, vous avez bien dormi, j'espère?*" ("Good morning ma'am, you slept well, I trust?") said Françoise in a tone of forced cheerfulness.

Mother seized the bull by the horns and minced no words, "Françoise, you need to know that it was I who specifically instructed Raimond *not* to trim the duck's wings. I knew the duck would escape, but that's exactly what I wanted. I knew you were determined to slaughter that duck so you could serve it to us. I didn't want Alain to see this happen, and the only way I could avoid the problem was to have the duck fly away. Alain must now find consolation in the fact that the duck is free and living in the wild where it is much happier. I think Alain will find that a lot easier than having to eat his own beloved duck. I will buy you another duck the next time I go marketing. It will be plucked and ready for you to cook, which Ploof was not. Raimond was only following my orders. Is that quite clear, Françoise?" Mother could be eloquent when she spoke French.

"*Oui, Madame,*" Françoise said, sounding displeased and looking surly as she left the room.

Mother had been so convincing in her speech to Françoise that I asked her, "Did you really know about clipping the wings and tell Raimond *not* to do it?"

"Well, more or less," she replied. "Yes, I knew long ago that all barnyard ducks have to have their wings clipped, but I didn't really think of it last night, nor did I tell Raimond to do anything. I simply didn't give the matter any thought, and for once, my carelessness has produced a fortunate result. And yes, I told Françoise a white lie. However, it was all part of the *greater good*, which in this case, means saving Raimond. Moreover, another part of the *greater good* is you not having your beloved duck plucked and popped into the oven, don't you think? You know Françoise, Alain. She would have done it at the first opportunity. She can't be trusted *not* to cook anything that's edible, and Ploof was eminently edible."

The glow from my experience at the Baichant farm still lingered, so I remained reasonably placated, despite the overwhelming deluge of white lies, greater goods, conjectures, and facts unflattering to Gypsies. When I joined Brenda at breakfast and told her my saga, she couldn't make heads or tails out of my morning's adventures and seemed surprisingly indifferent to the loss of Ploof.

Raimond, too, was confused by the morning's events. He could hardly believe his restoration in the eyes of Françoise, for it seems Mother neglected to tell him of the white lie she had told on his behalf. Raimond now asked me for my version of the morning's events, which I recounted in full, including the matter of my own and Mother's white lie to Françoise.

Somehow, my narration upset and displeased Raimond and put him in a state I had never seen before. Was he embarrassed by being found ignorant about the need for wing clipping, or had he known about it and felt guilty for neglecting to act on it? I wondered where the truth really lay.

Late in the morning, Raimond's inner turmoil came to a boil, and he told me, rather abruptly, that later on he would go to the fair and give that Gypsy a piece of his mind. He invited me to join him. After lunch and Raimond's Sunday siesta, the two of us set out on foot for the fair. I had the vague feeling that Raimond might succeed in making the Gypsy give me back my duck, which left me with mixed feelings. Raimond, on the other hand, knew exactly what he was after. He wanted to see justice done. As we walked briskly along, Raimond asked me if Ploof had any special identifying marks, and I told him about the missing web.

When we reached the fair we went straight to the stall where the rabbit race was held. The same Gypsy was there, touting bets on his rabbits. Raimond went up to him and told him he wanted to inspect the ducks in the cages because he had reason to believe one of them was ours.

"Anybody can tell me a story like that and think he has the right to walk away with a duck that is rightfully mine," replied the Gypsy testily.

"I have proof," said Raimond solemnly, "but I must see the duck up close to show you the proof." But the Gypsy was adamant in his opposition and wouldn't let us go near the cages, which contained several ducks, including three mallards, the same number as there were yesterday.

His voice now tinged with anger, Raimond said, "All I want to do is take a close look at your mallards' feet—if no webs are missing, none of the ducks is ours, and I will go away and leave you alone." A crowd was gathering to watch the men argue.

"I see," said the Gypsy. "A duck somehow loses one of the webs on his feet, and he automatically becomes yours!" replied the Gypsy derisively. The assembled crowd laughed, and Raimond's face flushed with anger. A few taunting words from the onlookers suggested that the crowd wanted the two men to fight it out.

The Gypsy was a sinister, tough-looking type and a big, burly fellow to boot. Raimond, a man of short stature and slight build, was no match for the Gypsy, I was sure. I didn't like the look of things and knew something had to be done. Suddenly, I had an idea. "There's Ploof! I see him! I see him! Over there!" I exclaimed excitedly. Pointing to a distant stall across the pasture, I shouted, "Come with me, Raimond! It's my duck all right!"

I grabbed Raimond's hand with both of mine and tugged it forcefully. Raimond came reluctantly, muttering to the Gypsy over his shoulder, something to the effect that he'd be back to settle the score.

When we had reached a safe distance from the Gypsy, Raimond protested, "I was trying to get your duck back, Monsieur Alain!"

"It's all right, Raimond. I know I can't have Ploof if Françoise is going to cook him the first chance she gets. Besides, Madame Baichant has promised me she will let me feed her mallards anytime I want. I can admire and play with her ducks all I want, and Françoise won't come and kill them," I said.

But Raimond wasn't listening. "That Gypsy is a sneak thief who steals from little boys. I won't let him get away with his tricks," he said, still seething.

"You're going to get badly hurt if you fight with that Gypsy, Raimond. He's twice as big as you are, and he looks ferocious to me! Please don't go back there, Raimond. I don't want you hurt because of a duck I can't even have—please, Raimond!" I pleaded. I started to cry. At the sight of my tears, Raimond calmed down, took my hand, and we set off for home in silence.

He was walking fast, too fast for me. I was trotting to keep up with him. I could see by Raimond's grim face that he was still tied in knots. I tried to break the silence, "Perhaps Madame Baichant was wrong, Raimond! Perhaps Ploof didn't fly back to the Gypsy," I said. "And perhaps Ploof is free, down by the lake in the meadow, with all the wild ducks that always hang around down there."

Raimond slowed down noticeably, and after several more paces, he started to talk about the two fish he had caught the day before and how he had seen wild ducks on the lake. "I'll keep an eye out for Ploof and tell you if I see him," he said, smiling at me for the first time that day.

The day I went out searching for Ploof was the turning point in what had been, until then, a rather unexciting summer. From then on, I went to the Baichant farm almost daily to feed the ducks and the rest of the menagerie of barnyard creatures. Michelle and I soon became fast friends. I think she craved the company of other children as much as I did. Brenda joined me only on the first two visits of the many I made to the farm. I think Brenda felt nervous around Michelle, who had an obstreperous streak, and Brenda may have been squeamish about the crudeness of life on a farm. I, on the other hand, was at the peak of my "piglet" phase, this being the same year I had been expelled from the Ecole Sugerre for painting myself all over with ink, and I was totally fascinated, if not smitten, by the rough and dirty farm life.

Mother's old injunction against associating with *pauvres gens* (poor folk) may have been on Brenda's mind. I never discussed the status of Madame Baichant with Mother so I can't say with certainty that she thought of her as *pauvres gens*. But the possibility that she viewed her this way was strong in my mind. My own rough idea of *pauvres gens* ("lower class" in England) were people who led a wretched life and worked at wretched jobs. I couldn't see how the term applied to Madame Baichant. She had a magnificent and productive farm, ran it extremely well, and it seemed to me that it was a noble and worthy way to work and live. In fact, I had by now switched my future career goal from locomotive driver to farmer—a prosperous one to be sure— owning a large, model farm. I even spent time on rainy days making elaborate drawings and plans for this ideal farm, allocating acreage to various crops and laying out the designs of farm houses, barns, and barnyards.

It's possible Mother had a more complicated explanation of the term *pauvres gens* than the one I had. But as far as I was concerned, it didn't matter. The subject of my playing with Michelle never came up. What's more, I don't think Mother had the slightest notion of how much time I spent there that summer. Having some doubts about her approval, I scrupulously avoided mentioning the subject.

Helping my cause in this matter was Mother's sudden passion for golf, which she had played previously without much enthusiasm. It started to grow after she no longer had the beach close by to entertain her. That year, she became what the French

229

called "*enragée du golf*" ("mad about golf"), spending morning and afternoon at the golf course taking lessons and playing with a new group of friends. She must have assumed that Raimond and Françoise were keeping an eye on Brenda and me, which was not really the case. Raimond certainly knew I was at the farm (I discussed with him almost everything I did in great detail), and I suppose he could see no harm in it. Brenda stayed home, playing with her dolls and the little stove and never expressed any curiosity about my activities at the farm, although she was well aware of them.

Six days a week, Mother left the house with Brenda and me at eight thirty in the morning to drop us off at our gymnastics class in Hardelot. After a round of golf, Mother drove us home in the late morning, and we seldom went back to the beach after lunch. Occasionally, Mother took me to an afternoon sand castle contest, where she left me to my creations while she returned to her golf game. Thus, on most days, I was free to go over to the Baichant farm in midafternoon to play with Michelle, who, because she was up before six most mornings to help her mother, took a long nap after lunch.

My duck-feeding privilege soon evolved into feeding all the animals and doing various other farm chores. I was grateful to have something to relieve the monotony of our isolated existence. Michelle and I became inseparable. She and Madame Baichant always greeted my arrival with obvious pleasure, and Madame Baichant lavished praise and profuse thanks for everything I did, though I suspect that my contribution to their work effort was minuscule and perhaps more of a nuisance than any real help. Michelle did a great deal to help her mother, and I usually pitched in at whatever Michelle was doing, whether it was feeding their five pigs or the other animals, picking vegetables for the next morning's run to Hardelot, or planting seedlings for winter vegetables.

Madame Baichant was a real chatterbox while we worked and she could be quite funny; I enjoyed listening to her and asked her questions whenever she stopped talking. It was while planting winter vegetables that I asked Madame Baichant where she sold her vegetables in winter, for I knew that Hardelot was uninhabited at that time of year. "I have to take them to Boulogne once a week," she replied. "Fifteen kilometers is a long way to go just for a few turnips, sprouts, and cabbages. A wholesaler in Boulogne crates them for me and sends them to *les Halles* [the big produce market] in Paris. The worst part for me is the long cart ride, often in cold, rainy weather. It's two hours each way, and I'm alone on these trips because Michelle is in school. I'm always so thankful when summer shows his face!" Madame Baichant's winter work sounded pretty wretched, and I wondered if one could be *pauvres gens* on a part time basis, or even on an hourly basis. After all, she came home every night to her warm, cozy house that I viewed as the perfect dwelling. The farmhouse appeared to me so complete and self-contained; it had everything she needed and nothing superfluous or frivolous. No electricity or running water to be sure—but Madame Baichant seemed to manage fine without them. I couldn't think of her as living a wretched life once she was back in her home.

Michelle worked in spells of twenty minutes to half an hour in length and always asked her mother if it were all right to take a break. She was never refused and usually returned to her tasks within a quarter of an hour without being asked to do so.

With Madame Baichant's blessing, Michelle and I ran off towards the adjacent pasture, where several haystacks provided endless fun. One of the haystacks had a ladder propped against it and was crumbling on one side, forming the ideal "playstack." We climbed its fifteen-foot height and then slid deliciously down into the loose, deep hay at its base. All the haystacks were loosely stacked and it was possible to bury ourselves completely within the vertical wall of hay in the lower part of the stack. I enjoyed the delicious excitement of wondering whether I would be discovered as Michelle repeatedly passed close to where I hid, and there was also the feeling of dismay when she gave up and walked to another haystack to search. I eventually solved that dilemma by instituting the rule that after the seeker had passed near the hiding place twice and missed it, the hider had to jump out, startling the seeker and ending the round.

Between chores, another place Michelle and I played was in the barn, where the hay was stacked almost to the roof and where an assortment of beams and posts made it possible, though challenging, to climb this Everest of hay. Playing in deep, soft hay was sheer joy.

It was during one of these hay romps, in the seclusion of the barn, that Michelle once pulled my pants off, declaring in no uncertain terms that she had no little brother and that she was curious. "I'll let you look at mine if you like," she added coyly. It seemed a fair enough bargain. We took turns exploring, touching and examining each other and were both very intrigued and amused by my becoming aroused, not to mention mysteriously and pleasantly excited in a strange way by our activities. We were both ignorant of the facts of life, and our investigations, though close to the subject, resulted in no enlightenment. One thing Michelle and I knew was that we would be in major trouble if we were caught doing this. I have no idea how we knew this, for I have no recollection of any adult ever discussing such matters with me or warning me against what we were doing. But know it we did. So, motivated by the fear of consequences, we soon returned to less prurient and safer games. But the mysterious and delicious tension we both felt when playing this way tempted us to repeat these clandestine games a few more times that summer. This was one aspect of my visits to the Baichant farm that I did not discuss with Raimond.

The last chore of every afternoon at the Baichant farm was one I grew to anticipate with utmost pleasure. It was when Michelle went to Lili's pasture and brought her back to her stall in preparation for the next morning's run to Hardelot. Michelle could do this task by herself but always invited me to join her. Earlier in the day, when Lili returned from the long morning's round of deliveries in Hardelot, she was unhitched and walked to a pasture a mile from the Baichant farm. There, she grazed contentedly in the company of several horses belonging to other Condette farmers. All the farm horses in Condette were of the Boulonais breed. They resemble Clydesdales in stature and are huge, powerful and handsome workhorses, gentle and intelligent, usually a dappled grayish-white (as was Lili) but sometimes a very dark brown, almost black.

When we reached the horse pasture, Michelle called Lili's name in a singsong tone. (The horses, unlike the cows, had different names.) Lili stopped her grazing, looked up as if to verify that she had heard Michelle call, and in a slow, unhurried gait, came towards us. The big challenge of this operation was for the two of us to mount the huge mare. Michelle used a willow branch to coax Lili through the gate, which she then closed and latched. With a little more coaxing, Lili was induced to stand beside and close to the gate, which consisted of a frame made with several widely spaced horizontal planks. The planks served as ladder rungs by which we climbed to a height level with the horse's back. Standing precariously on the narrow edge of a plank near the top of the gate, and a good four feet from Lili's spine, Michelle took a great sideways leap. She landed awkwardly on the center of Lili's broad back and scooted herself forward so I could use the same landing site. "Come on," she said. "It's easy!"

I clambered uncertainly up the gate and stood near the top like a diver nervously hesitating to take the plunge.

"She won't wait forever!" exclaimed Michelle, providing me with the best of all possible incentives. I jumped, but jumped too far, and slid off headfirst on the far side of Lili, who continued to stand still, apparently indifferent and possibly oblivious to my debacle. Although my outstretched arms took the brunt of the fall, it was quite a drop. I picked myself up, dazed and not sure I was still in one piece. With Michelle insisting that it was essential that I try again right away if Lili were ever to tolerate my riding her, I climbed the gate once more. On the second try, I landed flat across Lili's back with my nose pressed hard against her smooth coat. I lay there for a moment noticing the distinct and not unpleasant odor that horses exude, knowing I hadn't achieved my goal. Then, with much squirming, I finally succeeded in righting myself and assuming the semblance of a riding stance. I must explain that being astride Lili was almost like sitting on a flat floor. Her back was so broad and the curvature so slight that it would be stretching the truth to claim that my legs dangled on either side of her. "Hold onto my waist," said Michelle, who then let out two staccato yelps that sounded like, "Youpe! Youpe!"

This was Lili's cue to start moving. Michelle's yelps had been worthy of a command for a cavalry charge at full gallop, but I was pleasantly relieved to discover that Lili was in no hurry. Lili's coat was slippery, and as she swayed from side to side, I slid first left then right, teetering on the brink of falling off with each stride of the horse. My situation was precarious in the extreme for all I could do was hold onto Michelle who was sliding around as much as I was. Michelle had the dubious advantage of being able to clutch onto Lili's mane. It was a tribute to Lili's generous and gentle nature that we completed the journey without falling off.

I was gloriously intoxicated by my position of great and majestic height, and by the thrill of power that comes from being aboard a nearly unstoppable craft. I was sure that a maharajah felt this way when riding his elephant through the jungle in India. There were also the moments of acute suspense—wondering whether Lili would make the small course deviations necessary to avoid the low branches looming across our path. The branches would have swept the two of us off her back as surely as Lili's tail swept away the flies that alighted on her.

Once, when Michelle let me ride in front, I discovered to my surprise and dismay that there was actually no way to steer our huge steed. Pulling one way or the other on her mane did not cause the slightest change in Lili's inexorable course. She was self-directed by her own instincts and by an eventual reward consisting of a couple of carrots, delivered upon a safe return to her stall.

When we approached the farm, Lili automatically headed for a pile of hay in the Baichant farmyard. There, she came to a stop and Michelle and I dismounted by sliding off her into the soft hay. Lest anyone think that Lili was motivated by innate goodwill and intelligence in this last step of her performance, let me point out that she wasted no time in starting to munch noisily on the hay, and that it took considerable effort to persuade her to continue the journey to her stall. The horse had no halter, so all we could do to coax her in that direction was to tantalize her with two small carrots, which Michelle had tucked in the ample pockets of her smock for the purpose. Lili was a pushover for carrots, willing to forego a mound of hay for the two tiny succulent morsels.

Once Lili was safely in her stall, I dashed home and climbed into a warm bath which Françoise always had drawn and waiting for me. Mother never saw my soil-caked knees and hands, or the sandbars of black sand in the bottom of the tub after it had been drained. For all she knew, I had spent an angelic afternoon staying spotlessly clean, seeing to it that Brenda's dolls had a gentle father and a good diet of carefully prepared doll meals.

The summer slipped by in this idyllic way until the day when Monsieur Baichant appeared for his annual visit, riding in a cart that was the twin of Madame Baichant's. Unlike hers, which always gleamed, his was a mess, spattered with a year's worth of mud and manure. Michelle had warned me of his arrival and the purpose of his visit. He had come to slaughter three of Madame Baichant's five pigs. Michelle invited me to this ritual which, she said, *"Te montrera bien des choses,"* ("Will show you a thing or two.")

Monsieur Baichant had brought along a helper, a furtive, sinister-looking man whom I shall refer to as "Beady-Eyes" because his eyes were set very close together and were, in fact, like two small, black marbles in his triangular, rat-like face. He glowered at Michelle and me with those mean little eyes, as if he didn't think we had any business being spectators at this slaughter. Madame Baichant was nowhere around. Michelle greeted her father with *"Bonjour Papa!"* but her words elicited no reply. Monsieur Baichant acted as though he were angry at her and said not a thing to her the whole time we were present. Michelle and I stood in silence watching every move the two men made.

Aside from taking a few swigs from a bottle of red wine, the pair wasted no time. Entering the pig sty, they set about tackling one of the animals. The pigs, usually placid enough, were soon aware that something out of the usual was afoot and, panicking, led the two men on an unmerry chase around the sty. The men eventually succeeded in holding one of the pigs down long enough to pass a small noose around its hind legs. Once the noose was drawn tight, they dragged the pig to the barn where they left it lying and squealing deafeningly as they went about rounding up various implements they needed for the next step. This included two large galvanized tubs, which they placed beside the pig, and a block and tackle that Monsieur Baichant carried up the hay ladder and hooked to one of the barn's rafters. Then the men hooked the other end of the tackle to the rope around the pig's hind legs.

After another swig of wine, both men now pulled together on the tackle's rope and slowly raised the two hundred pound pig until its snout hung slightly more than a foot off the ground. The animal's loud squealing continued unabated while all this was in progress, but when it reached a full hanging position, the squealing turned into a series of long, mournful moans, as if it accepted the futility of further struggle. The men placed one of the tubs directly beneath the pig and the other tub off to one side of it, and took time for another gulp of wine as the pig continued to moan.

I didn't actually see the act, only its result, for Beady-Eyes was standing between me and the pig. He had with him a small, sharp knife that he used to slash a short incision in the pig's neck. When he stepped back, I saw a jet of wine-red blood spurt sideways into the tub beside the pig. The pig let out one short, sharp squeal at the stab, but then fell silent, though it was still alive, for I saw its ears twitching steadily for quite some time. *"Il ne sent rien!"* ("He feels nothing!") declared Beady-Eyes, as if trying to justify his deed. The men took turns on the bottle of wine while they watched the slowly diminishing stream of blood in silence. The pig's ears finally stopped twitching. *"Voilà, il est mort!"* ("That's it, he's dead!") said Beady-Eyes definitively. A minute later, the jet of blood ceased and turned into a trickle that went down the pig's snout and into the second tub beneath it. The slow bleeding continued for several minutes.

All this time, Michelle and I watched, transfixed in horror. I wanted to run from the scene, but, as if hypnotized, I was unable to do so. Once it was initiated, I had to know the outcome of this dreadful ritual. Eventually, the dead pig was lowered, dragged along the ground and then lifted into Monsieur Baichant's filthy cart. Michelle told me the slaughtered pigs would be taken to a *charcuterie* (pork specialty shop) in Boulogne and that her mother would get half the proceeds of the sale.

I didn't wait around for the slaughter of the other two pigs, and I could see that Michelle, too, was shaken. I told her I had learnt enough for one day and invited her to come to our house, something she had never done. When we reached the back of our garden, we played listlessly on the swing that hung from a large weeping willow tree. We were both upset, and the fun had gone out of everything.

Feeling as if my little paradise had been desecrated, I didn't go back to the farm for several days. When I finally did, it was late one afternoon, and the purpose of my visit was to say goodbye. The summer vacation was ending, and we were leaving for Ville-d'Avray the next morning. When I told Madame Baichant of our imminent departure, Michelle started to cry. She begged me to stay, promising that she would never make me watch a pig slaughtering again. I put my arm around her shoulders and tried to convince her that the pig slaughtering had nothing to do with my leaving. When that had no effect, I tried reassuring her with the promise that I would be back the following summer.

Madame Baichant asked if it were all right if she kissed me goodbye. *"Oh oui! Bien sûr, Madame Baichant!"* I replied, as I went to Madame Baichant and hugged her affectionately. Then I hugged and kissed Michelle, who, at this very moment, didn't seem as tough as I always took her for.

I asked Madame Baichant if I could pull a carrot to give Lili as a farewell present. She assented, but said she and Michelle were sitting down to supper and that I would have to go by myself. Michelle was still sobbing quietly, and Madame Baichant went to her, held her and stroked her hair. Putting my hand on Michelle's arm and giving her a light squeeze, I said a subdued goodbye to her and left their house.

I went to the vegetable garden, pulled a couple of carrots, and went to Lili's stall, which was almost dark because the sun had set. When I entered, the horse turned and took a few lazy, clopping steps towards me. Lili was facing the open door, and I could tell she knew I had some carrots, even though I held them behind me in one hand. I teased her a little before feeding them to her and then watched her munch pensively. I stroked the soft gray suede of her nose, acutely aware of how much I enjoyed the feel of it. *"Au revoir, chère Lili,"* I said wistfully.

Dan enjoying the quiet, Villa Champs de Mai, Condette, 1937

Villa Champs de Mai, after addition of dormers, Condette, 1937

CHAPTER 9

An Elf in the Drawing Room and Watery Dangers.

Not long after our return to Ville-d'Avray in the autumn of 1937, we received by post an invitation to Monique's birthday party. We hadn't seen the Poujets since their dog had bitten Brenda, and not long after that incident, Madame Poujet had seen fit to ostracize me because I had been expelled from school on account of the face-inking incident. She had also rejected Brenda, who was completely innocent of any misdeed. Her spurning the two of us had been rude and forceful. So Mother, Brenda and I were quite taken aback by her olive branch. Mother wasn't sure we should accept the invitation, but I insisted that Charlie Poujet was my only friend in Ville-d'Avray and that we had suffered long enough. Mother gave in and bought an expensive doll's dress for Monique's birthday present. I thought it outrageous that the dress was far fancier than anything Brenda owned, and I told Mother that she was overdoing the forgiveness.

Our reunion with Charlie and Monique was tense at first, but after a few minutes, the four of us acted as though nothing had ever happened. The party was unremarkable, except for the fact that Brenda and I were the only guests. If we had chosen not to come, there would have been no party.

Six-year-old Charlie was not the most stimulating of companions for me; he was almost two years my junior and timid about playing most of the games I proposed. I longed for a larger circle of friends of my age such as I had enjoyed during those two magic summers when we rented villas in Hardelot.

Not long after Monique's dull party, a new boy closer to my own age appeared on the scene in the most unlikely fashion. I had never paid any attention to a property that was beyond a short section of our garden wall, for I had never noticed any sign of life coming from that direction. One day, however, while playing near there, I had the impression that I was being watched. I kept scanning the top of the wall and eventually caught a fleeting glimpse of a small, much-tanned face, topped by a mop of curly blond hair. I called out and received no answer, but I was sure I had seen a boy looking down at me. My curiosity aroused, I ran to the tool shed and, with Raimond's help, pulled out a ladder and propped it against the mystery wall. When I reached the top, I saw a boy about my age staring up at me and looking as though he were expecting me. He greeted me casually, saying, *"Bonjours, je m'appelle Jacob. Et toi, tu t'appelles comment?"* ("Hello, I'm Jacob. And you, what's your name?").

"Alain," I replied. Jacob then apologized for spying on me and explained that his family had just arrived in their new house and he had been anxious to discover what his neighbors were like.

Jacob's new house was known in our household as "*la maison Américaine.*" Anything far-fetched or unusual was often accused of being American. This house certainly met these criteria. Its entire south side, which faced across the back garden towards our common wall and away from the street, was made entirely of glass. The large glass panes didn't have the usual window framing and there were no opaque panels separating the wide expanses of glass; nor were there any visible means of support, either for the glass or for the upper stories. From my vantage point atop the wall, Jacob's house was just a glass box with no apparent roof. Through the glass façade I could see everything inside: armchairs, sofas, tables, beds, kitchen counters and the cooking stove were all on display as if in some big furniture shop.

Until the day I climbed that ladder and met Jacob, I had never seen the house, but Raimond, while pruning our cherry tree near this wall, had given it careful scrutiny. As he served us lunch one day, he described the glass façade and the lack of a roof. "We all know that roofs must have a slope so the rain will run off," Raimond said, "but I could see nothing by way of a roof above the third story. Through the glass I could see from the lighting of the third story that it must have an opaque ceiling—so, where is the roof?" Raimond asked, sounding perplexed.

Mother replied that Father, while looking down from a skyscraper during a recent visit to New York, had noticed that most roofs in America were flat. Father had been told that these flat roofs were made of paper and tar, implausible and incredible as that sounded. This roof anomaly may be why Raimond had dubbed the mystery house next door *"la maison Américaine."*

We had seen a different aspect of the house from the street it fronted, the rue de Marne. From there, all we could see was a solid concrete wall, three stories high, about sixty feet long, and three small, square windows, set somewhat randomly in the wall. The two ends of the house were also flat, unbroken concrete surfaces with no openings visible from the street. A high steel gate led into the garden that was completely hidden from the street. We couldn't see any roof overhang or even a rain gutter from the street side of the house. Mother commented that the place looked like a bomb shelter, and wasn't exactly *"pittoresque"*.

When Jacob peered over the wall into our garden, his vantage point had been from a small tree which grew beside the wall. He now proposed that I use this tree to descend into their garden. "Its branches are close together, ideal for climbing," he said reassuringly.

With some difficulty, I repositioned the ladder so that it was directly opposite Jacob's little tree. Then I talked Brenda into joining me in this perilous crossing. When I reached terra firma on his side of the wall, Jacob seized my hand and shook it vigorously. The French are fond of shaking hands and do so at the drop of a hat. Jacob's effusive greeting brought to mind the way Stanley was reputed to have greeted Livingstone in the heart of Africa, a story Mother had recently recounted to me. His more than cordial handshake gave my expedition into his garden the aura of a grand and daring exploration. Together, Jacob and I helped Brenda down from the tree.

Jacob appeared to be as impressed by his new house as I was, and he was anxious to show it to us. It turned out to be even stranger than our original impression, for once inside, Brenda and I were amazed to see that walls between rooms extended neither to the floor nor to the ceiling. Instead, the walls, such as they were, cantilevered—or "sprang"—from the outer, street-side wall of the house, like partitions in a public toilet. These floating wall partitions were found on all three floors of the house.

Passage from room to room (zones might be a better term) was along an unbroken aisle that ran the length of the glass façade on each floor. There were no doors to impede anyone moving from one area to another or to provide a modicum of privacy. The only rooms that had doors were the bathrooms which were all on the street-side of the house and had small windows overlooking the street. The house design was the open plan style in the extreme. Many years later I learned that, far from being of American design, what we had dubbed "*la maison Américaine*" was actually an early work of the great French architect Le Corbusier and that it was nearly the famous architect's professional undoing. His clients hated living in it. It sat empty for many years before the first owners found a buyer for it. In the end, they virtually gave the house away, probably to Jacob's family. The first owners tried to sue Le Corbussier but were laughed out of court when they had to admit that they had enthusiastically approved his plans. Although Le Corbussier won the case, the publicity of the unusual trial was not good for his business, and he did not become one of France's (and the world's) most celebrated architects until the late 1940s, though he was well known among architects before then.

Jacob's room contained nothing more than a cot, a plain dresser, a chair, and a small table. The furnishings throughout the rest of house were as minimal as those in Jacob's room. I asked him when the movers would arrive and was surprised to hear that they had already come. Brenda asked him where he kept his toys, and Jacob replied that he had none, because his parents didn't believe in toys and expected him to read books instead. "Playing with toys is such a waste of time," Jacob asserted with conviction.

I asked to see his books, and when he told me he didn't have any, I volunteered, "I suppose your parents don't want you to have your own books."

"That's right," Jacob replied smartly. "I get to read their books when they're finished with them."

"Do you have many friends?" I asked, desperately trying to find common ground.

"Yes, I had a friend when we lived at our last house in Paris."

"At that house, what did you do when your friend came over to visit you?" I persisted, almost sure I knew the answer.

"He, too, liked to read books, so we were very good friends. The two of us sat and read my parents' books, sometimes aloud to each other. Would you like to read the book I've just finished? It's a good book. I enjoyed it more than many others I've read recently."

We walked to another room, and from a large bookshelf that covered the entire back wall, Jacob pulled out what, in those days, I called *"un livre de grandes personnes,"* ("a book for grownups"). It had no pictures, not even an intriguing cover, just a single-word title which was meaningless to me.

I riffled through the pages of the book Jacob handed me, searching for pictures. But, of course, there were none so I put it down. Deciding I had gone as far as I could in this charade, I proposed that we all go back over the wall so I could give Jacob a tour of our house. I was sure that when he saw my electric train, it would pique his interest, and he would discover how much fun it was to play with toys.

Jacob said that he was all alone in the house, but since he could probably make it back before his parents returned, he thought he could risk a visit to our house. The three of us climbed the little tree, clambered over the wall, and descended the ladder on our side.

As soon as we entered our house, Brenda lost interest in Jacob and scampered upstairs. Jacob made a beeline for a large bookshelf that he had spotted through an open door to our drawing room.

I was quite taken aback; I hadn't planned on showing Jacob the drawing room, which was unofficially off limits to me, especially if I were in the company of anyone my age. Jacob started a careful scrutiny of the titles on the shelves, pointing out a few which he said he had read or that his parents owned, and exclaiming with surprise at the large number of English titles. Then he found a book that intrigued him and asked if he could read it. When I told him I would have to ask Mother, he replied he wanted to sit down right here and now and that he wouldn't bother anyone just sitting and reading in our drawing room; he couldn't see why my mother's permission was needed for that. I had to agree, so I told him I was going to the garden to ride my bike, and that he could join me and ride Brenda's bike or stay indoors and read. He chose the latter.

That evening, Mother told Brenda and me that she had experienced the shock of her life. She had been upstairs when I had arrived with Jacob and didn't know he was in the house. She had walked into the drawing room and gone straight to her desk to write a letter. "When I sat down at my desk I suddenly noticed this little blond elf sitting silently on the sofa reading a book—I couldn't imagine who he was or why he was there—any normal child would have said something when I came into the room! When first I saw him, I had gasped, but that did not distract him from his reading. He was totally absorbed in his book and ignored me completely.

"I sat silently at my desk, waiting to see what he might do, or to see if I were dreaming and might perhaps awake from this strange dream. He seemed so real that I cleared my throat to see if he would look up. Still he didn't move and continued his reading. Eventually, I said quite loudly, 'Who are you, and how is it that you are here in my drawing room?'

"He looked up, not looking at all surprised to see me, and just said, 'I am Jacob Gourlain, and I am enjoying one of your books. May I take it home to finish it? I promise I will treat the book with care, as if it were one of my parent's, and I will return it as soon as I am finished. It was Alain who brought me here— are you Alain's mother?'"

Mother continued, "He was so calm—not at all nervous or shy—straightforward and completely natural. I have never seen a young child with so much composure. He was reading Zola's *Germinal*, which I hadn't enjoyed reading and which Daddy didn't care for either. So without hesitation, I told him he could have it—Jacob was overjoyed.

" 'Oh Madame!' he answered in his soft, sweet little voice, 'You are too good! I don't want to impose on your generosity that much. I will return it as I promised. I thank you a thousand times!' He was a charming child, and I took an immediate liking to him."

At that point, Mother invited Jacob to have afternoon tea with us and called me in from the garden. During tea, Jacob and Mother talked about books the whole time. Mother was amazed at his knowledge of many current best-sellers, and I was crestfallen that Jacob was turning out to be someone who wasn't likely to be much of a friend for me, however much Mother admired him. It was a strange feeling, for I had taken a strong liking to him. I envied his calm self-assurance, and couldn't help admiring his lack of any conceit. I really wanted Jacob as a friend, but I couldn't see how he would have the slightest use for me. I found my situation very unsettling.

After tea, I insisted that Jacob come up and see my electric trains, which he did courteously but a little grudgingly. We watched my little locomotive go around its track five times, and I offered to let him control the train, but Jacob said, "It's quite interesting at first, but after a while, I find it a little monotonous." It was obvious that he was not in the least interested in electric trains or play of any sort. He excused himself politely, explaining that he had better head home before his parents returned. I escorted him back to the ladder, which I climbed after him so that I could hand him Zola's *Germinal* once he was safely in the little tree.

A week later, Jacob telephoned Mother to say that he was coming over to return the book and to ask if Alain would please put the ladder in the same place against the wall. I had never used the telephone and was in awe of his prowess. Jacob stayed for tea, once again entertaining Mother and borrowing a book. This happened regularly, once a week until we left for the seaside that year.

Sometime in May, Jacob invited Brenda and me, and Charlie and Monique (whom he had met at our house on one of his book-exchanging visits) to a party for his eighth birthday. I had celebrated my eighth birthday only a month earlier, and on that occasion, Jacob had gone to our drawing room after tea and read a book while the rest of us went out to play in the garden. The Poujets, Brenda and I now wondered how Jacob would entertain us, since he didn't believe in any sort of play. Would the four of us go to his house, be asked to sit down on the floor and expected to read grownup books as he sat absorbed in a book of his own?

On the day of the party, Charlie and Monique used Raimond's *passerelle* to come to our house before heading for Jacob's house. The four of us then used our ladder and the little tree on Jacob's side of the wall to make our way to *la Maison Américaine* via the garden approach rather than by the street entrance. At first, the persnickety Monique refused to climb the ladder, saying that we would all see her knickers as she climbed. I pointed out to her that if she were the last to climb up, the only one to be treated to the sight of her knickers would be our dog, Jock, who was sitting patiently at the base of the ladder, probably wishing he, too, could go to the party. We left Monique behind, sulking and asserting that it was not ladylike to climb ladders. When Charlie, Brenda and I had crossed over, Monique decided to join us after all. We were all standing around the base of the little tree as she descended it and had a generous glimpse of her knickers, which were pink and bordered with lace, very elegant, and obviously intended to be seen. I made no comment though I was dying to do so.

Madame Gourlain, smartly dressed in a tailored suit, thought our method of arrival was most original and immediately made us feel at home by joking and teasing us gently about it. The only other guest at the party was Jacob's former Parisian neighbor and friend, Samuel. The six of us sat down to a sumptuous, catered *goûté*, highlighted by a cherry tart on which were eight lighted red candles. Monique had to explain to Jacob that he was supposed to make a wish before blowing out the candles. Jacob asked her why and, when we told him because it was his birthday, he replied, "That makes no sense—it's completely illogical!"

Le gouté was followed by the opening of three presents, which, not surprisingly, turned out to be grownup books. Jacob was visibly pleased and assured us that he had not read them, something which had been a matter of some concern for our mothers. Madame Poujet and Mother had both struggled with the difficult task of choosing a book that was advanced enough to please Jacob and that he wasn't likely to have read.

After the opening of presents, the six of us went outside and, to our amazement, Jacob proposed a game of hide-and-seek. However, we had a problem: there was nowhere to hide. The Gourlain garden was a rectangle bordered by their house and the walls of three neighboring properties. The rectangle was a lawn with no bushes and no plantings or adornments of any kind. But the lawn, if one could call it that, had not been mown or tended for some years and was now a field of deep hay, still a bright green because it was May. I proposed that if we agreed to play the game on our hands and knees, the hay, which had grown to a height of three feet, would conceal us completely. We could pretend we were a family of moles playing hide-and-seek, but instead of burrowing through the earth like moles, we would burrow through the tall hay.

Everyone thought this was a marvelous idea, except Monique who objected on the basis that she would be displaying her knickers while scrambling on all fours. I explained to her that she could choose between watching us or playing with us, and that we had all seen her knickers as she descended the ladder, and thought they were quite beautiful—indeed, a treat to see—why was she so worried? Monique chose to watch.

The game turned out to be a huge success, and Jacob even conceded he was having fun. Before too long, Monique, seeing all the fun she was missing, joined us and probably discovered that we more or less ignored her knickers.

Eventually, we created a maze of well beaten-down tracks through the hay, and under my tutelage and directions, the game evolved into a cross between prisoner's base and hide-and-seek, which was even more fun. Madame Gourlain came out on three occasions to announce that it was time for the guests to go home, but each time there were howls of protest from Jacob, who asked her to let us play one more game. I had made a convert and Jacob had been corrupted. We went home pleasantly satisfied with the way the party had turned out, and even Monique went home with knees and palms stained green by the fresh hay.

From then on, Jacob often came over our wall and asked to be included in whatever game Brenda, Charlie, Monique, and I were playing. Our little gang also went over the wall to Jacob's lawn and played some more *cache-cache aux taupes* (mole-and-seek). I don't know what his mother thought of this, but she never protested our appearance in their garden, and Jacob remained a good friend until we left Ville-d'Avray. He was definitely more fun than Charlie.

After the war, I heard from Raimond that the Gourlains had disappeared during the war and had never been seen again. "They had to go into hiding," Raimond said, adopting a somber tone, and adding, "They were Jewish, you know. No one knows where they went or if they were caught and put in an internment camp—perhaps killed."

I may not have had many friends, but Father certainly did. Among some of his closest were Mormilly (the man who crashed the plane) and Thiérry de Tapleine (who drove us home that day in his elegant Delahaye). These two men were frequent guests at our house. Mormilly and Thiérry were inseparable friends, though they made an unlikely pair. Thiérry was a man of small stature, frail, refined, dapper and soft spoken, whereas Mormilly was tall and heavy-set, had a booming voice, and was a good-natured diamond-in-the-rough. Mother, who disapproved of uncombed coifs said of Mormilly's untidy shock of curly blond hair, "*Ses cheveux lui donnent un air de méchant garçon—un peu farouche*" ("His hair gives him a naughty boy look—a bit farouche"). Mormilly never wore a tie and was a bit of a rowdy, but he wasn't out of control. The two men were dedicated *boulevardiers* (playboys) and inveterate bachelors, who liked nothing better than spending a night doing the cafés and nightclubs of Paris. Father occasionally joined them, telling me a decade later that these "evenings with the boys" were some of the wildest and most enjoyable evenings he ever had.

On one such occasion, Aldridge, Father's boss and also a close friend, joined them. Aldridge had just acquired a new Rolls Royce, which his chauffeur had driven to Paris. He boasted over dinner that it was such a powerful and fast car that he could probably reach Biarritz by dawn.

Biarritz is on the Atlantic, a few miles from the Spanish border and over five hundred miles from Paris in the days before the autoroutes. The main roads linking principal cities or towns were, for the most part, well paved, dead straight, and at night, completely deserted. Speed limits did not exist.

Mischievously, Mormilly, Thiérry and Dan turned on Aldridge and proposed a bet of a thousand francs each that he could not make good on his boast. Aldridge was not one to back down on anything, so he accepted the challenge. They agreed that for Aldridge to win three thousand francs, the Rolls Royce had to reach Biarritz by dawn the following morning, and the other participants in the bet had to go along for the ride. The three challengers would each win a thousand francs from Aldridge if his car didn't make it by sunrise. By the time the salad course was served, Aldridge had managed to communicate to Pavitt, his chauffeur who was waiting outside, that he should have the car's petrol tank filled and be ready for a long drive. Since no one hurries dinner in Paris, they finished a six-course meal in a leisurely fashion before setting off on the race.

The four men and Pavitt left Paris a little after ten in the evening. Pavitt was visibly taken aback when Aldridge climbed into the car and casually said to him, "To Biarritz, Pavitt, and step on it!"

After a brief pause, Pavitt regained his composure and said, "Yes, sir," and off they went.

Dan sat in the front seat to act as navigator, and the three other men were in back, telling stories and jokes, smoking cigars, and enjoying fine old brandy from the car's wet bar. Dan studied the map under a special map light in the car's ceiling. The shortest route would cut across the northwest corner of the Massif Central, a broad mountain range dead in the center of France. The roads would be twiddly (as Dan called them) and steep in places, so this route was obviously out of the question. Instead, Father proposed a route that followed the valley of the Loire westward, eventually turning south at Poitiers, then on through Bordeaux, and thence along the coast to Biarritz. This route crossed no mountains and, except for Bordeaux, passed through no large cities that would delay them. They all agreed that this seemed the best route.

In spite of Pavitt's velvet-touch driving, they were making good time on the deserted boulevards leading out of Paris. Nevertheless, Dan soon recognized a problem. Pavitt was slowing and sometimes even stopping at intersections! He was following the rules of the road used in England, and they differed significantly from French rules.

In those days, stop signs did not exist in France. More importantly, no driver ever ceded the right-of-way to any car on his left (with the corollary that he must cede to all drivers on his right). At intersections, the French driver just charges on, with sharp glances to his right for approaching cars, but absolutely certain that any driver on his left will stop for him. This worked fine because it was fully accepted as the cardinal basis of driving and as basic as driving on the right.

Dan pointed out to Aldridge in French (so Pavitt wouldn't understand) that they would never reach Biarritz by dawn with Pavitt obeying English rules of the road. He asked if it would be all right to explain the French system to Pavitt. Aldridge assured Father that Pavitt would listen to instruction of this sort without offense, so Father proceeded with this vital task. Pavitt listened calmly without comment or question and continued driving in the English style, as though Dan had never said a thing.

Dan was now in a quandary. If Pavitt continued in this fashion, Aldridge would lose the bet unfairly. There was something else gnawing at Dan. He had already sized up how nicely the car performed and knew there was a good chance of reaching Biarritz by dawn if they didn't waste time making unnecessary stops at every intersection. In fact, he was itching to prove it. He confronted Aldridge with his dilemma and proposed that he be allowed to drive instead of Pavitt and that he be placed on Aldridge's side of the bet. In other words, Dan would split the winnings with Aldridge if they reached Biarritz by dawn. It would be two against two, with everyone either winning or losing a thousand francs. At the time, a thousand francs would have purchased a modest used car in good condition, so the stakes were not trivial.

This last discussion was in English, and before Aldridge even had time to mull over the offer, Pavitt brought the car to a sedate and proper stop, got out, walked around to the passenger side, opened the door with an elegant bow, and said to Dan in a quiet and respectful tone, "She's all yours, sir. My heart's not been in this scheme right from the start. I look forward to seeing how it turns out." Dan looked at Aldridge and saw him gesturing with his hand outstretched, palm up, that the switch of drivers was fine by him.

Dan took the driver's seat and insisted that Mormilly sit beside him to act as navigator, warning him that if they had to backtrack due to faulty navigation, the bet was off. Mormilly agreed, and with Pavitt now sitting on the jump seat in back, they sped off. Good navigation and pre-planning were crucial whenever they arrived at a town where the *grandes routes* ended at the town's outskirts, forcing them to wend their way through crooked streets that dated back to medieval times. Fortunately, they had the excellent *Guide Michelin* that provided a clear street map for every town of any size. Mormilly did his homework carefully, well before their arrival at any town along their route.

Dan was an excellent driver. He never had even a minor accident during his entire lifetime. He loved to "scorch" as he called it, but he never took undue risks. Driving a car in good condition at extreme speed on a straight and deserted road did not constitute such a risk in his view. Years later he told me that on this trip, he had the car at well over a hundred miles per hour on the straight-aways. "This was most of the time—I don't think we met more than two oncoming cars on the whole trip and we had to overtake only one. We did hit numerous rabbits, which upset Pavitt no end. He was, I think, more upset about the mess on the radiator than about the rabbits. Pavitt wanted me to slow down, so the rabbits could get out of the way, but I explained to him what I knew all too well about rabbits in car headlights. The bright headlight beams mesmerize them. If I stopped, I'd also have to get out of the car and shoo them off the road! Quite out of question, of course."

The car had a huge petrol tank, but no one knew how far the car would go on a full tank at this speed or whether the petrol gauge reading could be trusted. The gauge was at the halfway mark when they reached Poitiers, about halfway into the trip. It was three in the morning. While driving through the deserted town, Dan spotted a lone petrol pump on the sidewalk. Although the house to which it seemed to belong was shuttered, he could see light coming through the shutter's louvers at an upstairs window.

He stopped at the pump, got out and shouted in the direction of the lighted window, which produced no reply. Pavitt remained in the car sound asleep—by far the most effective antidote to a state of sustained terror—but Thiérry, Mormilly and Aldridge left the Rolls in order to stretch. After conferring about their dilemma, they decided they needed something small to throw at the window with the lighted louvers. By the light of the headlights, the four men started looking for pebbles, but found nothing. Thiérry eventually volunteered his gold cigarette lighter. After four throws, Mormilly made a direct hit on the shutter. He made three more throws and two more hits before eliciting a response.

The louvered shutters opened and a man visible only in silhouette, but unmistakably naked, stood at the open window and announced boldly, *"Nous sommes au moment le plus précieux de la vie—je vous en prie, fichez-nous la paix!"* ("We are at one of life's most precious moments—I beseech you, leave us the hell alone!") He then disappeared back into the room, closing the shutters behind him.

"Try hitting the shutters once more and offer him fifty francs to come down," said Aldridge. Then after a pause, he added, "We are about to discover just how precious this moment is."

Mormilly returned reluctantly to his dubious task, this time yelling out the offer as loudly and distinctly as he could, that he needed petrol, and that he was in a desperate hurry. The shutters reopened, and the man said, *"Il me faut cents francs et pas moins! Et je veux les voir avant de descendre."* ("I'll take a hundred francs and nothing less! And I want to see them before I come down.")

"There you are!" said Aldridge. "Now we know the precise value of life's most precious moment." Standing in the headlight beam, he pulled out his wallet, counted out the sum demanded and waved the sheaf of notes.

As Aldridge did this, Dan called out a proviso, "And come down immediately or the bribe reverts to fifty francs."

In less than a minute, the front door opened. The man, wearing only dressing gown and slippers, walked straight to Aldridge and grabbed the hundred francs out of his hand before anybody realized what was happening. All the yelling and commotion had finally awakened Pavitt, who quickly grasped the situation, jumped out of the car, and went to work connecting the pump's hose to the car's fuel tank.

The pump was an older hand pump, the kind with two glass cylinders at eye level, one of which *le garagiste* filled to its five-liter capacity by swinging a large handle back and forth. When the glass container was full, his hand on the handle met resistance. He stopped pumping and rotated a small valve handle set between the two glass cylinders. The petrol then drained slowly out of the filled glass cylinder into the car, as *le garagiste* resumed the hand pumping to fill the second glass cylinder. It was a laborious process, requiring at least a minute's work for each filling of a single glass cylinder. The Rolls was voracious, and it took well over fifteen minutes to fill its tank, during which time *le garagiste* tried unsuccessfully to renegotiate the bribe for his off-hours service. *"En attendant, elle se refroidit et s'endort là haut! Sûrement ça vaut que'que chose!"* ("In the meantime, upstairs she's cooling down and going to sleep! Surely that's worth something!") *le garagiste* lamented.

After paying *le garagiste* for the petrol, the men resumed the race, reaching the Palace Hotel in Biarritz at ten minutes after seven. Thiérry and Mormilly staunchly maintained that Aldridge had lost the bet since it was after seven o'clock, but Aldridge argued that they had reached the outskirts of Biarritz before seven. Mormilly, probably in a dazed stupor, had made his only navigating mistake when providing directions for the last kilometer leading to the Palace Hotel, where they had planned to have a good breakfast.

Over croissants and coffee, Aldridge persisted in his argument. "The selection of this hotel as the finish line was after-the-fact. Since we have just forgiven Mormilly for his inattention after we reached the city limits of Biarritz, you must allow us some leeway in the definition of 'reaching Biarritz.' Besides, you will note that I originally said 'before dawn,' and that the sun was still below the horizon when we reached the hotel." Later, they checked a newspaper and saw that sunrise was at 07:12 (the race took place in November), so it seemed that Aldridge had a good case.

The friends enjoyed their breakfast but never managed to agree on whether Aldridge and Dan had won their bet fair and square. They argued good-naturedly over this matter each time they got together thereafter, but never settled the question. Aldridge was in admiration of Father's driving skills and said, "Right from the start I never really thought we would make it— even during the trip, with you driving like a professional racing driver, I still had my doubts!"

Father managed to catch a plane back to Paris later in the morning and was able to attend an important business meeting in Paris that afternoon. Mormilly went to the local aerodrome and wangled a seat as copilot on a military plane bound for Paris. Aldridge and Thiérry stayed in Biarritz to gamble at the casino. Upon hearing Pavitt declare that it would take him two days to complete the return trip, the two of them took an express train back to Paris, leaving Pavitt to drive back alone at his leisurely British pace.

Some years later, Mother chuckled at this last detail in Father's retelling of this incident. "Of course Pavitt couldn't go fast," she said. "His name is Pavitt! In French, *pas vite* means 'not fast.' "

In the autumn of 1937 I returned to the Dennis School and started what would be an exceptionally good school year for me. My relationship with fellow students and masters was on an even keel for the first time in my scholastic life, and I liked every aspect of daily school routine, even when things went a little haywire.

That winter, it was bitterly cold for ten days. The old mansion that served as our school building had no heating, and the so-called classrooms were so cold that a glass of drinking water left there overnight froze solid. Sitting all day in those glacial classrooms without any kind of heating was out of the question. Mr. Dennis called a school meeting in the palatial drawing room, which was only slightly warmer than the classrooms in spite of a fire blazing in its huge fireplace. There, he announced to the assembled school, "We could send you all home, but that would be highly inconvenient for your parents, who are expecting us to keep you productively employed throughout the day. My plan is to move tables and chairs from the classrooms into this drawing room."

Bundled up in overcoats and mufflers, and wearing our wool *bérets* inelegantly pulled down over our ears, the eighty of us spent the first hour of that school day hauling chairs and tables from the classrooms to the drawing room. Then we scrambled amicably to find places as close as possible to the hearth, where a hearty fire was kept ablaze all day. By late afternoon, the room, warmed by eighty boys and seven masters, managed to acquire what the British students among us called "a jolly good fug."

Mr. Dennis' scheme had created a one-room schoolhouse with eighty students. At first, the masters tried teaching us in the usual group fashion, but the arrangement was too noisy and it wasn't working. So he switched us to the "rainy-afternoon-mode," in which all eighty of us listened to one of the older boys reading aloud from Dickens's *Great Expectations*. Each day we sat there bundled up, listening to the story, watching the steam from our breaths, and staring at our blue knees protruding from our overcoats. I don't think any of the boys owned a pair of long trousers, and wouldn't have worn them if they did. After a week, the cold eased up, and we went back to using individual rooms for each class, but it was still cold, and we continued to wear our *bérets* over our ears and our overcoats all day long for two more weeks.

It was at about this time that Mother decided that I should take something she called "*le solfège*." Twice a week I attended *une école de solfège* (a music school) in neighboring Saint Cloud. Dictionaries (both French and English) describe "*solfège*" as the act of going up and down the musical scale (vocally). The school in question had us doing somewhat more than just that. Yes, we did sing do, ré, mi and so on, backwards and forwards, and played the scales—endlessly and monotonously on the piano.

One of our exercises involved something that looked suspiciously like fractions, a part of arithmetic that I hadn't yet covered in school. In a state of extreme boredom, I found that playing with these quasi-fractions (on paper) was quite amusing. We were told that a little black golf club with one flag dangling from the top of it represented an eighth note. If it had two flags at the top of it, a sixteenth note, or half the value, in time, of the eighth note, and that it took two such sixteenth notes to equal the eighth note. Each time a flag was added to the little golf club, it cut the note in half once more, so a little club with four flags was a sixty-fourths note. I was catching on to fractions fast and I started using notes with numerous little flags—sometimes as many as seven flags, which was a five-hundred-and-twelfths note. I found it fun to add all these tiny fractions within a measure, adjusting their various sizes and number so that their true arithmetic total came to the value of the larger fraction found at the start of the musical line. This was exactly what we were supposed to do, but we were expected to use fewer and larger fractions, which the teacher could verify without doing a lot of extra arithmetic with pencil and paper.

The music teacher thought I was deliberately trying to annoy her, which really wasn't the case. I defended my calculations as correct and challenged her to persevere in her verification of my work. After the second lesson involving such exercises, during which I grew even more proficient and adventurous with my fractions, the teacher must have reached her limit. When Mother came to fetch me, she announced that she could no longer stand it and that she didn't want me in her school.

Attending this music course had required that I miss two afternoons a week at the Dennis School, which I much preferred over the music school, so I was secretly jubilant over what I had unintentionally achieved. Nevertheless, this was my third expulsion from a school. Mother, who was neither amused nor sympathetic, asked me crossly, "Alain, are you planning to spend your life being expelled from schools?"

At the Dennis School, we sometimes had Boy Scout outings instead of sports or games. On these occasions, which began after the first period in the morning and after the *petits pains* recess, we would ride a bus to some bucolic setting in *la banlieue de Paris* (the countryside around Paris). There, we prepared an elaborate meal out "in the field," (actually, out in the woods). The Scout Master prided himself on being a great chef. He was French and not part of the regular staff of the Dennis School. On each of these expeditions, he brought along three small cast-iron cooking stoves and several sacks of soft coal, all of which he tied onto the bus's rear luggage rack. The stoves were the most important items on the trip, absolutely essential for *un repas sérieux* (a serious meal). This was no mere picnic, and it was a lot more than just an outdoor "weenie roast."

Whenever a scout had participated sufficiently and successfully in the preparation of a specific gastronomic delight, the Scout Master awarded him one of several scout badges that could be earned for each of various dishes. I believe this was the only basis for which scout badges were awarded in this troop. I don't know if this was the universal scout practice in France at the time, but it wouldn't surprise me if it were.

Unfortunately, I never had an opportunity to do anything that might earn me a badge. I was the youngest and smallest scout (I was actually *un louvteau*, a cub scout), and although it was never mentioned, the whole school seemed to know that I was permanently enjoined from using the elegant penknife which hung from my belt. Most of the boys were aware that there was little I could do to actually prepare food under these circumstances. They therefore assigned me to the task of inserting coal into the stoves, sparing them the problem of handling the food with soiled hands. The stoves were small, and were kept burning at a high temperature, so all I did on these outings was the stoking of the fires. Given my proclivity for blackening myself, I didn't lack enthusiasm for my assigned task. Regrettably, there was no badge awarded for stoking.

Nevertheless, I made an effort to remain clean. I was, after all, seven years old and, armed with my newly acquired reasonableness, I was convinced that if I did my part in this effort, Divine Providence would do the rest and somehow intervene between me and any large amounts of clinging coal dust. However, in spite of sound intentions, all reasonable care, and my fervent belief in Divine Providence, our cooking excursions left me even filthier than an afternoon of games at the base of the smoke stack when the wind was blowing the sooty smoke our way.

At the end of four happy terms at the Dennis School, Mother announced that the place was distinctly unhygienic and that I would not return there next fall. I was bitterly disappointed and pleaded with her at length, but to no avail.

Despite the fact that class assignments usually required a lot of hard work, there was never any unpleasant pressure. I had looked forward to every day at that school and it had been a remarkably satisfying experience. I couldn't believe that some dirty rings around a bathtub could topple such a good thing. I don't think Mother ever appreciated how much I learned at the Dennis School and how much I loved it.

In June of 1938, we went back to Villa Champs de Mai in Condette. I was barely out of the car before I headed up the grassy track to the Baichant farm. Michelle and her mother greeted me with open arms and hugs. Over the winter, Michelle had outgrown me by two inches and now seemed sturdier and more feral than ever.

When I returned to the house from my happy reunion, Mother asked where I had been. I told her without hesitation that I had been at the Baichant farm. "Since when have you been so close to the Baichants that you have to leave us before the car is even unpacked?"

I replied with my third official white lie, that I wasn't close to the Baichants. I belatedly remembered how careful I had been the previous summer to keep my activities at the farm covert, and I was furious with myself for being so careless.

During the next few days, I deliberately played it safe by not going over to the farm, hoping the matter would fade from Mother's memory. However, the issue was revived a week later when Mother was taking a walk and crossed paths with Madame Tourneau. The Tourneaus were our neighbors to the west; the Baichant farm was east of us.

Like us, the Tourneaus had been new residents of Condette the previous summer. They used the same communal grassy track to reach their house as we did to reach ours. They passed our house on the way, so we could hardly avoid seeing them occasionally. I was mystified as to why we had never spoken to them even though the family had three boys. The youngest was probably the same age as Brenda, and the eldest was clearly older than I. But in the middle was a boy who might have been only slightly older than I was. I longed to have the three brothers as playmates, but mysteriously, they always seemed to move out of "greeting range" whenever I made a deliberate attempt to run into them.

On this first face to face meeting of the two neighbors, Mother told Madame Tourneau that she had seen her three sons and thought it would be nice if they all came over for *le goûté* so we could get to know each other. However, Madame Tourneau responded frostily to the idea and said bluntly, "I thought your children preferred to play with the little farm girl next door to you, and since I don't want my boys doing this, I told them to avoid your children."

Mother was stunned and replied, "But my children don't play with the little farm girl—where did you get that idea?"

"I beg your pardon, Madame," replied Madame Tourneau haughtily. "I saw your son on several occasions as I drove past the farm, all smeared in mud or cow dung and apparently enjoying himself thoroughly in her presence." Mother, brought up short, returned to our house in a fury and ordered me into the drawing room. Being called for *tête-à-tête* in the drawing room was always a sign that there was trouble afoot.

"I now understand why you were so anxious to run over to the Baichant farm on the day we arrived," she said crossly as I walked into the drawing room. "How often do you go over there?"

I noted her use of the present tense and was able to reply truthfully, "I haven't gone over there except once, on the day we arrived."

"What about last year? Did you become smeared in cow dung when you went over there? How often did you do that?"

"I never got smeared in cow dung. Who would do a dirty thing like that? Sometimes I got muddy if we were planting vegetables on a day after it rained."

"What were you doing planting things at a neighbor's farm? And how often did you do this?"

"It started when I went over there to feed their ducks, which Madame Baichant said I could do after I lost Ploof. I saw them working in the vegetable patch, and I had nothing to do here at our house. It looked like fun, so I started picking vegetables with them. Michelle is lots of fun to play with, and I like her."

"Did Raimond and Françoise know about this? And was Brenda with you?" asked Mother. Then came the next white lie. The "greater good" I felt, was saving Raimond.

"I don't think Raimond and Françoise knew—I didn't tell them about it. Brenda didn't go over there, except once. She didn't like it and never went back after that." At least that last statement was more or less true.

"Well, it's going to have to stop. I had a talk with Madame Tourneau, and she doesn't want you playing with her boys if you're also playing with Michelle. And of course, it's more appropriate that you play with them. So, from now on, I don't want you to play with Michelle or work at their farm, planting things. Is that quite clear? I will punish you if you go over there."

I was stunned, but I could see that Mother had already made up her mind about Michelle and wouldn't budge. I dreaded telling Michelle and Madame Baichant that henceforth I was to avoid them. I was wretchedly miserable and angry over the matter, and I was in a sulky mood for several days after this exchange. I postponed indefinitely a farewell visit to the Baichants, clinging to the faint hope that Mother would relent and let me resume playing at the farm. I pestered her daily, saying that I was bored stiff and that there was nothing to keep me busy or amuse me here in Condette.

I tried to befriend the youngest Tourneau boy through a hole in the hedge, but he just ran away as if he had seen a ghost. I told Mother about this, and she said she knew the Tourneau boys had been told not to play with us. "What a shame, really," she said, "but it will change after a while if you stay away from the farm."

For me, the real shame would be when I had to face Michelle. When we drove by the farm on our way out, I always squinched down below the level of the car window, so I wouldn't see Michelle or be seen by her.

It finally dawned on Mother that I was not my usual bouncy self, and she took me to a doctor in Boulogne, who could find nothing wrong with me except possibly my tonsils which, though not inflamed, were larger than they should be.

After the doctor's appointment, Mother visited a nearby antique shop; she was still furnishing the house and never missed an opportunity to discover a hidden gem while rummaging in the piles of bric-a-brac at the back of such shops. On this occasion, she stumbled on a set of miniature golf clubs. The set even included a well made and appropriately sized leather golf bag to hold the small clubs. Mother bought it on the spot, declaring, "This is how we're going to keep you busy and amused."

The next morning, she took Brenda and me to the Hardelot Golf Club, but the instructor refused to give us golfing lessons, insisting that we were too young.

"Very well, I will teach them myself!" replied Mother indignantly.

We played nine holes, but we were observed replacing divots on a green. When we returned to the clubhouse, Mother was politely asked not to let Brenda and me play on the course. She was miffed, but not defeated.

That afternoon she set off across the huge cow pasture in front of our house carrying a sack of empty tin cans gleaned from a cache Raimond kept in the garage. Mother also carried a spade and several straight sticks, which she had asked Raimond to round up for her. Brenda and I followed Mother around the vast meadow and watched as she dug small holes a couple of hundred yards apart from each other and spaced around the periphery of the extensive pasture. In each hole, she placed a tin can flush with the roots of the grass, taking care to press pieces of the removed sod back into the space around the open mouth of the can. Close to each can, she inserted a stick into the ground and on the upper end of the stick she tied a brightly colored rag. *Et voilà!* In the space of two hours, Mother had created a golf course! She spent the next week playing this nine-hole course with Brenda and me, giving us pointers and encouraging us in this difficult game.

After a week or so, we were enjoying golf, and Brenda and I both had scores of around 120 for the nine holes. The course had its share of obstacles.

The cows had cropped the grass to a little over an inch high, but the terrain was pockmarked with mole holes and the imprints of hooves made when the ground was soft due to rain, so when the ball rolled, it seldom moved in a straight line. Twice, the ball completely disappeared into a mole hole. The meadow was generously dotted with tussocks of marsh grass, which the cows did not seem to relish. Well nourished by manure, it grew in healthy clumps all over the place. Golf balls had a nasty habit of landing or bouncing right into the heart of a tussock from which it was nearly impossible to play them.

Other hazards included the cows, who refused to let us play through, and who stood in the line of play so long that we eventually had to play around them. We were strictly forbidden to play over a cow or a herd of them, even if that was the most direct path to the next hole. There was also the little lake in the middle of the pasture and patches around the lake where the grass was so waterlogged that we sank into it as if in quicksand. There was no end of diversions on the little course, but they kept the game from being dull.

After church one Sunday, Brenda and I decided to play a quick round of golf before lunch. Since we had to be properly dressed for Sunday lunch, we decided to play in the clothes we had worn to church, so that we wouldn't have to change clothes back and forth all morning. Brenda was wearing a white organdy dress, her very best.

On the seventh hole, my ball landed near a meadow muffin and rolled onto its hardened surface, coming to a stop at its center (meadow muffins dry and harden with age). Mother had emphasized that—unlike croquet, where one is sometimes allowed to relocate the ball if it's impossible to play—in golf, one has to play the ball wherever it comes to a stop. Brenda and I agreed that mine was a tricky shot, but not impossible, and that I had no choice but to play it from this unusual tee. I rehearsed my swing several times without hitting the ball, as Brenda, who stood facing me some ten feet away and to my left, chuckled mischievously at my predicament.

I bravely swung my club, but it went low. The hard surface and dry appearance of the cow pie turned out to be only superficial, and a spray of the softer underlying material went flying in all directions, but mainly in the direction of Brenda. As I stood, stunned and appalled at the sight of Brenda's ruined dress, she immediately accused me of deliberately spattering her with meadow muffin and ran home wailing. Filled with regret and fear, I headed reluctantly towards our house. I could see Brenda already laying out a case against me, charging me with malice aforethought, and I dreaded Mother's reaction.

By the time I reached home, the tears of remorse that ran down my cheeks were also tears of genuine fright and apprehension. Indeed, it turned out Brenda had done her dirty work well. Mother was livid and berated me savagely before I even started to tell her my side of the story. I had never seen her so angry. I kept protesting my innocence but could make no headway swimming against her tirade of angry words. She wouldn't listen to anything I said—in her mind, it was an avoidable act. I hadn't avoided it out of pure mischief, and that was the end of the story as far as she was concerned. My tears and wails of repentance failed to assuage her anger or spare me from a vigorous spanking on my bare thighs. The worst part of this horrid tale was that Brenda declared that she would never play golf with me again and, without her companionship and a little competition, I had no choice but to retire from the game at the age of eight.

Our visit to the doctor earlier in the summer had reminded Mother that she still had to do battle with my tonsils, which she had failed to conquer when the surgery in Ville-d'Avray was dangerously botched. I also think she may have been trying to kill two birds with one stone: having an operation would keep me out of mischief for a good two weeks. In those days, patients were kept in bed that long for the most minor of surgeries. While she was at it, Mother decreed that Brenda's tonsils would also be removed, though I have no recollection that Brenda was having any problems with hers. Mind you, I wasn't having any problems either. Still, those vicious tonsils were there, lurking in my throat, waiting for an opportunity to attack, and had to be exterminated. The Boulogne doctor was all for my surgery, and it was agreed that Brenda and I would be "done" at the main hospital there.

Raimond accompanied Mother, Brenda, and me to the hospital. Brenda and I drew straws to see who would be the first to have the surgery. Brenda drew the short straw, but refused to go first, so I gallantly offered to do so, taking care not to mention to her that this was, in fact, the better place in line, since it shortened the anxious waiting. Following the surgery, Raimond carried Brenda and me, still unconscious, to the car; we were still under the anesthesia when we reached home. Everything had supposedly gone well this time. But in my case, the tonsils "grew back," and a third assault was made on them three years later.

The first few days following our double tonsillectomy in Boulogne are a blur. I do remember that on the first night after the surgery, I couldn't sleep because of the pain in my throat and that Father brought me a glowworm in a jar to help take my mind off my suffering. When the glowworm failed in its mission, Father stayed up a good part of the night, reading chapter after chapter of *Winnie the Pooh* to me.

A welcome distraction from the numerous miseries of that summer was a superb, mahogany canoe. Father's old army friend, Uncle Hill, was frequently a house guest at Villa Champs de Mai and, as a token of appreciation, he offered to buy us a sand yacht. But for reasons I have always felt were misguided, Father asked that he change the gift to a canoe. Father claimed a canoe was safer and that we would therefore enjoy it more. The canoe came equipped with a sail, leeboards and a rudder. Canoes are tippy even without a sail, and as a sailing craft, it's hard to imagine anything more prone to tipping over and therefore unsafe.

We car-topped the canoe to Hardelot and then carried it across the sand to the water's edge, where Father spent most of the morning rigging the sail, rudder and leeboards. The wind usually came up during the morning, and by the time he was ready to sail it, the sea was too rough for a canoe, forcing him to cancel his plans. Some mornings, the wind didn't come up at all, so the sea was calm enough for the canoe, but it was no use trying to sail it. In Hardelot, there was either no wind or too much wind, and seldom anything in between.

On windless days, Father sometimes took us out for a brief paddle without the sail. I remember these awkward outings and how, with every move Father made, I could feel the canoe quiver with his nervousness. On one occasion, he took Brenda, Mother, and me for a canoe paddle. I was sitting motionless in the bow, enjoying the ride, when all of a sudden, the canoe tipped over. Mother, who wanted to see how far we were from shore, had apparently turned around too vigorously and leaned a bit too much to one side. Fortunately, Brenda and I were wearing inflatable life preservers so we had a pleasant, if unexpected swim. Father was visibly upset by the incident, even though the water was only three feet deep, so that he and Mother were easily able to right the swamped craft and walk it back to shore.

This incident convinced Father that canoes, like sand yachts, were extremely unsafe, and he resolved that he would never take us out again. I was quite sure that sand yachts were not nearly as dangerous as canoes and told him so. Father didn't appreciate my observation and only said, "What do you know about it, Sonny?" The irony was that I knew a great deal about it, having watched sand yachts sailing along the beach for hours on end, often in strong winds. I had never seen anyone injured in spite of witnessing numerous capsizes at high speed, in which the passengers were flipped harmlessly onto the relatively yielding sand surface.

Our beautiful canoe sat upside-down on sawhorses inside the garage until Uncle Bob and his family came to stay with us for two weeks. He apparently loved to sail as did his two children, Peter and Betty. For a month every summer, Bob's family rented and sailed aboard a large, comfortable sloop on the Norfolk Broads, a labyrinthine river delta in eastern England. Uncle Bob had brought his 16mm movie projector to Condette and showed us films he had taken on their sailing holidays. It was obvious from his home movies that Uncle Bob and Peter were excellent sailors.

At the time of their visit to Villa Champs de Mai, Peter was fourteen and Betty was sixteen. Their entire family admired our canoe and longed to try sailing it, asking repeatedly if they could do so. On the weekends, when Father was there, he never offered to let them go out sailing. During the week, when Father was in Paris working, Mother was desperate in her efforts to entertain them and seized upon their request with enthusiasm. I was greatly excited by the home movies and even more so about the prospect of sailing with experienced sailors. Mother agreed to this outing and my going with them, but only on condition that I would wear my inflatable life preserver the entire time.

Uncle Bob had heard about our various canoeing misadventures from Mother and carefully planned our sailing expedition to avoid such problems. He chose to sail the canoe at Étaples, where the estuary of the River Canche provides relatively wave-free water, even in a decent wind.

Raimond found an old piece of carpet to protect the roof of Uncle Bob's huge Delage motorcar and, with some difficulty, the two men and Peter loaded the canoe on top of it. The canoe was quite heavy and the flat roof of this boxy car was so high off the ground that only Uncle Bob, who stood six-and-a-half feet tall, could hoist it into place. Raimond and Peter, at the other end of the canoe, couldn't lift it high enough and had to resort to using a step ladder. Anticipating the unloading process when Raimond would not be present to help, Mother had them strap the ladder onto the top of her tiny Simca which would accompany the big car to the launch site. Uncle Bob referred to the Simca, almost concealed beneath the cumbersome ladder, as "the fire engine brigade."

When we reached Étaples, Uncle Bob and Peter had the canoe ready to sail in ten minutes, as though they had done it daily for a living. I had donned my inflatable life preserver even before leaving the house in Condette. I wanted to make it quite clear I intended to heed Mother's injunction and wasn't taking any chances on their developing qualms about taking me on this voyage. Mother didn't seem to notice and made no comment as Uncle Bob matter-of-factly told me to get into the bow of the canoe when it was time to set sail. Uncle Bob removed his shoes and sox, gave them to Gladys, rolled his flannel trousers to just below the knee and gingerly clambered into the stern of the canoe. As he did so, I felt the bow rise perceptibly. Mother, Auntie Gladys, Betty, and Brenda waved us goodby and drove off to nearby Le Touquet in Bob's car to shop the boutiques in that posh seaside resort.

With Uncle Bob puffing contentedly at his pipe and controlling the rudder lines, Peter amidships in charge of the lateen sail, and me officially designated the bow lookout, we sailed easily and pleasantly up the River Canche, which became tree-lined and picturesque as we proceeded inland. The riverside trees and meadows were a lush green, as were the reeds and water plants that bordered the river. I loved the abundant and overpowering greenness of the scene. I was ecstatically happy as we glided along at a good clip, helped by an incoming tide and a good tail wind. We eventually sighted a stretch of shore with a small beach where we landed the canoe in order to enjoy the picnic lunch that Françoise had packed for us.

Uncle Bob strongly resembled Father, except that he was much taller, stronger, and heavier, though not fat. He differed from Father in one other important way: he was very relaxed and easygoing. This characteristic quickly earned him my devoted admiration and firmly established his position as my favorite uncle. Uncle Bob consumed most of a liter of red wine with his lunch, after which he had a snooze in the deep grass under the shade of a tree. It was the first time I had ever heard anyone snore, and for years thereafter, I believed that only giant people like Uncle Bob snored.

While he slept, Peter and I tried to catch some minnows, using the picnic basket and a piece of string as fishing implements. In our quest, we wandered downstream from the beach where we had landed. At a place where the shore consisted of a steep earth embankment, I stood too close to the water's edge, causing the bank to crumble, and fell into the river. It probably wasn't very deep, but it was too deep for me to touch bottom. True to my promise, I had never removed my life preserver, so I started to float easily downstream in the current, which had changed direction when the tide turned during our lunch. Peter ran along the bank, calling out and instructing me to paddle towards the shore. But the life preserver was so large and awkward that I found it impossible to make much headway by dog paddling. Although the coast was still a long way off, I wondered if I would be carried out to sea before anyone could rescue me. For the moment, I wasn't too worried and watched as Peter ran ahead of me along the bank. He finally came to a bend in the river where it widened and the shore once again became a gently sloping beach. There he entered the water fully dressed. Peter waded out to meet me as I floated towards him and he was able to grab my outstretched hand. He managed to drag me back to shore, even though the water almost reached his shoulders.

We both agreed that it would be wise not to tell his father about my tumble into the river. When we returned to the picnic site, we found Uncle Bob just waking up, and were taken aback to hear him say quite casually, "Hullo, have you chaps been swimming? What a splendid idea!" We were both still sopping wet, and I was amused by the fact that it didn't strike him as odd that we were both fully dressed. Except for the fact that we were barefoot, we had on basic British schoolboy outfits: gray flannel knee-length trousers, gray flannel shirts, and Peter was even wearing his knitted school tie— hardly swimming attire! Uncle Bob was either very relaxed after all that wine, or perhaps he thought it was none of his business if Peter and I chose to go swimming in our street clothes.

We rounded up the picnic things, clambered back into the canoe and pushed off. We now headed back towards Étaples, doing a lot of tacking back and forth across the River Canche, which wasn't much more than two hundred feet wide where we were sailing. An outgoing tide helped us against what had become a blustery head wind. Uncle Bob was kept busy shifting his great weight an inch or so each time a gust was upon us. I marveled at how nimbly he did just the minimum necessary shifting and how well he had the situation in hand.

We eventually reached the place along the shore in Étaples from where we had set out. Uncle Bob looked at his watch and announced that we still had plenty of time and that we would continue our course towards the sea, past the colorful fleet of fishing smacks tied along the fishing pier in Étaples. I was thrilled that our voyage wasn't over yet.

After we sailed past the hustle and bustle of the fishing boats unloading their catch, Uncle Bob crossed to the south edge of the widening estuary where the bordering reed beds made the water less choppy. Once there, we glided along swiftly on a close reach, parallel to and near the edge of the reeds.

The tranquility of our journey was unexpectedly broken by a great roar that grew louder and louder. Suddenly, we had a glimpse of its source as a large airliner loomed over the reeds, coming straight for us. We were at the north end of Le Touquet aerodrome and directly beneath the flight path of any aircraft taking off. The gigantic plane was barely off the ground and rising ever so slowly as it lumbered ponderously towards us. We ducked instinctively, and I could swear the huge craft passed over our mast with only a few feet to spare. The blast of air from the plane's prop wash caused the canoe to lean violently, and water came cascading over the side as we teetered perilously on the brink of a capsize. Peter released the sheet, nimbly climbed onto the high side, and the canoe righted itself, but not before taking on a sizable amount of water.

"Jolly good show, Peter," said Uncle Bob in his usual calm, unexcited monotone, and resumed the contemplative puffing on his pipe. Up to this point, sitting in the bilge, I had stayed dry, but now I was sitting in more than three inches of water, which sloshed back and forth like a miniature tidal wave within the canoe. Uncle Bob and Peter, on wicker seats, sat slightly above the water in the bilge. We were barely afloat, with only a few inches of freeboard. Oblivious to our plight, Peter exclaimed excitedly that the plane had been a Handley Page Helena airliner, a huge four-engine biplane used on the Imperial Airways route to India. Animated, and still ignoring our precarious condition, he continued, "For the trip to India, it has to land about every five hundred miles to refuel. It has sleeping berths for eight passengers, as well as a cabin for twenty more seated passengers. What extraordinary luck to be right here as it was taking off! It was worth getting a little wet just to see that magnificent machine from this vantage point!"

He could well speak of getting a little wet—he wasn't sitting in three inches of water! But in truth, I agreed with Peter; it had been a remarkable sight, though I would have preferred a side view instead of the bottom view.

We had no bailing can, and there was no beach nearby to which we could repair to dump out the water, so we had to turn around and head back to our launching site. The canoe was now sluggish and low in the water, and barely moved upstream in the outgoing current we were bucking, but a beam breeze was strong enough to afford us some slow progress. The trip back to our launching point took a long time and gave me the opportunity to work furiously at bailing with a small celluloid goblet I retrieved from the picnic basket. We weren't in danger of sinking, but I didn't want our voyage to end and desperately hoped that if, through my efforts, the bilge could be dried before we reached home port, Uncle Bob would turn us around and we would sally forth once more.

The water level in the canoe went down perceptibly, and my efforts elicited a low-key "Jolly good show, Alan" from Uncle Bob. I was eventually thwarted in my struggle to achieve a completely dry canoe by the fact that Uncle Bob made the canoe stern-heavy. Most of the remaining water congregated under his great presence and out of my reach. By the time we made homeport, I could claim that at least my end of the canoe was dry.

The ladies were on the beach awaiting our return. It had been a magnificent day. For many years thereafter, I reflected on it as the greatest day of my life. In Condette on the morrow, life seemed more humdrum than ever.

In another effort at keeping me busy, Mother enrolled me in a swimming class. The lessons took place on the beach in Hardelot every afternoon when tides were suitable. The Penguin Beach Club had built a wooden tank about thirty feet square and five feet deep, well below the high tide mark where, twice daily, the high tide filled and flushed it with clean seawater.

Six sturdy posts incorporated into the pool's construction supported three parallel cables which spanned the pool. Pulleys, one on each cable, rolled along the length of the cables and, by means of a short tether connected to a canvas belt around a swimmer's waist, kept him from sinking. The student swimmer swam back and forth the length of the pool hauling the pulley behind him. However, the system had a major design flaw. Since the cable sagged in the middle, swimmers who were supported at the right level at either end of the cable found themselves somewhat lower in the water when they reached the center of the pool. I watched several students start to panic as they approached the cable's mid-point. They thrashed about, coughing, sputtering, gulping cupfuls of seawater and screaming for help. If things got really bad, Monsieur Cridoux, the instructor, reached for a long-handled boat hook and used it to drag the struggling swimmer to the edge of the pool as though retrieving an errant skiff. Cridoux tried tightening the cables to reduce the sagging, but the cables, which were really just thin ropes, usually broke under the added strain, often in mid-lesson, creating even more chaos for the hapless swimmer.

Beginners used the two outer lanes (cables) so that Monsieur Cridoux, outside the pool, could walk along beside the student swimmer, haranguing him as he struggled to propel himself from one end of the pool to the other. Monsieur Cridoux, who taught only the breast stroke, counseled the swimmer to breathe in time with his arm movements and to keep his heels together as he brought his feet forward. We never saw Cridoux swimming in his marvelous pool, and it was widely rumored that he could not swim.

Making matters worse for the swimmers were the numerous uninvited spectators who lined the edge of the tank, kibitzing, joking and laughing at the plight of the harried students. The swimming lessons were a new feature at the beach that year, and despite the horrors just described, taking lessons in this tank was a surprisingly popular pastime. Few people in Hardelot knew how to swim, and mastering this skill was viewed as one of life's great achievements.

For several days before my scheduled lesson, I watched the proceedings at the pool with no small misgivings. On the day of my lesson, I showed up well prepared, wearing my well-proven inflatable life preserver. I rebuffed Cridoux's assurance that his cable and tether system achieved the same purpose as my preserver and insisted that I be allowed to use it. Monsieur Cridoux, reluctant to loose a pupil, permitted me to wear my preserver on condition that I would also use the tether. It was the only way he could keep me swimming in one lane of the pool, he insisted.

Using both devices, I found I had so much stuff around my upper body that moving my arms in the prescribed fashion was out of question. However, I struggled along using a crude dog paddle. Cridoux allowed me to "swim" this way for half an hour on the middle cable, where I didn't interfere with his other pupils in the two outer lanes. He made no pretense of giving me lessons, but each time I showed up, he would say, "One day, Monsieur Alain, you will decide not to use your life preserver, and then I will teach you to swim like a grownup."

Cridoux's inventive pool—made of stout, interlocking wood panels, braced on the outside, and colorfully painted—leaked copiously at all the joints, so that by the next low tide, it was just about empty. While awaiting my turn for a lesson, or after the lesson, I kept myself amused by damming the rivulets that flowed down the beach from the leaking pool. If I could round up some cohorts to help me, we sometimes built an extensive, crescent-shaped dam around the pool's lower end. The resulting reservoir substantially reduced the number of kibitzing spectators, who found they had to stand in several inches of water if they wished to make fun of the swimmers.

The walls of the pool were anchored to a concrete slab which formed its base. Cast into the sand, this slab kept the wooden pool from floating away when submerged at high tide. Despite this massive anchor, the pool walls were destroyed by a heavy storm in August and were never rebuilt. I was sorry about this; I always stayed at the beach for the rest of the afternoon after my harrowing half-hour swims, and the pleasure I derived from my damming operations more than compensated for the misery of my immersions.

Back in Condette, I was becoming braver and was venturing out on my bike up the grassy track to the paved road and on into the village of Condette. No one had ever told me not to do this, and I now felt I could handle the traffic, which was a lot busier than the traffic in Hardelot where I had ridden my bike around town with impunity two years earlier.

I was returning from one of these sorties one afternoon, tearing along at maximum speed, when I passed Michelle, who was standing by the side of the track. Throughout this mostly wretched summer, I had managed to avoid seeing or being seen by Michelle. "*Bonjour, Alain!*" she yelled cheerily as I passed her. I was quite taken aback.

Although I knew I was supposed to ignore her and was going fast enough that she might well believe I hadn't heard her, I slammed on the brakes, turned around, and rode back to where she was standing.

"I've waited all summer for you to come over and play," she said quietly, without recrimination.

"I wanted to come over, too, but Mother said I must not see you or play with you any more," I said sheepishly.

"I know that's why you didn't come. Mother said she thought that was the reason. *C'est bien triste* (it's very sad)," she said pensively. Then, brightening up, she said, "I'm on my way to get Lili. Do you think you would get caught if you came with me?"

I thought about it for a moment then said impatiently, "So what if I do get caught! I don't care!" I really felt that the whole summer had been a prolonged sentence for a crime I hadn't committed and that I was now entitled to commit the crime in question. I dismounted my bike and, with Michelle beside me, walked it back up the grassy track to the place where the path leading to Lili's pasture forked off to the right. On that little-used and overgrown pedestrian path, I found a break in the bordering hedge, hid my bike there and walked on with Michelle, who took me by the hand. It seemed like old times, and I suddenly felt exhilarated and much lighter, as if a great burden had been lifted from my shoulders. I was so relieved to know Michelle was aware that my absence had not been because I didn't care for her, and I was really looking forward to the ride on Lili.

Michelle urged me to be the first to mount Lili and to ride in front. I rediscovered all the thrill and fun of rides on this magnificent mare. I also enjoyed the feel of Michelle's hands around my waist and her body pressed tightly against my back. The mile-long trip back to the Baichant farm took us along the deserted path, so I had no fear of being caught with her. Before the path rejoined the grassy track to our house, we found a tree with suitable overhanging branches, which I used to dismount Lili. I thus avoided the risky part of the journey—the grassy track where Mother or Madame Tourneau drove the car on the way in or out. When we parted, Michelle said, "If you come with me again, you can ride in front every time." I promised her I'd be back.

During the remaining few weeks of the summer, the swimming pool in Hardelot no longer existed, so I seldom went to the beach in the afternoons. I was thus able to enjoy the company of Michelle, whom I liked a great deal, and indulge my passion for riding Lili. Almost daily, I waited for Michelle at the start of the deserted path so that I could accompany her to the horse pasture. All I did was walk, albeit hand-in-hand, with Michelle to the pasture and ride Lili most of the way back before hopping onto my bike for the rest of the trip home. If asked, I was prepared to say that I was not playing with Michelle. I was only riding the Baichant horse back to their farm. I suspected Mother probably wouldn't have bought that subtle distinction, but luckily I never had to use it. Those twenty or so rides with Michelle were my secret triumph over a summer filled with loneliness, boredom and longing.

Alain, Jacob, Brenda, and Raimond, la Closerie, Ville-d'Avray, 1938

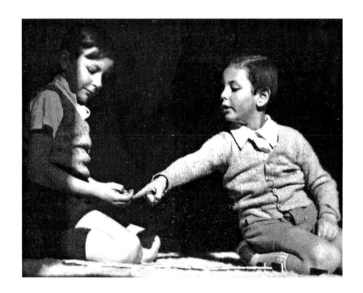

Alain and Jacob ("the little elf"), Ville d'Avray, 1938

Uncle Bob, Alain, Jenny, Brenda, Betty, Peter, Auntie Gladys, in
Condette, 1938

Alain, Jenny, and Brenda, at the beach in Hardelot 1938

CHAPTER 10

A Russian Paramour, then an Older Woman

The autumn of 1938 found my parents in a quandary. I usually returned from the Dennis School looking as though I had been working as a chimney sweep, and for this reason, Mother was adamant that I wouldn't go back there. For his part, Father was steadfast in the belief that I should continue attending an English-speaking school. Yet there seemed to be no other such school in Paris.

The previous summer, Father had gone to America on another business trip, and this journey greatly influenced the selection of my next school. On the return voyage aboard the *Normandie*, two fellow passengers at his dining room table were Mr. and Mrs. Derosier. They were the founders of the American School of Paris, and Mr. Derosier was its Headmaster. He was French, educated in France and the United States, and she was American, schooled in France. Father found them extremely likable and was impressed by their warmth and wisdom. As a result of this meeting, Brenda and I started attending the American School of Paris in the fall of 1938, she in first grade and I in fourth grade. The school was intended to cater to American families, but most students were from French families seeking a bilingual education for their children. The school's curriculum covered both languages and both cultures with about equal emphasis.

I took an immediate liking to the school. In contrast to the gloom and austerity of the French schools I had attended, my new school was modern, bright, and airy. My classroom was on the top floor of a five-story building and had once been a penthouse apartment. The room's large picture windows looked out onto rooftops and church spires and, in the distance, the Eiffel Tower. I was especially entranced by the look of our classroom in the mornings, when the warm glow of the sun bestowed on the room a special luminance. Basking in this warmth, I wondered if I were growing like our greenhouse vegetable seedlings which, according to Raimond, only grew in the warmth of the sun. If he were right, I was going to do a lot of growing in this classroom. Being as small as I was for my age, this was no minor consideration.

The warmth and joyous luminosity I so loved vanished after lunch because there were no windows on the west side of the room. On one of those unilluminated, non-growing afternoons I made my second contribution to school architecture (the first being the hanging moon for the benefit of daydreaming students). My new concept was based on sound engineering and was totally feasible, though perhaps a little extravagant.

I had seen locomotive turntables that redirected massive steam engines from their main track onto a shorter section of track. The shorter tracks radiated outward from the turntable, like the spokes of a wheel, into a round storage shed called a "roundhouse," where the locomotives were stored and repaired. It seemed to me reasonable that if such a turntable could rotate something as big and heavy as a locomotive in any desired direction, why not a classroom full of children? Just place one of these turntables onto the roof of the school with a crane, then build a classroom on top of the turntable—*et voilà!* The classroom would turn slowly by means of a small motor. By having the classroom track the sun and retain its light and cheerfulness all day long, I would have the benefit of more growing time.

Except, of course, when it rained. However, since this was an American school, there was no lighting problem on rainy days. We had fluorescent ceiling lights, and they were almost as bright and cheerful as the sun, or so I thought at the time. I only hoped they were as good for growing as was the sun. At two of the French schools I had attended, little light came through the small windows when it was cloudy, and teachers were so stingy with electricity that lights were never turned on in daytime, even on the gloomiest of rainy days.

Probably from Raimond at home, I had come to believe that anything new and different, or anything *American,* just had to be better. And although it was true that my present American classroom was superb compared to any I had known, I saw no reason why I couldn't dream up other novel improvements it might have. The turning classroom that tracked the sun was the first of several concepts that followed in quick succession.

In my fourth grade room, the first hand-crank pencil sharpener I had ever seen created quite an impression on me. In my new, ideal classroom, each student would not only have a sharpener at his desk, but each sharpener would have a little motor, so we wouldn't have to crank it by hand.

I had never seen a student desk like the one in which I sat. It was a comfortable, one-piece, modern desk with the writing surface arranged as an extension of the armrest. In my improved classroom, each desk would be on its own smaller turntable, and it too, of course, would be motorized. Thus, when the teacher referred to a large map of the United States on the wall to our right, every desk would turn to the right, and students would face the map head-on for a better view.

Day by day, I envisioned more refinements for my wonder classroom. One of these improvements came to me after my first visit to the dentist, where I noted how his chair went up and down. If our school desks went up and down like the dentist's chair, small students, like myself, could see over the heads of larger students when the teacher, Miss Miller, wrote along the bottom edge of the blackboard. Then, after the teacher complained about our illegible handwriting, it occurred to me that each student should have a typewriter at his desk so that Miss Miller would no longer be deluged by a sea of scribbles.

I started to make drawings of my ideas. This was no small undertaking, as I needed to make numerous separate sketches of each of the details, along with a main plan showing the whole thing. I had once watched my grandfather, who was an architect, drawing the details of a house he was designing, and he had patiently explained the process to me. At the time, I hadn't paid much attention; nevertheless, it seems my grandfather's methods had, in fact, made an impression on me.

I was able to do this sketching in school because my desk was at the rear of the classroom. In this class, Miss Miller stayed at her podium the whole time—a pleasant change from those French schools where the teacher roamed the aisles ready to pounce on any student engaged in a misdeed. I probably looked quite diligent as I worked on my drawings, and in fact, that's exactly what I was. The privacy of my design work was also facilitated by an improbable concept called the "honor system." In theory, we were honor-bound to tell on students who were doing anything wrong. This, I believe, was meant to relieve the teacher from the burden of watching over her students. Sitting where I did, at the back of the class, there were no students to observe my activities and I was able to sketch with impunity.

I took my drawings home and showed them to Raimond, who somehow came by the impression that this was how my classroom was in reality. He may have been pretending, but since it was from Raimond that I had acquired the notion that everything American was novel, marvelous and techno-modern, it's possible that he really believed me. Either way, I was having such fun impressing Raimond that I decided to impress everyone else with my incredible American classroom.

Mother listened to my descriptions, sounded convinced and pumped me for further details, as Raimond had done. Soon, everyone on the home front was admiring my drawings and asking me about my incredible new school. Each day I came home armed with new embellishments and sketches, explaining that there were so many wonderful things in this classroom that no one could possibly present them all at one try.

The real classroom's drapes operated with pull cords, another refinement I had never seen before, and which struck me as particularly ingenious. As I told it, however, the classroom's drapes had motorized pull cords, and Miss Miller had a switchboard at her desk that operated all the curtains by remote control.

Other exotic items materialized in my dream classroom: a telephone, a radio and, for learning songs, a phonograph. Then, I dreamed up a large translucent globe of the world that turned slowly by means of a motor and was lit from within. A blue light illuminated only half the globe to show where it was nighttime. A white light, also inside the globe, lit the other half showing where daylight prevailed in the world. Since the lights within did not turn with the globe, the moving passage of night and day around the world was clearly illustrated as the globe revolved slowly.

All who heard my descriptions were amazed and looked as though they believed all of it. I wallowed in their admiration for my drawings, reveled at having an audience intrigued by my every word, and decided I would invent another story that I would tell while at school. There I was assisted in my endeavor by an American classroom practice called "show-and-tell." For me, it turned out to be just "tell" since I could hardly bring what I was describing to class.

Several students had their turn at show-and-tell ahead of me. Among them was an Arab student called Youssef. He told the class that he had a pet camel at his home in Morocco. Youssef demonstrated how he clicked his tongue loudly against his palate, so that Dramba, his camel, would kneel down for him to climb aboard. No one could top his story—that is, until I came up with my tall tale.

I had recently seen the film "Mowgli, the Elephant Boy." The film had made a lasting impression on me, and I had become obsessed with elephants. My plans for a future profession had shifted from being a prosperous farmer in France to being an elephant herder in India. Other aspects of my story probably came from reading Kipling's *The Jungle Book* in which several animals had strange, long names such as "Rikki-Tikki-Tavi." When my turn came to show-and-tell, I declared in all earnestness that my family had once lived in India and that when we left India, I was allowed to bring one of my pet elephants to France with me. The elephant, whose name was Bajawanda (Baji for short), now lived in an oversized stable on our estate. Baji ate a ton of hay each day and did so many tricks that it would take the rest of the afternoon to describe them all. The class clapped enthusiastically, and I started to tell them how Baji could be made to do a handstand on his forelegs, but Miss Miller interrupted me and said that I had told quite enough for one day.

A week or so later, Mother announced that Miss Miller had asked her to come in for a parent-teacher conference (another American novelty). This piece of news made me extremely nervous. Had Miss miller discovered my untruths? Would she punish me for telling a huge lie to the whole class? Would Mr. Derosier expel me from a school I liked so much? Had I exceeded the limits of reason? How could that be? I was eight years old and well into the age of reason. Wasn't I immune to being unreasonable?

When Mother returned from the conference, I heard her call me in a cold, severe tone from downstairs, "Alain, please come to the drawing room. I need to talk to you." My heart sank. Those words and that tone of voice usually implied trouble.

When I entered the drawing room, Mother was sitting at her desk and said, "Miss Miller wanted to know more about our life in India." I stood silent not knowing what to say. Then she added with a deadpan expression, "And she showed me your turning classroom. It's every bit as wonderful as you said it was!"

"You saw it?" I replied incredulously, not knowing whether the game was over or whether Mother expected me to keep up the pretense.

"No, Alain, unfortunately I didn't see it. And I'm not sure which is the biggest fib, Bajawanda or the turning classroom. They're both marvelous little tales, but I hope you didn't think anyone would believe you!"

"Then why did everyone act as though they believed me? It's not fair that they tricked me that way!"

"It seems to me *you* were trying to trick them. All of us let you go on with your stories, waiting to see when you would trip yourself up. Those who tell fibs usually trip up because they have to keep telling new fibs to make the first one hold up. When a fibber trips up, we all think it's funny, and we have a good laugh at his expense. But if the fibs are such that they hurt someone, we punish the fibber."

As a result of this little homily, I decided there were dangers in being taken too seriously when I was just having fun. After that, if someone smiled knowingly when he inquired about my elephant, I would happily spin a new tale about Bajawanda. But if anyone sounded serious when asking about Baji, I would admit that Bajawanda was just a story I made up for the sole purpose of outdoing Youssef.

The questions about Bajawanda did not continue for long. The real reason for the parent-teacher conference was that the teacher felt I wasn't doing my class work properly and not keeping up with the other students. That may have been because I had spent so much of my class time drawing up the details of the turning classroom. However, since I was only eight years old and most of the students in fourth grade were about ten, Mother and Miss Miller decided to bump me down to the third grade, which was in the Junior School and across the street from the building that had my enchanted classroom on its top floor.

The students in the third grade were friendly and welcoming, as was the teacher, Miss Cabinalice (her name rhymed with Alice). However, the change was as severe a blow to my morale as it was to my pride. I no longer spent luminous mornings in the penthouse classroom doing some much needed growing in the warm sun and admiring the distant Eiffel Tower. My new classroom was nice enough, but it received only a few meager beams of sunlight in the late afternoon. They filtered through autumn-yellow chestnut leaves and were too sparse to really illuminate the room or induce much growth. I felt I was doomed to spend another year without growing.

This classroom looked out onto a forlorn, scruffy city garden where we played during recess. I carefully chose my seat in the rear of the room, so I could look out through the window at the garden or, more precisely, past the garden at the occasional passing of a bus on the street beyond. I replaced my wistful gazing at the

Eiffel Tower by a careful study of Parisian buses. I was especially fascinated by their little rear balconies and much intrigued by the "lavatory chain" that dangled back there, so passengers could pull it to let the driver know they wanted to get off. It struck me that bus riders literally "flushed" themselves out of the back of the bus.

My new classroom was cheerfully decorated, a first for me. The walls were covered with the artwork of previous students and, as the year wore on, with our own pictures. That too, was a novelty, in contrast to the French classrooms I had known, in which the bare walls had always been a dull gray and looked as though they had not known fresh paint in a hundred years. My new classroom also had travel posters, maps, and a large chart on which the daily performance of each pupil was noted by pasted-on stars of different colors.

Each of us had a row on this chart, and at the end of each day, Miss Cabinalice added a star to each student's row. She awarded a silver star for "above average," and a gold star denoted "absolutely the best," as she put it. Each day, she awarded only one silver and one gold star. A black star was for poor performance or bad behavior requiring disciplinary action. All other colors, at least twenty in all, denoted "satisfactory," and we were free to choose any of the colors if we qualified for that category. Each student soon established a solid row of his favorite color or, sometimes, a pattern of repeating colors.

I found no incentive for earning honor stars. I felt they were a lifeless, muddy imitation of true gold and silver—insipid and fake. The gold stars were actually a brownish yellow with a little metallic sparkle thrown in to redeem their basic drabness. Likewise, silver was just plain old gray if I blurred my vision by squinting. I much preferred the bright tones of the "satisfactory" stars and studiously avoided any scholastic effort that might earn me a gold or silver star. Once, I earned a silver star and I remember exclaiming aloud, "*Zut alors!* How did that happen?" Miss Cabinalice looked puzzled by my reaction, but didn't ask me about it. Nor did I volunteer any explanation. Grown-ups—Raimond excepted—never seemed to understand the way I thought. It was just too much trouble trying to get through to them and so often fruitless.

Actually, we received two identical stars every day. Miss Cabinalice pasted a second matching star on our forehead, so our parents could see how we were doing on a daily basis. The stars on my forehead created a minor problem for me. When I reached home in the late afternoon, it was time for my bath, and the star was invariably washed off before Mother and Father ever saw it. Raimond, who always knew what really mattered, stuck the star back on my forehead after my bath, using a paste made of flour and water, to the despair of Mother. At bedtime, Mother insisted on soaking off the star with a damp washcloth, maintaining that it wasn't healthy for me to sleep with a star on my forehead. I suspect she didn't approve of my eating supper with a star on my forehead either, but she knew she couldn't push me that far.

One of the highlights of the day was when a teacher from the Senior School, Mr. Spafford, drove us home at five o'clock. About eight students lived in the same general area as Mr. Spafford, and we all squeezed quite comfortably into his spacious V-8 Ford sedan, an exotic car in France at the time. I remember how much I enjoyed the unusual sound and power of its engine. The car literally bounded up the hills of Ville-d'Avray in high gear, whereas Mother's little Simca ground slowly up these hills in first. The Ford had another extravagant feature, a radio, but all we could receive on it was classical music. This exasperated Mr. Spafford who complained that he wanted to listen to "jazz." I asked him what jazz was, and he answered that he was hard put to describe it. When we didn't listen to the radio, Mr. Spafford led us in an assortment of songs. Among the many titles from various nations were "Au Clair de la Lune," "It's a Long, Long Way to Tipperary," or our favorite, an American song, which I have never heard since. The refrain went like this:

I went to the animal's fair,
The birds and the beasts were there.
The old raccoon
By the light of the moon
Was combing his golden hair.

The monkey he got drunk
And climbed up the elephant's trunk.
The elephant sneezed
And fell on his knees,
And that was the end of the monk, the monk,
And that was the end of the monk.

At school, during recess, I reclaimed my role as an organizer of games. I still remember the names of some of my faithful lieutenants and colleagues. Jean-Louis was a slightly chubby and jovial French boy who could be depended on through thick and thin. Boris was skinny, furtive looking, and the son of White Russian refugees. He was clever at coming up with devious and sinister plans once the games were in motion but had to be watched for overdoing it. Jimmy Retter was an American boy who refused to obey the rules I established and who frequently disrupted the games with his unruliness. Retter's tendency to create mayhem extended to his classroom conduct. On the classroom chart where performance stars were posted, nearly all of the ones beside his name were black. Worse yet, he boasted about it!

Though I alone undertook the organizing of the games, I was not necessarily the captain of one of the two "camps." Organizing meant deciding on rules and modifying these rules if flaws emerged in the game plan. As official game organizer, I also decided who did what and where, defined boundaries between camps and settled disputes. I loved to experiment with rule changes to see if I could make the games more exciting. I sometimes urged the stopping and restarting of games if rules or boundaries turned out to be impractical or unfair. By and large, my peers tolerated this, and no one ever protested my assuming this role. At the start of recess, all the boys gathered around me to see what game we would play and what new rules applied, if any. Prolonged debates about rules occasionally took place. The debates were surprisingly orderly and sometimes lasted through the whole recess period. In fact, the activity should rightly have been called "the game of debating about game rules."

Our games were more sophisticated versions of those I had organized two years before at the Ecole Sugerre. The usual scenario involved two warring camps, taking prisoners by tagging them in certain specified zones of the playground, and rescuing them by "untagging" in other designated zones. The games involved a lot of running and chasing, or being chased, but no rough stuff—indeed, no physical contact, except for the tagging. I usually added a theme to the game by having the camps pretend to be Robin Hood's Band of Merry Men, versus the Sheriffs of Nottingham, or the American Escadrille Lafayette versus the Red Baron's Squadron, or just Pioneers and Indians. It amused me that the themes seemed to be what my peers especially enjoyed and for which I was most appreciated. My own view of the themes was that they were icing on the cake and of no great consequence to the game. What mattered to me were judiciously chosen boundaries between camps, how well the rules worked, and whether they were fair and the game fun.

Among the students who participated in our games was Olinka, another White Russian, who became a tomboy after I convinced her that the boy's games were more fun than no games at all, which is what the rest of the girls seemed to prefer. All the other girls steadfastly refused to play the boys' games despite my numerous entreaties. It wasn't just the power I was after—that too, of course—I honestly believed that the more players there were, the merrier the game would be, and why wouldn't girls enjoy running, chasing or being chased, and triumphing in battle as much as the boys did?

Olinka's conversion to my cause was the result of an amusing incident. An iron grill fence separated the playground from the street, and its gate was usually locked. One day the gate was left open, and a large German shepherd came into the school playground. This breed was widely used in France as guard dogs, and they had a reputation for being fierce and nasty. When Olinka saw the dog, she became terrified and started screaming for help as she ran towards a woodpile in a corner of the playground. Out of forty children present, the dog singled her out and ended his chase barking at her heels as she scrambled up the woodpile. She climbed high enough to be just out of his reach, and pleaded to be rescued as the dog growled and snapped at her heels.

I remembered that Raimond had once said that if you talk forcefully and in a tone of authority to a fierce dog it wouldn't attack you. I placed great trust in what Raimond said, so I immediately decided to put his dictum to the test. With apprehension, I marched up to the dog and, in as gruff a voice as I could muster, I snapped at it, *"Ça suffit!"* ("That's enough!") To my amazement, the dog stopped barking. I followed up with, "Go on—go away!" in French, of course, for that's all a French dog can understand. Appropriate shooing motions accompanied all this. Raimond was right, at least as far as this dog was concerned. By now, Miss Cabinalice was on the scene and joined me in coaxing the dog through the gate and out of the yard.

Then I returned to the woodpile where the frightened Olinka was still calling for help, protesting that she couldn't get down. I helped her down by holding onto each of her shoes in succession, and each time, guiding it to a place in the pile where she would find a safe foothold. Upon reaching terra firma, Olinka exclaimed, "Alain, you are so sweet!" and promptly put her arms around my neck and kissed me affectionately.

Among the boys who had gathered to watch the proceedings was the infamous Jimmy Retter, and he began taunting me with, "Alain likes girls—Alain prefers girls!"

Grasping at anything to save face, I boldly declared that Olinka was really a spy and working for our side, and that although I had found the kiss somewhat distasteful, it was in reality an important secret signal. At the time the dog had entered the playground, I happened to be the commander of a squadron of World War fighter pilots, so my story wasn't all that far-fetched.

"Isn't that right, Olinka?" I said, nodding my head up and down discreetly as I put the question to her, hoping she would notice my gesture and play along. "Now you must join our squadron and fly away with us," I continued with a tone of urgency and authority.

She apparently realized my predicament and replied, "Yes, I am your spy. But Alain, you must tell me exactly what a spy does, because I have no idea." I heaved a sigh of relief when I saw that Retter failed to notice the implications of her remark. The others had missed it too, or were just too impressed by my improvisation, and went along, curious to see how a girl would work out. Olinka did just fine and could run as well as the rest of my squadron, just as I had thought she could. She had long, slender, muscular legs which I had noticed and admired as she descended from the woodpile.

Raimond had saved the day once more, on two counts, not only in the matter of staring down dogs, but also by telling me about spies and the secret signals they use. He had recently described to me at some length the exploits of Mata Hari and other spies.

Thereafter, Olinka frequently took part in our games. In truth, I had greatly enjoyed her kiss but received no others, despite my efforts to find another plausible basis for this honor. As is usual in such situations, my sustained and thwarted longing soon caused me to develop a secret crush on Olinka.

One Saturday, when Father had taken Mother to London for a weekend vacation, I told Raimond—the only person I really trusted in such matters—of my secret liking for Olinka and asked him to take me to her house for a visit so we could play together. He couldn't have been more sympathetic to my cause and immediately agreed to my request. My guess is that he welcomed a rare pretext to be out of the house and away from Françoise for a few hours. He might also be able to spend an hour or two in a café while I was visiting my paramour.

I knew Olinka's last name, and luckily, Raimond found that there was only one Valnikov in the Paris directory. I also knew the district where she lived, and fortunately, the Valnikov family was listed in the *arrondissement* that included this district. Without further delay, Raimond and I set off on a circuitous trip requiring that we take a train and two bus rides. When we reached Olinka's house, unannounced, Olinka's mother was more alarmed than pleased by our arrival at her door. This may have been because Raimond was still wearing his yellow and black-striped butler's waistcoat, a bright red wool scarf around his neck, and no jacket. (When we set out on the trip, even I had thought his attire a little *outré*, but never thought it might cause a problem.)

"What is the purpose of your visit?" Madame Valnikov asked bluntly.

"Olinka and I are very good friends at school, *Madame*, and I thought we could play together," I replied earnestly. She eyed me suspiciously and turned to Olinka who had arrived at the door while we were talking.

Olinka seemed dumbfounded by my arrival. After a pause, she said in a pathetic tone, "Alain, all I have to play with are my dolls, and this house has no garden, so we can't go outside and play hide-and-seek or anything like that."

"C'est rudement dommage" ("It's a great pity"), I replied, caught off balance and unable to think of anything that might save the day. Then I added tersely, "I'll see you back in school on Monday. *Au revoir."* It was all over in a flash. Raimond murmured some apologies to Olinka's mother for having burst in on her the way we did, and we left with our tails between our legs.

On the way to the bus stop, Raimond, (whose own plans may also have been thwarted) volunteered that both of us were "guilty of not making sound plans," and he proposed that we not mention this incident to Mother. I readily concurred. I felt quite let down but soon found consolation in standing on the back balcony of the bus going home. Kids weren't allowed to be there, but Raimond passed a small bribe to the conductor who conveniently overlooked my presence in this magical place. Raimond knew how much riding on the bus's balcony meant to me, and now, puffing on a Gauloise Bleue, he pointed out the various sights we were passing. He was enjoying the ride as much as I was. When we approached our stop, Raimond asked me if I wanted to pull *la chasse d'eau* (the lavatory chain). When he saw how excited I was by this offer, he lifted me up so I could reach it. I gave the chain two smart tugs that resulted in satisfying clangs at the front of the bus. My day had been redeemed.

One aspect of the American School that amazed all non-Americans was the fuss they made over American holidays and celebrations which dominated all else for weeks on end. Halloween, Thanksgiving and Valentine's Day were never mentioned at any of my previous schools, nor did I know what they were. As for Christmas and Easter, neither had caused even a small ripple in the routine at my other schools, except for the vacations they engendered. French schools didn't seem to feel it appropriate to expend valuable class time over special occasions such as these—at least in those days.

At the American School, we carved faces in pumpkins and cut out paper turkeys that eventually festooned the walls of the classroom. It all seemed very strange to me. I remember Jean-Louis's mother coming to pick him up after school, looking at all the decorations and the related activity still in progress, and commenting, *"Mon Dieu! Ce n'est pas sérieux tout ça!"* ("My God! This is all so frivolous!").

Then came a school play, something else one didn't see in French schools of the time. Brenda had the lead role as a fairy princess. Mother made her an exquisite costume which looked like a bridal gown. My sister stole the show, not only with her costume, but also with her singing. For my part, I acquitted myself quite well as a gnome. I and several other gnomes formed a chorus and our roles required us to perform an elaborate song and dance routine. We rehearsed long hours each day for a whole month. Rehearsal took place under the direction of Brenda's teacher, a veritable witch of a woman called Miss Trotmi. In our final public performance there wasn't a false step or spurious note because we knew Miss Trotmi would have devoured us alive if there had been.

For this performance I wore a marvelous green satin costume, also made by Mother. The superb quality of the costume's design and its workmanship pleased me no end but embarrassed me in the company of my fellow gnomes who had far simpler, and even poorly made outfits. I have never liked feeling conspicuous in a crowd.

While there were many *divertissements* that year, I covered no new territory in math and French and did moderately well in these subjects because of extensive drilling at my other schools. My English spelling improved a little, and we received a smattering of American geography and history. The school conformed to American standards, which were much less stringent than French standards, and I found it easy to achieve passable grades for the first time in my life. Looking back on it, I suspect I probably would have managed quite well if I had stayed in my luminous fourth grade classroom—if only I hadn't become so absorbed by my drawings and daydreaming. However, I might not have enjoyed life as much as I eventually did in third grade, and I feel that this "lost year" probably didn't adversely affect my overall scholastic career.

Nevertheless, during the first few weeks in Miss Cabinalice's class, I grew bored by the slow pace and lack of new work. I continued my habit of sitting in the back of the class. There, thanks to the honor system and Miss Cabinalice's preference for staying at the front of the class, I resumed what I call "the three D's"—daydreams, designs and drawings. I managed to avoid being caught at my three D's by listening with one ear. That way, I didn't get into serious trouble when the teacher addressed me. This policy and my design activity resulted in very marginal performance and conveniently earned me no gold or silver stars.

I was assisted in my drawing endeavors by the fact that the classroom had a hand-cranked pencil sharpener to which we could go as often as needed. It amazes me that Miss Cabinalice didn't notice how much more frequently I went to the sharpener than anyone else. I had discovered that sharp pencils make for better drawings.

I was secretive about my drawings and showed them only to Raimond, but I never mentioned that I was doing my sketches during class time. He was always interested, providing constructive critiques and asking pertinent questions about them. Thanks, in part, to Raimond's coaching and critiques, these drawings were becoming increasingly elaborate and refined. I planned the layout of cars, even fussing over the placement of knobs and switches on the dashboard and numbers on the speedometer dial. This fastidiousness also applied to locomotives and various types of aircraft, from airliners to a special "gypsy flying boat," which was my favorite design that year.

My gypsy flying boat was a plane well equipped for travel to exotic places. Onboard I could sleep in a bunk, cook and enjoy five-course meals, and write down in notebooks all the discoveries I made each day as I traveled around the world. My plan was to land each night in some new place and camp comfortably aboard my flying boat. The plane was amphibious so I could land equally well near an oasis on the Sahara desert, on a wild stretch of the Amazon, or on some flat, country meadow in Europe.

Lindbergh and his wife were doing something like this in a seaplane, as reported in the *National Geographic* magazines, which I devoured each month. Their specially fitted Lockheed seaplane seemed woefully inadequate since it had no living quarters, and all they carried with them were a few sandwiches, which they claimed was all they had room for. By their own account, the sandwiches were usually stale and moldy and they complained about having to sleep in flimsy, leaky tents when it was raining, or on sharp rocks along some craggy shore near their landing site.

What brought this outburst of creative designs to a halt was another parent-teacher conference. Mother and Miss Cabinalice knew that I was mostly going over old stuff and were baffled as to why I wasn't doing better. A few days later, Raimond provided Mother with a clue to the mystery by telling her how impressed he was by the drawings I was doing. He had been sworn to secrecy, but probably thought it applied only to the subject matter of the drawings. I'm sure he never intended to betray my confidence—Raimond wasn't like that.

Mother tipped off Miss Cabinalice, who came off her podium one day and caught me working on an important set of aeronautical drawings that were lying on top of my desk. She quietly asked me what I was doing. Remembering Mother's homily on fibbing, I made a clean breast of the whole matter. Continuing in her quiet, pleasant voice, Miss Cabinalice asked me why I made so many drawings.

"I'm so bored that I can't help being in the moon—that's where I find all my best ideas," I said to her in those words. "And then, some of my ideas seem so good to me, that I just want to draw them so I can look at them whenever I need to."

Miss Cabinalice listened patiently and told me she wanted to see all my drawings during recess. But for now, I should give up being in the moon or making any further drawings in class. Later that afternoon, we went over my collection of drawings in detail, and Miss Cabinalice showed as much interest and enthusiasm as Raimond had. She went on to explain that I could probably do the class assignments very fast if I really paid attention to the matter. And if I did that, she would allow me to draw during any leftover time, while some of the other students were finishing their assignments. Then she awarded me a silver star for the day.

I told Miss Cabinalice that I didn't want the silver star; I wanted a green one instead.

"Is that because you feel you don't deserve a silver star?" she asked casually.

"No, I just don't like gold and silver as colors for stars," I replied.

"Oh, I see!" she said. "But since I now know the color you want instead of silver, you must also tell me what color star I should give you if you deserve a gold star"

After some deliberation, I settled for a bright, lemon yellow star.

During the drive home in Mr. Spafford's car that evening, I was in a trance. I couldn't believe I hadn't been expelled, jailed, slapped on my thighs, or subjected to verbal abuse.

Miss Cabinalice was a young, stunningly beautiful, Panamanian woman. Despite her Latin American origins, she had flowing, golden blonde hair and very blue eyes. Her complexion was quite dark, which I assumed was a deep suntan, the result of living in a sunny country, and she always wore the most elegantly tailored suits. What I liked about Miss Cabinalice was something I had never seen in any teacher until then. She was lively, enthusiastic, funny, entertaining, warm and, best of all, a good listener. I was no expert on the subject at the time, but

I don't remember that she had any trace of an accent in either English or French, both of which she spoke fluently, though Spanish was her native tongue.

I wondered why it had taken me several weeks to notice her charms, and I said so to Mother, to which she replied, *"Encore une fois, tu étais dans la lune mon cher!"* ("Once more, you were in the moon, my dear!"). My daydreaming was now a major source of concern to Mother, and she was determined to stamp it out any way she could. She berated me whenever any evidence of it occurred, or used sarcasm or ridicule to make me feel foolish for indulging in daydreams.

Mother developed a bad habit of her own. She refused to believe things I told her about school, or anything else, for that matter, unless it conformed well to what she expected or liked to hear about the subject. And she constantly accused me of inventing. *"Alain tu inventes!"* became a household refrain. This infuriated me because I had taken her lecture on fibbing to heart, and wouldn't for anything in the world allow myself to be caught in another major untruth. Well, perhaps the occasional white lie, but mother herself had shown me their use and value. Her attitude caused me to clam up about all my ideas and daydreams. Raimond was the only person to whom I could talk freely.

Brenda was in a classroom next door to mine. A curtained French door connected the two rooms, and from what we could hear through that closed door and its heavy curtain, it was clear Brenda was not as fortunate with her teacher as I was with mine. Miss Trotmi, a French woman with a shrill voice and a sour demeanor, was a real virago. Whenever Miss Trotmi's caterwauling reached a crescendo—a daily occurrence—Miss Cabinalice rolled her eyes in mock wonder, to the immense amusement of our class.

My admiration for Miss Cabinalice became an infatuation. I was transfixed by all she said and did. She made everything fun, even things I used to think of as dull. Eventually, she could do no wrong or boring thing, and everything she said or explained seemed crystal clear. I would have followed her over a cliff. The very sound of her voice was music to my ears. I was completely spellbound by Miss Cabinalice.

I decided that thirteen years hence, when I reached the magical age of majority (when it would be all right to do anything I wanted), I would ask her to marry me. No one, not even Raimond, knew of my great love, so afraid was I that something would topple my fantasy. Surprisingly, I even succeeded in keeping it from Miss Cabinalice, who showed me no particular attention or favoritism, as evidenced by the stars on my chart. By the end of the school year, I had only three honor stars, which for me were, of course, green and yellow; most of the other students had four or five honor stars, and a couple of students had over a dozen.

The Olinka affair had never ripened to include fantasies of marriage, so my infatuation for Miss Cabinalice had no effect on my friendship with Olinka. After the failed trip to Olinka's house, my crush on her waned significantly, but I still admired her and regarded her as a good friend. Olinka's presence always lit up the scene for me, so I continued to invite her to join in our games, which she usually did.

In June, there was a prize-giving ceremony attended by the senior and junior schools and all the parents. They awarded a prize in the form of a book to the best student in each grade. An engraved frontispiece in each book attested to the student's achievement and grade point average for the year. Almost every adult associated with the school gave a speech before the awarding of prizes, and their speeches seemed to drone on interminably. I was distraught and in a wretched mood because it had dawned on me that next year I would no longer be in the junior school and in Miss Cabinalice's class. Indeed, I would be lucky if I caught an occasional glimpse of her at lunchtime when she brought her class across the street to the school dining room in the main building. The fact that I would be back in the luminous classroom seemed small consolation for the loss of Miss Cabinalice in my daily life.

I even wondered why they didn't have teachers move up a grade each year with their students so that such cruel separations would not occur. I talked myself out of that idea when I realized that such a scheme would doom Brenda to endless years at the mercy of the terrible Miss Trotmi.

I was deep in my somber reverie when Boris, seated next to me, nudged me in the ribs and whispered furtively, "Hey! That's you! Go on up and collect your prize!"

I had been in the moon again and had no idea what the prize was for. Jean-Louis, seated next to me on the other side, had gone up to collect the prize for best student in our class. That had come as no surprise—his row on the chart had so many gold and silver stars that they were beyond counting—but what on earth was my prize for? How embarrassing to win a prize and not even know the reason for the award!

I stumbled sheepishly up to the podium where Mr. Derosier, the headmaster, seized my limp hand, shook it vigorously, congratulated me, and handed me a huge bronze medal in a velvet-lined jeweler's case. I thanked him and went back to my seat, still baffled. The medal was engraved with the words:

SCHOOL SPIRIT
ALAN HOLMES
A.S.O.P.
1939

The other side of the medal depicted an angel with excessively large wings. With her left hand, the angel daintily held up one corner of her pleated skirt. In her right hand, which she held out, was something that looked like a garden cutting wedged between her thumb and flattened palm.

Neither the medal's inscription nor the figure on it made any sense to me, and I was sure there must be some mistake. I was now paying close attention to Mr. Derosier, hoping he might award a second medal to someone else and thereby shed some light on medals in general.

When the awarding of prizes was finally over, Mr. Derosier made an announcement that struck like a spear through my heart.

"It is with sadness and great regret that we bid adieu to Miss Cabinalice, who will not be coming back to the American School of Paris next autumn. She is going to marry her fiancé, who is a doctor and lives in Panama."

As soon as the ceremony was over, I bolted out of a side door of the assembly hall so no one would see me crying. I found an empty classroom and let go, wailing and sobbing uncontrollably. I don't know how long I was there, but I finally calmed down and went to the washroom to clean up my tear-stained face.

There was one more thing we third graders had been told to do. We were supposed to gather in a side hall and march back across the street to the junior school under the care of Miss Cabinalice. There, we were to collect our belongings, and wait for our parents to pick us up.

In the hall where we were supposed to gather, I found that my class had already left. I ran out of the building onto the sidewalk and then to the nearest street corner where our class always went in a group to cross the street. The rue d'Auteuil was a wide and busy artery, and I had never crossed a street with so much traffic all by myself. To make matters worse, it was now rush hour. I waited on the corner for a moment. Then, when there seemed to be a small opening in the traffic from both directions, I dashed across the street. Several cars screeched to a halt, and drivers cursed me, fists waving. Somehow, I made it across and walked down the street to the junior school entrance, where I saw Mother and Brenda waiting in the car, talking together so intently that they apparently had not seen my suicidal street crossing, nor noticed my approach. I rapped on the car window and yelled that I would be right back, and went into the school.

Miss Cabinalice was just leaving the classroom as I neared its door. "Oh there you are, Alain! Where have you been? I was worried sick about you—I assumed you were with your mother, but I haven't seen her either. Let's go in and get your books" she said, taking my hand and leading me into the strangely silent and empty classroom.

"May I see your medal?" she asked as we reached the desk where my belongings were stacked.

As I fumbled in my pocket for it, she said, "Why—you've been crying! Your eyes are red and swollen. What's the matter, Alain?" She paused, and I remained silent, not knowing what I would say. Then she added softly in a tone of genuine concern, "Is the medal the wrong color?"

It struck me as an odd question, but there was no hint of sarcasm or teasing in her voice. I suppose she just needed something to start me talking. I was still choked up, and now the tears were welling up again. She crouched down on one knee and put her arm around my shoulder.

Through my tears, I could see the concern and gentleness in her beautiful eyes, now on a level with mine. I managed to blurt out, "You're leaving and not coming back. And I like you so much." She put both arms around me and drew me to her. Standing there, surrounded by her warm hug and smelling the fragrance of her hair, the most wonderful feeling came over me.

Then she said in that quiet, sweet-sounding voice I loved so much, "If you write to me, I promise I'll write back. And someday, I'll come back to Paris with Eduardo, and maybe you can meet him. He's a wonderful man, and I'm sure you will like him." She rocked me gently back and forth as she held me.

Before leaving the classroom, she wrote her address in my notebook. "Anita Cabanales," it said, followed by an address, which she told me was her mother's home in Panama. She didn't know where she would be living after she was married, but using her mother's address would ensure that my letter would reach her, she said. I was puzzled and asked Miss Cabinalice if the name in my notebook was her mother's. "That's *my* name Alain! My name is Anita, and now that I'm not your teacher anymore, you may call me Anita." I thought for a minute how strange it was that I hadn't even known her first name, and was very puzzled by the name "Cabanales." In my mind, I went over the name "Cabinalice" and broke it down into "cabin" and "Alice," both of which I thought I knew how to spell and pronounce. Then I looked at my notebook and decided I might be able to accept "Caban" instead of "Cabin," but "ales" rhymed with "sales," and that couldn't possibly turn into "Alice"—that part just didn't sit right with me. However, I didn't want to disrupt the mood, so I asked no further questions.

Anita took my hand, and we walked out to the car. She said goodbye to Mother and waved as we drove off. I was crying silently but managed to hide the fact from Mother and Brenda. They were bittersweet tears, for the ecstasy of Anita's hug still lingered. That would remain a secret. I didn't want anyone trampling the memory with jokes or joshing. Before we reached home, I had regained some degree of composure and confided timidly to Mother that I didn't know why I had received the medal.

"In the moon again, Alain? Didn't you hear Mr. Derosier say that it was for the student who best understood what school was all about?" she asked, then added, "You can be very proud, Alain. Mr. Derosier also said that it was the first time the medal had ever been awarded to anyone in the junior school. I'm just a little puzzled as to how such a daydreamer could know so much of what school was all about! But you apparently do know, somehow, and I'm very pleased and proud of you, Alain."

I too, wondered how anyone could have thought I knew what school was about—any better than the rest of my classmates. School was about having fun at recess and occasionally learning stuff to please the teacher. Didn't we all think that? No, I suppose Jimmy Retter didn't, but everyone else did. I remained puzzled about the whole business, and it struck me as odd that I was being told I could be proud of something I didn't even understand. But it didn't matter that much. I lapsed back into a daydream in which I was still in the arms of Anita Cabinalice, savoring the scent of her flowing blonde hair.

Before leaving Ville-d'Avray for our third summer in Condette, I was very careful to pack the notebook that contained Anita's address. However, when we arrived at the house in Condette, the notebook wasn't where I had put it, nor was it in any of the other suitcases we unpacked. I asked Mother if she had seen the notebook, and she said, "Oh that old thing! I didn't think you needed your class notebook during vacation, and I needed the space to pack other things, so I took it out of the suitcase."

Mother couldn't understand why I was so upset over a used-up school notebook. I was uneasy about her knowing that it contained the address, lest she guess how strongly I felt about Miss Cabanales. Without disclosing my reasons, I risked pestering Mother until she finally agreed to ask Father to look for it when he went back to Ville-d'Avray. The house in Ville-d'Avray was not to be rented for another two weeks, and he was still going back to it every weekday evening after working in Paris. On each of the following two weekends, I awaited the return of Father with high expectations and every time he had forgotten the matter. So, despite the best intentions and a concerted effort on my part, the summer went by without the opportunity to communicate with my first great love.

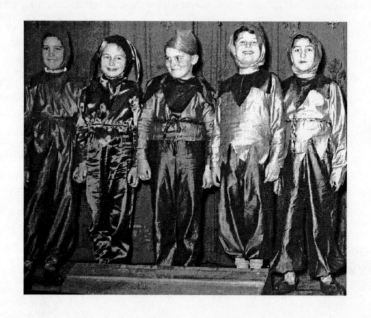

Alain (2nd from left) in school play (American School of Paris)

American School of Paris medal

The Angel with oversize wings

(medal shown smaller than actual size)

CHAPTER 11

Battles and the End of Fun

Early in the summer of 1939, Madame Tourneau appeared on our doorstep in Condette to invite us over for tea to meet her three boys. Mother was delighted. Madame Tourneau must have noticed that I had stopped associating with the Baichant girl the previous summer and was now prepared to let Brenda and me play with her three sons. We quickly became good friends with the Tourneaus who seemed as much in need of playmates as Brenda and I were. Jacques, the eldest, was thirteen and was almost as tall as a grown man. Pierre, two years older than I, was about normal in size for an eleven-year-old. Miquet was Brenda's age and slightly taller and heavier than I was. All three were intelligent boys, *bien élevés* (well brought up), as the French were fond of saying, but extremely shy and timid.

During the two summers the Tourneau boys had spent in Condette they had been to the beach in nearby Hardelot twice and had never taken a swim in the sea. They stayed indoors most of the time, reading books, playing board games, or fighting mock wars using their vast army of tin soldiers. I had never cared much for tin soldiers so I seldom joined my new friends in their elaborate set-piece battles, perhaps because to be proficient at their games required a lot of previous experience. Surprisingly, eight-year-old Miquet, who had been playing the games for three years, could sometimes beat his two older brothers. The boys re-enacted famous battles and based the positioning of their tin soldiers on information gleaned from a well-thumbed book showing the battle formations for Napoleon's great engagements.

The boys' several hundred tin soldiers were still not enough to represent all the soldiers mentioned in their history book, so they usually portrayed only a small sector of the battle. From that point on, it became a game of rewriting history based on a throw of the dice and some shrewd judgment on the part of each player. All I remember of this game is that when the opposing army fired upon one of the tin soldiers, dice were used to determine the warrior's fate. If the dice came up a six, the soldier had been killed. For a throw of five, the soldier was wounded and temporarily out of action for the next five rounds of dice throwing. If the dice came up any other number, the soldier was in luck; he had escaped being hit and was still in action, and it was his turn to fire back. These war games also involved an elaborate scoring system requiring reams of paper and a lot of arithmetic.

The Tourneau boys were a pale-looking threesome, probably because they were indoors so much. This seemed very odd to Brenda and me, for we were used to literally being pushed outdoors to play. Mother insisted that we were in Condette to benefit from the country air, and she did not tolerate any indoor pastime, unless we were in a torrential downpour. Even in light rain, we were expected to play on the wide, rain-sheltered terrace, bundled up in sweaters if it was a cool day. Despite these draconian rules, Brenda and I were definitely not robust, healthy children. If anything, we were both in delicate health, suffering colds, bronchial problems, and frequent ear infections throughout the colder months. In summer, however, we were healthy, and Mother maintained this was because we spent so much more time outdoors.

Brenda and I continued with our gymnastics class at the Hardelot beach club every morning, and in the afternoons, started inviting the Tourneaus to join us in various beach activities, including the sand castle contests. The Tourneau boys had never built sand castles or dams and were surprised to discover how much they enjoyed these activities. Madame Tourneau was so taken by their enthusiasm that she enrolled them in the morning gymnastics sessions and started sharing the driving to and from the beach with Mother. The ride in Mother's tiny Simca, one of the smallest mass-produced cars ever made, presented a certain challenge, for it had only two front seats that barely accommodated Mother and the adult-sized Jacques, with Miquet standing between his knees. Brenda, Pierre, and I stood tightly jammed together in the minuscule luggage space behind the front seats with our upper halves protruding happily through the open roof. This worked well on warm sunny days, but on cooler days, we had a choice. We could bundle up in our raincoats to keep warm as the car picked up speed, or we could ride with the roof closed, jammed in the tiny space like so many sardines in a can. The simile is apt since opening the roof of the car required that it be rolled back like the lid on a sardine can.

By mid-summer Madame Tourneau went so far as to rent a beach cabin, as our family did, for she discovered that she, too, enjoyed the beach and that they needed a base there.

Because the Tourneaus had never engaged in outdoor games, I was the one who proposed and organized everything when we played together, even though I was much younger than Jacques and Pierre. They were easy-going and seemed happy to have someone show them how to do things.

I also taught Pierre and Miquet to ride a bicycle and would have taught Jacques, but his knees wouldn't fit under the handlebars of my bike. After the two younger boys mastered bike riding, Madame Tourneau rented an adult-size bike in Hardelot for Jacques, and we took it down to the beach at low tide for his maiden flight, as Raimond had done for me. Before long, Madame Tourneau had to rent each of them a bike on a long-term basis.

One day, when neither mother was free to take us to the beach where a sand castle contest was to be held, I proposed that the five of us ride our bikes to the beach, a distance of six kilometers. We reached the beach well after the contest had started because the two youngest, Brenda and little Miquet, were exhausted after the first kilometer, and our expedition bogged down as Jacques and I spent considerable time coaxing the two of them to keep cycling. Once at the beach, it seemed pointless to enter the contest since we couldn't finish our sand castles in the remaining allowed time.

I had been the chief instigator of the failed plan and I felt an obligation to propose something else. Then I remembered the fun I used to have biking across tide pools. After a brief search for a suitable one, I demonstrated by charging at high speed through a six-inch-deep pool, creating a magnificent display of splashing and emerging sopping wet but triumphant. The Tourneaus had not worn their swim trunks as I had, and Jacques worried that his mother would be upset at the sight of their soaked-through clothing when they reached home. I assured him that they would dry off by then. Pierre was the first to yield to my cajoling and made a dash through one of the smaller pools. He was so elated over the experience that the two of us had no difficulty convincing the other two boys and Brenda to have a try.

After an hour of exhilarating fun, the five of us were confronted with the unpleasant prospect of the long, soggy trip home. Brenda and Miquet protested that they would never make it. I proposed that Jacques and I ride home and leave Pierre to watch over the two littlest. I assumed one of the two mothers was bound to be home by the time Jacques and I arrived, and she could come to pick up the other three with the car. In the meantime, Pierre's, Brenda's and Miquet's bikes were jammed into our beach cabin for the night, and I urged the three of them to play energetic games on the beach to keep warm as they awaited the arrival of one of the mothers. Everything went as planned. Madame Tourneau was the one who drove to Hardelot to pick up the rest of the team and she was all praise for my leadership and initiative in the afternoon's fun. She was also highly amused by the streaks of blue dye that extended down the boy's white, untanned legs. Their navy-blue shorts had dried as predicted, but the streaks down their legs revealed the true nature of the afternoon's activities.

Madame Tourneau must have been pleased about the way her boys were enjoying their summer. She seemed to have a soft spot for me, perhaps because of the contributions I made to their fun, and she always made a pleasant fuss when I arrived at her house. Among other special attentions, she regularly served me an extra large piece of cake with the afternoon tea when I happened to be there at teatime. When Miquet loudly protested the repetition of this blatant favoritism, Madame Tourneau justified it on the grounds that I alone was small for my age and needed the extra food to catch up. Miquet, though almost two years younger, was slightly taller than I was and more heavily built.

I ran into Michelle twice that summer. Now that I was accepted by the Tourneaus and playing with them regularly, I didn't want to upset the apple cart and go through another summer of ostracism and solitude, so I was nervous about having anything to do with her. On the first encounter, the Tourneaus had gone to the city of Lille for the day (where they lived when they weren't summering in Condette), and I had cycled into the village on a small errand for Françoise. I met Michelle on the grassy track as I was returning, and she invited me to fetch Lili and ride the horse home with her. I had such glowing memories of those rides on Lili that I couldn't resist her invitation, and felt relatively safe with the Tourneaus out of town. Those moments high atop Lili were as magical as ever. But my extreme anxiety over the possibility of being seen by Mother negated much of the fun the ride would otherwise have given me.

On the second occasion, also during a prolonged absence of the Tourneaus, and while on a stroll up the grassy track, I saw Michelle as she came out of her house. We chatted briefly and before long, I succumbed to her coyness and invitation to play games in the hay barn. Once in the barn there was no risk of being seen with her, I reasoned, but there was some danger of being spotted leaving the farm afterwards. However, I felt confident that I could exercise sufficient stealth to get away with my little adventure. In truth, I wanted to prove that I could choose my own playmates. Condette was a dull place without the Tourneaus to play with, and I craved a little excitement.

Michelle now towered over me by about four inches. She was not only taller, but had changed a lot in other ways. She seemed even stronger and tougher than before and acted as though she knew a lot more than I did. Two years before, playing in the hay barn meant only one thing—undressing, exploring each other, caressing, fondling and experiencing the incomprehensible and delicious feeling of being aroused. It was no different this time, except that Michelle kept on insisting that someone at school had told her something that intrigued her, and she wanted to find out if it was true.

"Si tu le mets là," she said, coyly pointing to her exposed behind, *"J'aurai bientôt des p'tites poupées, comme les chiens ont des p'tits chiots."* ("If you put it there, I'll soon have some li'l dolls, the way dogs have li'l puppies.") I was still utterly naive about the implications of what she was proposing, and it all seemed incredibly far-fetched and unbelievable. I told her so and asked her to repeat the explanation for her strange request, which she did, adding, *"Allez, Alain! C'est vrai, je te le jure! Fais ce que je te demande."* ("Come on, Alain! I swear it's true! Do as I tell you.") I pondered her words and decided that it had to be utter nonsense. Brenda had plenty of dolls, and I was reasonably sure that was not how she had come by them. All this debate had cooled my original excitement and had brought our initial fooling around to a stop. This kind of play never lasted long for fear that our prolonged absence from the outside world would arouse suspicions. The possibility of my being caught in Michelle's presence was small. Nevertheless, I now found myself in a state of acute anxiety. The absurdity of her proposition was all I needed to convince me that our play had lasted long enough. I made a move to put on my shorts and to leave.

Michelle wasn't taking no for an answer. When I refused her advances, she suddenly turned rough, wrestling me down in the hay, straddling me, grabbing one of my fingers and bending it backward in an effort to force me into doing her wishes. Her sudden and unexpected aggressiveness sent a wave of panic through me and gave me the strength I needed to push her off and wriggle free. I grabbed my clothes and tumbled off the hay pile. I made my escape without further incident, vastly relieved that I hadn't been seen with her. On the walk home, I marveled at how the long-promised age of reason finally had a firm hold on me.

This incident inoculated me against wanting anything further to do with Michelle. From then on, I had no qualms about greeting her cheerfully and turning down her repeated invitations whenever we crossed paths. But these smug encounters always caused a pang of sadness, for I had always liked Michelle and her mother. I also thought wistfully of the good times we had spent together two years earlier, and of the magical rides on Lili she had made possible.

Brenda's and my life now more closely resembled the way it had been during the two years when we rented villas in Hardelot. Once again, we frequently spent whole days at the beach. Much of our activities revolved around our bikes, which we parked in our beach cabin every night or at noon, when one of our parents picked us up and drove us home for lunch. There was no good bike riding to be had in Condette.

On a cloudy, cool day in Condette, I was being a chef and caterer for a dinner party that Brenda was throwing for her assorted dolls and teddy bears. I had originally set out to make a chocolate cake for Brenda's guests. I was kneading the dough, or, more correctly, rolling a rough blob of moistened soil back and forth between my two hands, when I found that it gradually hardened and eventually acquired the shape of a smooth and perfect sphere. It was while contemplating the various possible gastronomic interpretations for this *boulette*, which didn't so much resemble a cake as it did a chocolaty brown snowball, that it struck me that the *boulette* was in fact a superb projectile. I put it to the test against our garage door, where it left a thoroughly satisfying dark brown mess as it splattered on the hard surface. Real snowballs weren't as messy, of course, but the mess from this *boulette* was easily hosed off.

Before long, I perfected my technique for *boulette*-making into a fine art. The trick lay in adding just the right amount of water to the soil. With too little water, a *boulette* crumbled in my hands as I threw it; with too much water, it didn't harden and I had myself a mess so slimy I could barely throw it. The soil for *boulettes* could be found anywhere in Condette, but I obtained it from a "quarry" of my own in a remote corner of the garden where unsightly digging would not incur the wrath of Raimond nor that of Father.

I demonstrated my perfected mud ball making technique to the Tourneau boys, who soon joined me in the pastime. It was thoroughly satisfying to have these neat spheres appear out of a formless blob of mud, and we soon had quite a pile of them. We then directed our attention to the garage door, which eventually became totally brown. When we could no longer distinguish new impact sites on the garage door from old ones, we turned to throwing them at each other. It wasn't long before we decided we needed forts to which we could repair and take shelter as we made a new pile of ammunition. Thus was born the game of *la guerre aux boulettes* (the mud ball war).

We built the forts from old boards which Raimond had been saving for some as yet unspecified project. First, we dug a short, shallow trench in the ground. While one of us held a row of boards upright in the trench, we filled the trench with soil and built it up around the base of the boards to form a low, running mound from which they protruded. The upright row of boards was more or less resistant to being knocked over by an incoming *boulette* and constituted the defensive wall of our fort. The next step in the evolution of this game was finding ways to make the forts more durable. We tried different arrangements of the boards, sloping or angling them and tying them together with bits of string.

As in any war, the weaponry also evolved. I invented more sophisticated *boulettes*, special-purpose ones that deserved distinguishing names. I made plum-sized ones that I called "*piquantes*" ("stingers") because I could throw them fast enough that a human target would get a mild sting from the hit. In addition, there were the *pilardes* for which I also invented the name (probably from *piler*, to pile on). *Pilardes* were huge and heavy, about the size of a grapefruit, weighing well over a pound, hard to throw and slow, but perfect for toppling an enemy fort if the *pilardes* great mass could be made to fly that far. The game finally evolved into seeing who would be first to knock down an opponent's fort by the shear number of well-placed hits. The key factors in winning a mud ball war were ingenious fort design, a good aim, quality *boulette* production and the ability to produce them at a high rate while under enemy fire. Raimond watched the progress and development of this game with relish.

Unfortunately, our respective mothers didn't share Raimond's enthusiasm and took a dim view of all this. After our first full battle, the mothers issued a Joint Communiqué, that of August 30, 1939. It formally decreed that all *guerres aux boulettes* were henceforth outlawed. Upon being asked why they were issuing such a harsh edict, the mothers unanimously maintained that no amount of laundering could restore our clothes to some semblance of cleanliness after a major battle.

The Tourneau boys were extremely disheartened by the Communiqué, but I wasn't ready to give up so easily. Undaunted, I pleaded our case, first with Mother, then with Madame Tourneau: if our clothes were already so permanently soiled, then surely there would be no further damage done if we soiled the same clothes once more in battle. Since every participant already owned a set of clothes that permanently lacked "some semblance of cleanliness," why couldn't we play the game if we all wore those very same clothes on the prearranged day of battle?

Raimond, a non-participating supporter of this game and an enthusiastic spectator, lobbied on my behalf. *"Après tout Madame, Monsieur Alain a raison!"* ("After all Ma'am, Mr. Alain is right!"). Mother, and eventually Madame Tourneau, capitulated and jointly agreed to the countermanding Decree of August 31, 1939. In France, reason—cold logical reason—usually wins the day.

One dull, dreary, gray Sunday morning, not improved by an earlier trip to church for mass, I found myself badly in need of something to lift my spirits. I meandered over to the Tourneaus' house to see if I could set up a *guerre aux boulettes*. Monsieur and Madame Tourneau were off playing a round of golf. In spite of the fact their parents weren't there—the Tourneau boys had never done much without first obtaining parental approval—Jacques couldn't see any reason why we shouldn't play the game. After all, the original Mother's Communiqué had been countermanded in the presence of all concerned, and we knew the precise terms of the most recent decree. So we all went off to our respective rooms to don our earth-stained battle regalia.

I teamed up with Pierre, and Jacques headed up the opposing camp that included Brenda and Miquet. Brenda, who only occasionally joined in our boys' games, was on Jacque's team because Miquet was only proficient at making the small *piquantes*. However, Brenda was very good at making the medium (standard size) *boulettes* and could add balance to the distribution of useful personnel. Jacques, so much bigger than any of us, had a powerful throw that no one else could come close to matching. The strengths of the two sides thus seemed fairly well balanced.

Both camps considered themselves invincible and waged a propaganda war of words as we set about building our respective forts, which stood facing each other a little more than twenty feet apart. The span of this no-man's-land between the forts was chosen because it was slightly less than the distance that Pierre, our "*pilarde* cannon," could successfully lob one of those massive missiles. The established articles of war stated that no side could start manufacturing *boulettes* until the forts were built and war had been officially declared. When the forts were completed and both camps had their supplies of soil and water ready, Raimond blew my scout whistle, signifying that war was officially declared.

Kneeling behind our fort, I worked furiously manufacturing *pilardes*, while Pierre was lobbing them as fast as I could make them. Occasionally, I made a few *piquantes*. which I aimed right at Jacques, spoiling his aim and disrupting a steady barrage of the heavy *pilardes* that he might be conducting.

At one point, one of our *pilardes* actually fractured one of the main boards of their fort, leaving an open gap in their fortifications. This meant that Brenda and Miquet, kneeling behind their fortifications, were now subjected to hits from *piquantes* and splatter from the huge *pilardes*. Nevertheless, they struggled on, maintaining full tilt *boulette* production inside their damaged fort.

Jacques had an excellent aim and, on almost every throw, kept hitting the same board on our fort; it started to lean, and since we were not allowed to make repairs to the fort during battle, Pierre and I were now also vulnerable. Counterbalancing this setback, my *boulettes* were definitely of higher quality, bigger and harder, and therefore more devastating. Since neither Brenda nor Miquet could make a decent *pilarde,* Jacques occasionally had to cease his merciless lobbing to make a few good *pilardes* himself, during which time we continued to pummel his fort mercilessly. In the meantime, Miquet peppered Pierre with *piquantes* every time he stood up to throw a *pilarde.*

Every now and then, one of the *boulette* fabricators had to make a run with a pail to the garden tap for more water. With another pail, we also had to run to the "quarry" for more soil. Each time, the runners were exposed to hits from *piquantes.* It was a lively, heart-pounding game accompanied by wild shouts of triumph at a well-aimed throw, and yelps of protest and outrage when the enemy scored a direct hit.

This heroic and raging battle was still in full swing, and we were all well battle-scarred with chocolate-colored soil, when Mother made an unexpected appearance on the scene. She advanced into no-man's-land where she was in the line of fire between the two camps, causing an immediate ceasefire. We all stood up and peered over our battered fortifications, wondering if she had lost her mind. After a moment of silence, she intoned in a solemn voice, *"La guerre a été declarée!"* ("War has been declared!")

"I know," I said, holding back the temptation to laugh. "It's been going on for some time now. If you move out of the line of fire, it can continue, and you can enjoy watching the fight to the finish!"

"No, not your little play war. I mean that *we* have declared *real* war on Germany! The Germans are refusing to pull back from their invasion of Poland," she said, still in a very somber tone.

We stood there in stunned silence for a long moment. Finally, Pierre dropped the *boulette* he was holding. More silence followed. Then Jacques dropped the *pilarde* he had been about to throw. We continued standing still, not knowing what to say.

"Why don't we just continue our own little war?" I finally asked, trying desperately to recapture the wild, carefree spirit that had prevailed. But Jacques started to walk towards their house.

Pierre looked at me briefly and silently followed his brother. Miquet, who was still holding a *piquante*, threw it at me and dashed off to catch up with his two brothers.

I looked at Raimond who had been standing on the sidelines and whose face had turned ashen. "I will be conscripted," he said grimly and walked away.

The threat of war with Germany had rumbled across Europe for years, like distant thunder on a hot, humid summer day and, as in such weather, there had been an uneasy tension. Until now, we had been watching lightning flashes in the distance. Although it hadn't reached us yet, the storm was clearly upon us now; there was no longer any use pretending it wasn't.

In denial, I had tried to revive our game, but even at nine years old, I was acutely aware the news was grave. I had repeatedly heard grown-ups talking about the possibility of war. And I had heard all about the Germans. Father had fought with the British Army in World War I, twenty years before. Mother had spent four terrible years under the German occupation in Belgium. From her, I had heard numerous stories of horror and atrocities committed by *les sales boches*. She never referred to the Germans any other way. Father hardly ever talked about his war experiences, but what little he said suggested worse than Mother's descriptions. Raimond also told me stories of that war, though being too young by one year, he had missed conscription into the army. His brother and many of his friends had been killed in the war. At the Dennis School, we had read sad, poignant poems written by men in the trenches. Current newspaper and magazine articles frequently focused on the last war and on preparations for another.

In a distracted way, I watched the three Tourneau boys disappearing through a hole in the hedge that separated our gardens. I stood there, trying to imagine what war would mean to us. Mother broke my dreadful reverie by saying, "*Vas te laver,*" ordering me to wash up. I wondered why, of all things, she wanted me to do that. There was at least an hour before lunch. I now foolishly felt that I could savor a few more precious minutes of the fun I had been enjoying if I rebuilt my fort, and started to do so, ignoring Mother's instructions. Seeing this, she became angry and, in a stern voice, told me to do as I had been ordered. Why was she so angry with me? I wasn't the one who had invaded Poland.

I went up to my room and as I started to undress, I looked out the window and noticed how dark and menacing the sky had become. Like the sky, the news facing us overwhelmed me. I suddenly felt cold and started to shiver all over. Later, during lunch, we tried to eat but weren't hungry and said nothing.

In the confusing days that followed the declaration of war, the news reached us that Mr. Derosier had decided to return to the United States and that the American School of Paris would not reopen that autumn. Shortly thereafter, Father reasoned that Paris was likely to be bombed, and that we would be safer if we stayed at our summer house in Condette.

From here, on the north coast of France, we could easily board a ship to England if fighting similar to that of the World War I developed. We weren't very far from that war's battlefields. However, that eventuality seemed unlikely. After all, the Maginot line, which bordered France's entire boundary with Germany, was heavily fortified and vaunted as impregnable.

Searching for a school, Mother learned that a girl's school run by the Convent of the Sacred Heart in the city of Lille (closer to the German border) was relocating to an abandoned château right in Condette. To pay for the expenses of the move, the nuns were welcoming new students of either sex. Father wasn't at all keen on my attending a girls' school, but there wasn't any choice, other than the village communal school. Madame Tourneau had also decided their family should remain in Condette, so the three boys would also attend the convent.

School was not starting for another three weeks, so we set about preparing for life under war conditions. Anticipating shortages and the need for transportation without petrol, Mother bought each of us, including herself, a brand new bike. I had been riding old clunkers for years, all previously owned and dilapidated bikes. Mother had long held that anyone who habitually rode through tide pools didn't deserve a brand new bike. She made me promise that I would abandon what she called "this bad habit," something I was very reluctant to do. I refused to make the promise until she pointed out to me that, with the onset of autumn and cool weather, I wasn't going to be tempted to race through tide pools much longer.

The bikes she bought might have to last us many years and were not only new, but were equipped with everything that was available in the way of accessories. My new bike was a bright metallic red and far too big for me. Mother anticipated that the war might last four years, as had the previous war, and that I would grow into it. Even after Raimond had adjusted the seat and handlebar to their minimum height, I was barely able to reach the pedals.

My bicycle had a three-speed *dérailleur* (gear), something rare and exotic in those days, and it had a *porte-paquet*, a package carrier for my book satchel. It was equipped with a dynamo and headlamp that I would need in October, riding home from school after dark. In the meantime, I rode my new bike with the light switched on in broad daylight. This made pedaling quite a bit harder, but I viewed the extra effort as a small price to pay for the thrill of knowing that I was actually generating electricity through my own physical effort. I rode this bike during most of my waking hours and long after dusk, when I could better appreciate the results of my hard pedaling. I was in seventh heaven. There were, it seemed, some redeeming aspects to being at war.

Françoise, who probably dreaded the thought of her culinary skills being constrained, convinced Mother that we should stock up on many things that might become scarce. The larder was soon brimming with all the things the French consider essential: bottles of wine, smoked hams and sausages, olive oil, waxed cheeses, canned delicacies, dried peas, beans, onions and garlic, jars of lard, and bags of sugar and flour. We tried to imagine what things might become scarce or unavailable and set about storing what we could, even if we weren't absolutely sure they would be in short supply.

To protect these valuable provisions, Françoise placed a veritable minefield of mousetraps across the larder floor. The traps inevitably tripped when someone went into that dimly lit dungeon. All it took was one trap to trip, jump up, and trip another. In short order, most of them went off. As Françoise laboriously reset every trap, she cursed the guilty party, who was always Raimond. He frequently went into the larder on her orders to get something or other. He was at her beck and call all day long and bore the added misfortune of not knowing the exact location of all her traps.

Our house in Condette was strictly a summer house and would be hard to heat in winter. The day after the war was declared, Father went to Boulogne, the nearest large town, and contracted to have central heating installed. The contractor thought he was crazy because central heating was still almost unheard of in this relatively primitive part of France. There were wood burning fireplaces in the farm houses, but the fancier summer houses were unoccupied in winter and had absolutely no heating. Nevertheless, work started immediately because all able-bodied men would soon be conscripted, and getting anything done after that would become nearly impossible. Father explained to us that he had spent the entire four years of the previous war being cold and he wasn't about to go through that experience again. Furthermore, he had a backup plan under which he would move his office and part of his staff to Condette if the Germans started to bomb Paris heavily. Every room in the house would then be in use and in need of heating.

Madame Tourneau followed our family's example and installed central heating. She also bought new bikes for all their family, herself and Monsieur Tourneau included, even though the two of them had never ridden bikes.

As in the *guerre aux boulettes*, we were making numerous preparations before the war really got under way. One of these days, someone would blow the whistle and the real war would start. In the case of the *guerre aux boulettes*, the preparations had been full of excited anticipation, but these preparations filled us with anxiety, dread, and fear.

Alain, cold day in Ville-d'Avray garden, note 8-ft wall in background, 1939

Alain and Miquet, Condette, 1939

CHAPTER 12

A Bomb, a Trap, Two Sea Mines and a Sunset

A week or so after the declaration of war, a siren blew in midmorning. It blew intermittently in twenty-second blasts, each separated from the next by a few seconds' silence. Mother declared that this was just a test of the air raid alarm system, but the words had barely left her when Raimond came bursting into the drawing room to tell us that this was no practice alarm. "A practice alarm would take the form of a series of steady, two-minute blasts of the siren, Madame," he explained. "A real alarm is a series of twenty-second blasts such as we were experiencing." Raimond read the newspaper daily from cover to cover, and he always knew all there was to know about affairs of current import. Father was in Paris at the time, and Raimond had, it seemed, assumed the role of man-of-the-house.

"Mon Dieu, Raimond! Qu'est ce qui nous attend?" ("Good Lord, Raimond! What are we to expect?") exclaimed Mother, in a tone half joking, half serious. She knew that Raimond wouldn't joke about such a matter, but she found it hard to believe that the Germans had chosen the sleepy hamlet of Condette to launch the first air offensive of the war. After a pause, during which she seemed to gather herself, Mother asked limply, "What should we do, Raimond?"

Raimond, as usual, had a ready answer: "We must go to the high dunes. It's highly unlikely they will bomb us. But there might be a gas attack. They know the populace has no gas masks."

Raimond had said the dreaded words, and there was silence as we all pondered the gravity of what he had said. There had been speculation as to what the Germans might do now that war had been declared. The treachery of the German surprise attack on Poland suggested to many that, since they could hardly succeed with a sudden push across the Maginot Line, they might try using gas on the populace. Raimond now continued: "Unlikely as it might be, we'd be foolish not to take the simple steps that would save us from a gas attack. And to achieve that goal, we must go to higher ground. Poison gas is heavier than air and lies in the low spots. The high dunes are the only area with any altitude in Condette, but they are high enough to make a difference. Don't worry though—by the time we reach the dunes, the all clear will probably sound, and we will have had *une sortie agréable*. I propose to Madame that we leave immediately."

Mother pondered this proposal for a few seconds and agreed that it was the wisest course of action. There was one problem though. The tiny Simca could only take two adults and, counting Françoise, there were three. "I will ride Madame's new bike, so Françoise can ride in the car with Madame and the children," Raimond volunteered. The high dunes were only a mile away.

Just then, the phone rang. It was Madame Tourneau who had heard from her eldest son, Jacques, that this was a real alarm. He, too, read the paper daily. Madame Tourneau wanted to know if we were planning to do anything about a possible air raid. Mother told her of Raimond's plan, and Madame Tourneau said she would join us, adding that she and her three boys would leave immediately for the dunes in her car.

It was a cold, cloudy day, so Brenda and I quickly fetched our sweaters and raincoats and had just sandwiched ourselves behind the front seats of the Simca when a new crisis arose. Françoise had just started a roast beef cooking in the oven and was protesting loudly, *"Je n'abandonne pas mon rosbif! Ah non, pas ça! Jamais!"* ("I'm not abandoning my roast beef! Oh no, not that! Never!")

She continued her jeremiad, "How dare those Germans attack in the middle of my lunch preparation? What barbarians! Don't

322

they eat, those Germans? Is nothing sacred to them?" No amount of persuasion could induce her to leave her roast beef. Raimond knew the futility of continuing to argue with Françoise and climbed into the front seat of the Simca in her stead. As we drove off, Françoise, who stood at the edge of the driveway with her hands propped on her broad hips, called out that the roast beef would be ready for us when we returned.

"J'espère bien qu'elle a raison!" ("I certainly hope she's right!") exclaimed Raimond as we drove off. I pondered the two possible interpretations of his hope, and as to which of the two Raimond had in mind: first, that there would be no bad outcome to the alarm, or second, that the all clear would come before the roast would be seriously overcooked. I kept my thoughts to myself, worried that I might sound flippant and that it would look as though I had failed to grasp the gravity of our situation.

On the north side of Condette lay a ridge of high sand dunes topped by a forest of pine trees. It might be more accurate to say that a pine forest ended at the edge of a sandy bluff. These were the high dunes of which Raimond had spoken. When we reached the base of the bluff, we found the Tourneaus already there. Brenda, the three boys, and I removed our shoes and climbed the steep, sandy face of the high bluff where I proposed that we play the game of *rahzabuntchas*. A *rahzabuntcha* is a quaint pastime indulged in by the Belgians when they have access to sand dunes. Two people form a chariot team and race against another team (if there is one) by having one person on the team pretend to be the horse and the other to be the chariot. The one who is the chariot is pulled by his feet and slides down the sand dune on his (or her) posterior. If there is just one team, the participants take turns being the chariot, but of course, no contest is possible. The steeper the sand dune the better, and the faster the race. It was tremendous fun and a wonderful way to expend youthful energy as we climbed back up the sand dune before making each exhilarating descent.

Raimond, for his part, took off his own shoes, and neatly rolled his trouser cuffs up to his knees before climbing the huge dune. After a long, slow climb, he stood at the crest of the bluff, watching us play and looking as though he wanted to join us in the fun.

Before long, Raimond called out to us saying that a low-flying plane seemed to be heading in our direction. From the top of the bluff, he had a commanding view of the flat plain on which Condette nestles. He announced a few seconds later that it might be a German plane. We all stopped playing and stared briefly at the still distant plane, then scrambled up the dune as fast as we could for a better view. When Raimond warned that it might strafe us and that we'd better take cover, we ran into the pine forest and hid behind some of the larger pine trees. As the twin-engine plane passed low and slightly to one side of us, we could make out the black and white cross of the German insignia on its wings and fuselage. It was flying in the direction of Hardelot.

The two mothers, who had been sitting near the top of the bluff talking together and pretty much ignoring our playing, had also run for cover into the forest upon hearing Raimond's warning. Once the plane had passed, they returned to the comfortable armchairs they had scooped out for themselves in the sloping face of the sand dune and resumed their conversation where they had left off. By now, the sun had come out, and it turned into a pleasant day.

Raimond returned to his vantage point and once more lit a cigarette. As the teams were preparing for another race down the dune, Raimond suddenly announced: "We may have to come here at night, or it may be raining next time the siren sounds. We should build a shelter out of branches, something we could cover with a tarp, which we would bring with us every time we have to come here." The *rahzabuntchas* had exhausted me, so I was glad that Raimond had found a new way to pass the time, and I was excited at the thought of building a little house. The five of us marched into the pine forest where we started foraging for large fallen branches. We had rounded up several suitable main spars for the shelter when the all clear sounded. By now, it was lunchtime so we went home, leaving behind a pile of branches for our next visit.

"Une bonne sortie, comme je l'avais prévu," ("a nice outing, just as I had predicted,") declared Raimond when we reached home just in time for Françoise's delicious *rosbif bien seignant* (rare roast beef).

It was still September, and many of Hardelot's families had made the same decision as Father. They were staying on at their summer residences until it became clear how this war would develop. Monsieur Cridoux, the Penguin Beach Club director, saw an opportunity to extend his summer income, and announced that he would continue the morning gymnastics classes and, whenever the tide was favorable, the afternoon sand castle contests. He even invited the Seagull Beach Club, his arch nemesis and competitor, to join the Penguin Club at a specially discounted price when it became clear that the other beach club was closing for the season at the normal time. However, on most mornings, the weather was cloudy at the beach, and a distinct chill prevailed so that few Penguins and Seagulls showed up for gymnastics.

An afternoon sand castle contest had been scheduled on the day the lone German plane flew over Condette. Jacques, Pierre, and I set off right after lunch for Hardelot on our bikes, with our sand spades tied securely to the crossbars of our steeds. Brenda and Miquet didn't join us because they felt the long ride to Hardelot and back was too much for them after a morning of *rahzabuntchas*.

Jacques Tourneau, a bookish boy who was already wise to the literati fashions of Paris, dubbed us "Le Groupe de Condette" and discussed the need for a sand castle strategy as we cycled along. He proposed that we band together and build one huge sand castle to represent the medieval fortifications of Carcassonne in the south of France, probably the largest fortified town in the country. Raimond and Françoise's son, André, lived with his grandmother not far from Carcassonne, and Raimond had shown me postcards of the fortified walls and numerous towers with their ornate crenellations.

As we continued cycling, we all agreed that we liked the idea of a large jointly built sand castle, but I proposed we should call ourselves "Le Groupe de Carcassonne" since Carcassonne was more illustrious than tiny Condette, and the name itself had more of a ring to it than "Condette." I liked a name with a ring to it, I told the boys.

"That's not the point," insisted Jacques. "The name of a *groupe* should be obscure-sounding and of unknown origin if it is to catch the attention of great minds, such as those of the sand castle contest judges."

Since I had never heard of the Paris literati, let alone their antics, Jacques' assertion made little sense to me. However, for the sake of this civilized argument, I persisted: "The name Carcassonne is surely more obscure to people who regularly have to drive through Condette to get to the outside world." Pierre was on Jacques' side even though, like me, he had no idea what we were arguing about. By the time we reached Hardelot, we had enjoyed our lengthy argument and agreed we would sign our masterpiece "Le Groupe de Condette."

When we reached the beach, we found that about fifty of the young contestants and other passers-by had gathered in a tight cluster in the middle of the dry sand area above the high tide line. Since a decent sand castle can't be built in dry sand, a gathering at this location puzzled me. We immediately headed towards them, and Jacques and I pushed our way towards the middle of the crowd where we found some sort of discussion in progress.

There was an open area about twenty feet across at the center of the gathering, and in the middle of it was a metal cylinder about six inches in diameter. One end of it was buried in the sand and the other end, sticking up two feet above the surface, had four tail fins. The thing was painted sky blue and had some foreign words and various numbers stenciled on it.

Jacques immediately recognized what it was, and exclaimed loudly, *"Fichons le camp! Vite! C'est une bombe et elle pourrait sauter n'importe quand!"* ("Let's get the hell out of here! It's a bomb and it could blow up at any time!")

I'm sure others in the crowd must have known it was a bomb. What was surprising was that no one else had come to the conclusion that, although unexploded, it could still go off unpredictably. Jacques' words acted like an explosive in their own right. I've never seen fifty people run so fast. The scattered mob regrouped about a hundred yards from the bomb, and a woman announced she was going home to call the police. In the meantime, several curious children headed back in the direction of the bomb, and various adults had to chase after them and drag them back under noisy protest.

Monsieur Cridoux had been in the original cluster of people and was so rattled by the discovery that a bomb had fallen on what he viewed as *his* beach that he announced immediately that he was canceling the sand castle contest. Our Groupe de Condette let out a collective "*Zut alors!*" and I complained loudly that we had come all the way from Condette for the contest and that I couldn't see why it couldn't be held at some safe distance from the bomb. But Cridoux was adamant in his refusal, claiming that there might be other bombs buried deeper in the sand than this one. After a thoughtful pause, he announced that because of the danger of bombs hidden in the sand anywhere on the beach, he was closing the Penguin Beach Club for the duration of the war.

As Cridoux continued his speech to justify his momentous decision, Jacques commented loudly, "He's reflected long enough to realize that, in fact, he suddenly has a convenient and quasi-legitimate reason to close down the Penguin Beach Club and leave with all the dues he has just collected for the fall session." Several adults near us laughed, but Cridoux, who apparently didn't hear the comment, continued haranguing the crowd.

Jacques, Pierre, and I walked away and started to debate the subject of bombs hidden in the sand. We soon concluded that we had seen how far one bomb could bury itself in the sand and could see no reason why other bombs would go much deeper. Besides, most bombs were supposed to blow up upon striking the ground and this one had to be a fluke and a dud. We therefore concluded that there were no hidden bombs in the sand and that Monsieur Cridoux was *un peu dérangé,* or perhaps too strongly motivated to end all formal beach activities for the season. Undaunted, the three of us were anxious to start work on our fort.

Quite a few members of the original crowd were still milling about, muttering grumpily and wondering what to do now that their original plans had been shattered. I announced as loudly as I could that we were about to build the sand fort to end all sand forts, the fortress of Carcassonne, and that everyone on the beach was invited to join us in the this monumental enterprise. All within earshot cheered and agreed to join in our effort.

Jacques whispered to me under his breath that he had not the slightest idea of what Carcassonne really looked like. He was worried that, being the oldest among us, he would be expected to lead this endeavor. He would be doing so in a state of total ignorance, something he felt he could not in all conscience do. *"Regardes donc ce à quoi tu m'as engagé!"* ("Now look what you have committed me to!") he protested pathetically.

"T'en fais pas! Ils ne s'y connaissent pas plus que toi!" ("Don't worry! They don't know any more about it than you do!") I said, trying to reassure him. Then I added, *"Tu peux leur faire faire n'importe quoi. Ils n'y verront que du feu."* ("You can have them do anything. It's all smoke and mirrors.") I then advised him to look as though he knew what he was doing and to sally forth. But he still didn't know what he should or might do. So I turned to the crowd of some thirty kids and told them to follow me. When we reached a spot on the wet sand at least two hundred yards from the bomb, I started to drag my spade behind me so that it left a mark on the hard, wet sand as I walked along. My course wiggled in and out as I traced a badly distorted oval about ten yards across at its widest point. I dug a pile about a foot high on the line I had traced and told my cohorts to start digging a sand wall about the same height along the full length of this line. I underestimated their enthusiasm and abilities—in less than an hour, we had encircled the outlined area with a running sand mound almost twice the requested height.

We had just started building some towers along the wall when an extremely loud explosion and the sight of a brilliant geyser of fire about twenty feet tall interrupted our labor. We abandoned our digging and ran towards a place where a group of people stood about a hundred yards from what now looked like a volcano spouting fire, the intensity of which was already on the wane.

Two soldiers looking very pleased with themselves were standing in front of the crowd as we joined it. One of the onlookers called out to a member of our Carcassonne team, "Hey Paul! You should have been here! Those two soldiers just blew up a German incendiary bomb with a stick of dynamite. They lit the fuse on the dynamite and casually walked away. About two minutes later it exploded, and the fireworks started."

Paul turned to me and said, "You and your Carcassonne! I missed all the fun!" I felt very sheepish but said nothing. Someone commented that if the plane had been trying to hit one of the villas about a hundred meters away, their aim was exceedingly poor. The crowd laughed. A man said that the lone German plane that had flown over Hardelot during the morning's air raid had probably dropped the bomb; the beach had been deserted at the time.

The bomb's fiery eruption ended abruptly, and the soldiers returned to the spot where only wisps of smoke rose from the fragmented carcass of the incendiary bomb. Wearing thick gloves, they gathered up the various smoldering pieces of scrap metal, put them in a large, stiff canvas sack which they dragged to an army truck parked on the beach, and drove away.

When the excitement over the bomb subsided, most of the fort-builders, excluding Paul who curiously believed another exciting event would take place without him, indicated they wanted to complete the fortress, so we headed back to our diggings.

We started carving and detailing some crenellations and turrets on our fort, but I soon noticed that the sea was now much closer to us, for the tide had risen substantially during the hour or so that the explosion had distracted us from our task. I cried out for everyone to stop building towers and crenellations and start the urgent business of raising the wall higher, especially on the side of the approaching sea. "To the battlements! Carcassonne must be saved! Dig with all your might! Pile on the sand where the ramparts look the thinnest! Dig for your life!" My entreaties had the desired effect; the team returned to the task with renewed vigor.

Before long, the waves were lapping at the base of our fortress, and eventually the rising sea turned it into a beleaguered island. We fought valiantly for the next half hour, shoveling like mad in places where the action of the waves was causing the wall to crumble. Eventually, the sea gained the upper hand, and the waves lapped over the crest in too many places for us to repair. The wall was breached like a bursting dam. The break grew ever wider, and the water rushed in faster and faster until we were standing in cold water up to our knees. We waded to the shore's new location, about two hundred feet distant, and, before disbanding, our valiant crew all shook hands and agreed that it had been a marvelous and exciting afternoon. Jacques, Pierre and I set off for Condette wet, happy, and exhausted. As we cycled along, the three of us side by side on the deserted Condette road, Jacques admitted, "I was under the impression Carcassonne was all sharp-angled in outline, more like a star—I had no idea it was an oval-shaped fortification."

To which I solemnly replied, "Neither did I." The three of us laughed our heads off.

That evening, Mother made a rare long-distance call to Paris to tell Father about the air raid and the bomb. She also wanted to see if he wanted to change his mind about our staying in Condette. He replied that he had read in the evening paper about the lone German plane that had flown across northern France and dropped a single bomb on some unspecified beach. He was stunned to hear that Hardelot was the beach in question and wanted more details about the bomb. Mother told him I knew all about it and put me on the phone. I had the first phone conversation in my life as I described the bomb and its eventual demise to Father.

When I was done, he asked that I put Mother back on the line. Father told her that all of Paris was talking about this first act of belligerence on French soil by the Germans and that the evening papers were full of editorials postulating the motives for such a step. The consensus seemed to be that it was an exploratory flight to discover whether France had any defenses against an air attack. It was apparent that we had none; the plane had flown over the countryside unchallenged in any way. It was also conjectured that the German flight was intended to show the populace how defenseless and vulnerable we were. It seemed that, as a piece of propaganda, the plan had been quite successful. Others surmised that the pilot was deranged and had undertaken the flight without authorization. This theory was based on the fact that the plane had dropped one small bomb on a meaningless target as it flew towards the sea and that it was not observed returning from this flight anywhere along the coast of France or Belgium. Had the plane continued out to sea and gone down, unseen, into the ocean when it ran out of fuel?

Father decided that, mysterious as the incident was, there was no cause for alarm and that we should stick with the original plan to stay in Condette. The Germans were not going to waste their bombs on a small farming community like Condette. But he wanted Mother to go into Boulogne to see if the government was issuing gas masks, something they were already seriously talking about in England. A gas attack on Condette was highly unlikely, he explained. However, a cloud of poison gas could waft our way from some more plausible target, such as the harbor town of Boulogne, or even Étaples, where there was an airport nearby, as well as a small harbor. Furthermore, once we had purchased the gas masks, Father wanted us to take them with us whenever we went shopping in those places.

In Boulogne the next day, Mother spent all morning going from one government office to another without success in her quest for gas masks. No one seemed to have any idea what agency was in charge of issuing them to the civilian population, nor had anyone even heard of any plan to so. Mother finally found a private company that made and sold gas masks to individuals, but the company had a waiting list for their product. Days later, and after several trips, Mother was able to buy six of their most expensive model. Each mask came stored in a well made, imitation pigskin leather case, which was extremely large and surprisingly heavy. Raimond, Françoise, Brenda, Mother, and I hauled these around whenever we knew we would be some distance from home. On short errands or activities close by, we relied on being able to dash home as soon as the alarm sounded. And later, when we went to school, Brenda and I always carried the beastly things with us, cumbersome as they were.

Once armed with these masks, we saw no need to return to the high sand dunes to finish building our emergency shelter. But on the evening of the first air raid warning, Raimond described what might have happened if the bomber had dropped his incendiary bomb on the pine forest—the very spot we had planned to build our shelter. Raimond's scenario assumed that the bomb would have exploded as intended. His vivid description of the resulting forest fire (the first time I had ever heard of such a cataclysm) was enough to give me nightmares on several occasions. In these dreams, we were camping in our lean-to, and the pine forest was a raging inferno about to consume us alive. My bad dreams stopped when we were finally able to buy the masks and no longer faced the prospect of heading for the high dunes if an air raid alarm sounded.

The days grew colder, and we wanted to turn on the new central heating. But a promised coal delivery had never taken place. When Mother went to the coal merchant in nearby Pont-de-Briques, they told her that there was no coal allocated for private deliveries in this part of France, where most of the permanent residents, mostly farmers, relied on wood fireplaces in the winter. The coal yard was brimming with coal, but the owner maintained that it was destined for large institutions and commercial enterprises. Mother rummaged in her purse and dredged up all the cash she had and offered it to him *sous la table* (under the table), but he flat out refused her bribe, boasting brazenly that it was not nearly enough to tempt him.

Fortunately, our new furnace could burn wood as well as coal, and Mother immediately announced her intention to stockpile a large quantity of wood before the opening of school and before the onset of cold or wet weather would make wood gathering more of an ordeal.

Armed with a small bow saw, the Tourneau boys and I sought out fallen or dead trees in the forest of Hardelot, sawed what we could into small, manageable logs, and gathered smaller branches for kindling. We contrived to take home all this wood on our bikes, which was a slow process since we couldn't carry much on each trip, and the nearest spot for gathering wood was half-an-hour's ride from our house. Another solution was badly needed.

During the summer's shopping trips to the weekly outdoor market in nearby Étaples, one of my favorite haunts was a pawnbroker and bric-a-brac shop whose establishment was right on the square where, every Wednesday, they held the weekly open-air market. I had seen an old perambulator on sale there for twenty francs (about half the cost of a child's cheap bicycle in those days). I convinced Mother that this baby carriage would make a handy cart which I could tow behind my bike for hauling wood and pinecones. I had already discussed the project in detail with Raimond, who was enthusiastic about my idea and prepared to make certain alterations to the pram if we bought it.

Mother approved but declared that since petrol was now harder to obtain, we would have to cycle to Étaples to bring the perambulator home. Even if petrol had been abundant, I doubt we could have loaded the rather large pram into, or onto, Mother's tiny Simca.

Raimond volunteered for the excursion to Étaples, and Mother offered him the use of her new bike. Raimond had ridden a bicycle only once before in his life, many years earlier. This detail didn't seem to deter him from wanting to go on the expedition. He insisted he could ride well enough and valiantly agreed to command the enterprise.

We tied our gas masks to the bicycle frames so we wouldn't have them dangling from our shoulders and set out in high spirits immediately after lunch on our twenty-kilometer trip to Étaples. This was much farther (probably by a factor of three) than any trip I had ever undertaken on a bicycle, but with my new bike and its dérailleur, I was confident that I could go the distance. I could see that Raimond was a bit wobbly, but I reflected to myself that by the end of the trip, he would be an experienced cyclist and his wobbles would be washed out.

The road we used for most of the trip was the main road between Boulogne and Étaples, so it had *bornes Michelin* every kilometer. *Bornes* are literally milestones, or, to be strictly correct, "kilometerstones." They look a little like miniature, round-topped tombstones and stand twenty or so inches above the ground with the wide flat face of the stone facing the oncoming driver. What they tell you depends on the type of road you are driving on. For us, on an important but secondary road, there was only the distance to the next main town, which was Étaples. At first, we seemed to pass these kilometerstones with reassuring regularity, but after about a dozen kilometers, the time interval between these encounters seemed to increase alarmingly. I began to wonder if we would ever reach our destination. Raimond, not used to working his legs in this fashion, was also starting to flag.

When I complained to Raimond that it was hard to keep pedaling, he pointed out that I didn't need to have my headlamp on during daytime, and that turning it off would make the pedaling easier. "It takes energy to make electricity and the only place it comes from is your legs," he explained. Reluctantly, I turned off the light and had to admit he was right.

We finally arrived in Étaples shortly after four o'clock, only to find the bric-a-brac shop had just closed. Bitterly discouraged, we proceeded to a nearby café to drown our disappointment, Raimond with a glass of wine and I with a glass of water flavored with bright red grenadine syrup. *"Un rosé pour le jeune homme,"* the barman sing-songed, as he handed me my beverage. While sipping our drinks, we overheard a man lamenting that since the declaration of war, the junk business had fallen off—people seemed to be holding on to their old stuff, he said. The man had to be the owner of the eloood bric-a-brac shop. Raimond went over to him and, and after chatting him up, confirmed that he was.

At first, the pawnbroker balked at Raimond's request that he reopen his shop, maintaining that it was against the law for him to do so. But Raimond bought him *un coup de vin*, which in short order converted him over to our cause. Soon the man was proclaiming loudly that laws were for breaking, weren't they? He took a long time to finish his drink and wanted another, but Raimond eventually coaxed him out of the café and over to his shop.

Just as I remembered, the wooden pram was an elegant and superb machine. It looked quite *art nouveau* with the great loops of its spiral suspension springs supporting its gracefully curved bodywork high above the ground. Four very large, but thin-rimmed wheels added to the effect. Despite its light and airy appearance, the pram was huge, and the sturdy wood panels of its bodywork added to its considerable weight. Raimond commented that it must have been designed for twins. *"Non, non, Monsieur! Des triplets!"* exclaimed the pawnbroker. I was elated at finding it in such good condition and felt that our arduous journey had been well rewarded. I could hardly wait to bring the pram home and supervise all the changes I would talk Raimond into making.

It was after five o'clock when we set out from Étaples with my new pride and joy. We had brought some light rope for the purpose, and my plan, thoroughly reviewed and discussed before the trip, was for the two of us to ride our bikes side by side like a pair of dray horses, jointly towing the pram behind us.

We had only gone about a hundred meters when it became clear that the plan was flawed. Twice, the pram showed us it had a mind of its own and wandered off to the right, until it careened off the road, nearly pulling us with it. I persuaded Raimond that the only solution was that one of us should cycle beside the pram. Then, whenever it deviated too far off its proper course, the rider of the rear bike could yank the pram back into line by a sharp jerk to its handle. The rider of the other bike would continue his job as the locomotive in front. We set off again with Raimond in the lead position. This seemed to work, but the course-correcting yank (needed about every fifty meters) was an added burden to the rider in front and made it a jerky ride for the cyclist bringing up the rear.

Our progress was slow, and several long hill-climbs along the way made the going even slower. With ten kilometers still to go, darkness overtook us, and a large yellow moon made its appearance over the pastures that bordered our deserted road. I turned on my lamp to avoid the occasional potholes. I had been dreading the onset of this necessity; I hardly needed the extra drag that the dynamo created. Raimond, too, was growing tired, and we stopped frequently to exchange positions. When I was in the lead, our progress was substantially slower because the only way I could manage the load at all was in low gear, something Raimond's bike didn't have. Still, my brief intervals of towing afforded him a little rest. Even with my bike in low gear, I found that the time I could spend in the lead position was growing shorter each time it was my turn. Raimond eventually took over the lead position full time. I discovered that I could steer the pram quite successfully just by a steady pull from my right hand, instead of jerking it every now and then. As we continued on doggedly, I became convinced that before long I would fall off my bike from sheer exhaustion.

Describing our ordeal to Mother the next day, Raimond said there came a time when, in the rear position, I just stopped pedaling and coasted as he pulled me, the pram, and the drag of my dynamo, which dimly illuminated the slow progress of this tired cortege. Raimond said he had called out in protest, but could elicit no response from me. How he managed to keep going, I can't imagine. I must have been steering in a trance; I have no recollection of the last two kilometers after we turned off the main road onto the narrower side road leading to Condette. Raimond commented that when we reached home at eight o'clock, I was in a complete daze, as if hypnotized, still clutching onto the perambulator with my right hand, and with my bike still upright after we stopped. He had to lift me off the bike and carry me to bed. My eyes were wide open, but he was sure I was asleep. When he asked me if I wanted any supper, he said I just stared blankly.

Raimond swore he would never ride a bike again. Nonetheless, he immediately set to work straightening the pram's frame. The suspension frame to which the wheels were attached was slightly bent, as if it had been caught between a wall and a car that had backed into it. We hadn't noticed this detail in the pawnshop and it was probably the cause of our steering problems on the trip back from Étaples. Raimond, capable as always, was able to straighten the frame and repair a crack in the woodwork of the main carriage, undoubtedly caused by the same mishap. Raimond attached a light wood pole on each side of the pram, like the shafts of a horse-drawn cart, using screws to fasten them to the wooden body. The bike was connected to the two poles, which were bent slightly to meet at the bicycle's seat post. The result was a vehicle resembling a rickshaw.

I named the pram *"La Carrosserie Nationale,"* ("The National Coachwork"). In French, the name has a certain ring, and I relished the pompous sound of it. In keeping with the spirit of this grand enterprise, Raimond emblazoned its bold name in bright yellow paint and extravagant flourishes on the sides of the *carrosserie*.

When this magnificent carriage was ready, Raimond hooked it up to Jacques' bike and the Tourneaus, Brenda and I set off on the first of many wood gathering expeditions. Our little terrier-cairn, Jock, led the parade, reconnoitering the bushes on either side of the road for dangerous rabbits that might ambush our defenseless five-bike convoy. We felt more like a royal procession setting out on an important mission than the band of humble firewood gleaners that we were. The Carrosserie Nationale could carry seven or eight small logs and a bundle of kindling or a couple of burlap sacks full of pinecones. On the return trip, each of the five bikes also carried a single log tied onto the bike frames with string. Our team often made three or four round trips a day, and we soon had a good stockpile of wood for both households.

The golf club was now officially closed, but Mother continued to play there even if the unmown greens made the game somewhat challenging. Fortunately, it was a dry autumn, and the unwatered greens didn't grow much under these conditions. Since there wasn't another soul there, she decided that Brenda and I could join her in doing the occasional nine holes. Brenda was once again willing to play golf with me since there was no danger from exploding cow pies on the course.

It was during one of these clandestine games that we suddenly heard a terrible yelping sound. Mother volunteered that Jock had probably caught a rabbit. The fearful racket continued and was clearly that of an animal in pain. But it was obviously no noise a rabbit would make; besides, Jock was trained not to chase rabbits on golf courses. We agreed that Jock might be in some kind of trouble and stopped our game to look for him.

We found him just beyond a small knoll, lying on his side, his leg caught in a large animal trap, and bleeding seriously. Brenda, Mother, and I pulled and tugged at the trap's jaws for about ten minutes without succeeding in prying them apart. It was a huge steel trap of the type used to catch wild boar, measuring more than a foot across and weighing well over ten pounds. Jock continued his anguished yelping, and Brenda and I were soon in tears at the sight of our beloved Jock in so much pain. Mother finally decided we had to find a way to make a stretcher. Her plan was to put Jock and the trap on the stretcher in the hope that Raimond would be able to find a way to release him once we reached home.

But first, we had to contend with a stout metal stake to which the trap was connected by a massive chain. The stake was driven deep into the sand dune, and the three of us ended up on our hands and knees, feverishly digging it out of the sand with our bare hands. Once the stake was free, we were faced with having to carry Jock, the trap, the stake, and the chain. Mother, one of the most resourceful people I have ever known, now created a stretcher out of two golf clubs and her golfing jacket. We then struggled to place Jock gently on the flimsy stretcher along with the trap, chain, and stake. I could barely lift my end of the stretcher and its cargo.

We were about two miles from the house, but we had biked to the golf course and hidden our bikes in the bushes near a hole in the hedge bordering the golf course. Fortunately, the Carrosserie Nationale was still hitched to my bike because we had planned on gathering more wood on the way home. It now became an ambulance as we laid the comatose Jock, the trap, and all its attachments inside the spacious *carrosserie*. Jock had stopped yelping and lay perfectly still, his eyes glazed and lifeless. Only his short, quick breathing told us he was still alive.

When we reached home, Raimond took one look at Jock, decided the little dog was in shock and immediately went to work on him. He helped Mother and me place Jock, the trap and all its attached paraphernalia on the kitchen table and told us to lift the end of the table closest to Jock's tail so that the dog's head was lower than his rump. Jock appeared unconscious, but since he was still breathing, Raimond assured us that meant there was still hope.

Mother and I were left holding up one end of the table as Raimond went in search of a crow bar. In the meantime, Françoise found a couple of matching pans and placed them upside-down under the table's legs so as to relieve us from holding the table. I now turned my attention to petting the little dog's head and ears the way I knew he especially enjoyed it, and kept whispering in his ear, "*T'en fais pas, mon pauvre petit Joque!*" ("Don't worry, my poor little Jock!") I feared he would not wake and my eyes filled with tears. Brenda was crying so much that Mother had to take her to her room, away from the sight of the suffering dog, where she tried to console her.

Raimond returned with the crowbar and, without difficulty, pried open the trap and released Jock's leg. Raimond now set about cleaning the gaping wound left by the trap. Bare bone was showing, but, strangely, the wound was no longer bleeding. Almost all the way around Jock's hind leg, just above where the leg makes a sharp angle, jagged pieces of flesh dangled untidily and bone was showing. Using cotton balls soaked with a diluted peroxide solution, Raimond swabbed the open wound and rinsed it extensively with bottled water, making a large puddle on the tiled kitchen floor. He then tied the loose ends of flesh into a tidy bundle around the exposed bone with clean cotton string, so that the jagged ends of the wound were almost completely reunited. Several small pieces of flesh still dangled from his leg and didn't seem to fit anywhere. To my amazement, Raimond just cut these off with scissors, saying, "If I don't do that, he will die of gangrene." He then made a splint from a wooden date box cover and bandaged the whole leg.

Now that the surgery was over, I still feared that Jock would not awake from his sleep-like state. Once more, Raimond knew what had to be done. He went for a bottle of ammonia, poured some out on his handkerchief, and held the hanky next to Jock's muzzle. The result was miraculous. Jock snapped out of his trance and tried valiantly to stand up, but couldn't because of his splint and the tilt of the table. Raimond gently lifted Jock onto the floor, where the little dog stood motionless but was teetering on the verge of falling over. Françoise brought him his water bowl, from which he lapped noisily for a couple of minutes. My tears, which all this time had never completely stopped, now really started flowing as I cried and laughed with relief and joy.

Jock limped around with his splint for two weeks, and when it was removed, the wound was clean and nicely healed. The mishap left Jock with a permanent limp, but it didn't deter him from his usual boisterous scamper when he joined us on our wood gathering expeditions.

Soon after this incident, Raimond was ordered to report for military duty. He must have been almost forty years old, but even so, he would still only be *un simple poilu*, a simple foot soldier. Raimond was such a kind and gentle man that it was hard to imagine him as a toughened and effective soldier, though his recent performance in the treatment of Jock's mishap would certainly have qualified him as a medic in the army.

Anticipating the approaching winter, Mother knitted Raimond a dark gray balaclava and made a special trip to Boulogne to buy him thick wool socks, long woolen underwear and a pair of wool-lined leather gloves. Françoise made Raimond a *pâté de foie gras* to take with him so he could spread a little on his daily bread ration.

On the day of Raimond's departure, Françoise broke into one of her sudden rages against him, saying that he would be unfaithful to her while away. Frying pans were flying, and poor Raimond came sobbing to Mother. Knowing that she was safe from flying pans if Brenda and I went along, Mother led us into the kitchen and tried to talk Françoise into a state of relative calm. She pointed out to Françoise that the best way to ensure that Raimond would return faithful to her was to be sweet and loving to him at this sad and painful time. "Is throwing pans and shouting wild accusations at him any way to be sweet and loving?" she challenged, and then added in a dire tone, "When he's gone, you will feel terrible for the way you treated him!"

Françoise almost instantly switched from a raging fury to uncontrollable grief, now crying and wailing that surely Raimond would be killed. At this revelation, Brenda and I, already massively saddened by the prospect of his departure, immediately joined in the chorus of sobbing and wailing. Poor Raimond! It must have made his anguish so much worse to see us all in such a state. It was pouring rain as we watched him squeeze into the little Simca and head for the station with Mother at the wheel. Brenda, Françoise and I stood at the side of the driveway, crying in the rain, as the little car splashed out of sight. I was inconsolable for days after Raimond's departure and couldn't take my mind off the picture I had of him standing in a muddy trench under leaden skies, shells bursting all around him.

The opening of school helped ease the despair I felt after Raimond's departure. I can still picture Brenda and me riding our bikes to school in the rain, wearing boots and rubberized capes that covered even our handle bars, with little Brenda struggling to keep up and me circling back frequently to coax her on. It was a two-kilometer ride along a winding country road, and I was proud that Mother entrusted Brenda to my care for this journey. We came home for lunch, and in the afternoon, I went back to school without Brenda, who only attended school in the morning.

I didn't stay at that school for long, but I think that within any comparable time span I learned more than I have anywhere else, before or since. After the English-speaking Dennis School and the easy-going American School of Paris, I had a lot of work to do before I would be caught up to the level I should be for my age in a French school.

The nuns brooked no nonsense. Sister Martine, my teacher, was merciless with her knuckle rapping, which she administered whenever I looked up from my book. She also meted out this punishment if she found any sort of drawing or doodle on my paperwork, which was often. I eventually acquired the impression that she taught the class standing behind me and spying over my shoulder.

Sister Martine also refused to let me out for recess until my assignment was done, and done correctly, so I have no memory of ever enjoying a recess at that school. She wouldn't even let me go to the toilet, saying that my discomfort was my penance for being so slow and lazy. One day, after hours of bladder anguish, I had an "accident" when Sister Martine whacked me on the knuckles for the fidgeting brought on by my state of necessity. I suffered in soggy silence for fear of an even more horrible punishment that might befall me if she knew of my plight.

Every evening I had homework assignments which kept me up late into the night; I also spent most of my weekends doing homework. Mother, who thought I was finally being cured of being *"constament dans la lune,"* kept up the pressure on the home front. She maintained a sharp eye on me as I did my homework and reprimanded me if my attention strayed. At least she didn't beat me when it did, and thankfully, she allowed me to go to the bathroom.

Our main subject was French grammar with its endless conjugations of irregular verbs in all their moods and tenses; the subjunctive pluperfect comes to mind. In geography, we memorized the location of every *département* and river in France.

Another important subject was math where, in the six-week period I attended the school, I had to catch up on fractions, decimals, ratios, percentages, and the metric system. I had covered none of these topics during my two-year, English-speaking hiatus, but thanks to my designs, I was already well acquainted with the meter and the centimeter. And of course, my cycling expedition to Étaples had made me intimately aware of the kilometer. But French children of my age had studied and mastered the whole metric system thoroughly. When I say the whole metric system, I'm referring to its every nook and cranny. Does anyone ever use the *decalitre,* the *décigram* or the *hectomètre*? The math problems became more practical; I was now being asked (for example) to

342

calculate the weight of water contained in a dimensioned water tank—filled to 3.75 centimeters below its rim. The tank was round, so they also taught us the concept of the ratio *pi*.

Fortunately, math was not difficult for me. I found Sister Martine's explanations logical and straightforward. I seemed to understand the point of the matter at hand and was able to work with the new concepts almost immediately. While I found the problems fun and intriguing, I would have enjoyed the math more if Sister Martine hadn't been such a martinet. My good work in math bought me no reprieve from her ferocity. If I correctly completed my math assignment before the end of class and thought I would be released for recess, I was mistaken. There were always a few confounded conjugations that Sister Martine remembered I had to straighten out. This teacher knew only ruthless perseverance, and mercy was not among her virtues.

One Saturday in mid-October, Brenda, Mother, and I went to Boulogne harbor to meet Father who was returning from England by boat, as flights from London to Le Touquet (our local airport) had been discontinued. During the drive home, he calmly announced that in two weeks I would be going off to a boarding school in England. Mother was as stunned by this revelation as I was and immediately objected on the grounds that I wasn't ten years old yet—I still had a year to go before the preordained date of that dreadful eventuality.

"The present arrangement isn't at all satisfactory," Father asserted. He had long ago decreed that ten years was the age at which I should start what he called "serious schooling" in England. He was obviously unaware of what was going on under the auspices of the good nuns of the Sacred Heart. He may also have been concerned about my attending what was essentially a school for girls. Even though the school had successfully enrolled a small contingent of boys, most of the students were girls. I'm more inclined to suspect he had found a good pretext to do something he felt was already overdue.

That night after I went to bed, I overheard my parents' tense discussion of this matter. Mother thought that nine years of age was much too young for a boy to be sent to boarding school. "In fact, even ten is too young in my opinion." I heard Mother say reproachfully.

Father's reply was that in England, families of our standing sent their sons off to boarding school at the age of six. Mother's riposte was that we weren't standing in England, we were standing in France. It was the first and only time I ever heard my parents argue forcibly. I drifted off to sleep listening to them, confident that Mother would win this argument and that I wouldn't be going off to England until at least the following year.

The next morning, Mother looked like a limp rag; quite evidently, she had lost the battle. My heart sank. I had been told nothing about what English schools were like or what to expect, and the thought of being so far away from home, all alone among total strangers, was enough to fill me with dread. Overcome with anxiety, I begged Mother to plead once more with Father. She declared grimly that it was no use. He had his heart set on it.

In the meantime Father did his best to reassure me. He unpacked a glossy brochure displaying photographs of smiling boys having lunch, boys at ease on their beds reading books, boys playing soccer, boys playing rugby, boys playing cricket, boys at play in a room full of model trains, boys at work in a wood-working shop, and boys climbing into elaborate tree houses. Yet another photo showed a group of men all wearing black gowns and mortar boards, which Father explained was the teaching staff. In each photograph everyone looked happy and carefree. It appeared to be an idyllic place.

The school, Father explained, was situated on a heavily wooded two-hundred-acre estate in Surrey, where each boy supposedly built his own tree house. It sounded rather like the Dennis School I had liked so much. Both schools were English schools, and perhaps all English schools were run like the Dennis School, which I considered the best school I had known. The prospect of a whole room devoted to model trains was also a definite plus. My spirits lifted somewhat, but the idea of separation from the family still preyed on my mind.

Father told me that Aunt Lottie (his sister) had reviewed many other possible schools before becoming convinced that the Abinger Hill School was the best available. This was definitely another point in its favor, since I adored Auntie Lottie. She had discovered Abinger School through a close friend who knew the sister (matron) there. Auntie Lottie and Father had visited the school and had seen the train room, the carpentry shop, the swimming pool, the bright, cheery classrooms, the pleasant dormitories, and even some of the elaborate tree houses for which the school was famous. "You're bound to love it there, Sonny, and in a few days, you'll have masses of new friends," Father said reassuringly. This last statement was another strong point in its favor.

When Mother asked him why I had to go to an English school, Father's reply was, "The French and Belgians are quite good at a lot of things, but raising boys to be real men isn't one of them." It was clear I was going to Abinger Hill, and that was final.

I continued attending the convent school until the time for my departure in early November. One Saturday, we went to Boulogne and shopped for things on a list of items needed by boys attending Abinger Hill. Most of the items on the list could only be bought at a special school outfitter in England. Those items would be purchased under the supervision of Auntie Lottie when I reached England. For this purpose, three days in England would be set aside before I actually began attending Abinger.

Mother's purchases in France were limited to handkerchiefs, washcloths, towels, a hairbrush, a toothbrush, toothpaste, soap and a soap box, a clothes brush, and a pencil box. By way of a pencil box, I chose the very latest model that incorporated a built-in pencil sharpener and a small drawer for collecting the shavings. She also bought me a pair of shoes because the pair I had was somewhat worn, and there had been talk about shoe rationing. All non-consumable items on the school list were to have my name clearly and indelibly marked on them. Mother painted my initials on the clothes brush and the pencil box with white enamel wall paint, using a sable watercolor brush.

After the shopping, Mother took me to the basilica and found a priest to hear my confession, something she felt I had better take care of before leaving. For good measure, she bought me a small, triangular medal called a "scapular," and a small-linked chain so that I could always wear it around my neck. On the little triangular medal was a representation of Saint Christopher carrying the infant Jesus, overlaid in clear blue enamel. To have it blessed, we returned to the priest who had confessed me. He explained to me that as long as I had the medal on my person, I would never die in a state of sin. I took this to mean that as long as I maintained a small backlog of unconfessed sins on "my slate" (venial sins, of course, such as white lies), there was no way I would die. It was like an insurance policy against dying.

On the day of my departure, Father and Mother, Brenda and I, and of course, little Jock, drove to Boulogne, a busy fishing harbor as well as the port where we would board the ferry to England. The atmosphere in the car was tense. No one said a word. Mother had acceded to Father's decision under protest and was still utterly miserable.

As we approached the docks in Boulogne, I made an effort to break the silence, which was only adding to my gloom, by announcing that I really liked the smell of fresh fish which was now permeating the car. To this, Brenda unexpectedly said, "I suppose you would like your wife to wear fish perfume on your wedding day!" It was so unlike Brenda. I was often guilty of teasing her, but she had never teased me. She chose the wrong time to start. I turned around and punched her in the arm, not hard, not enough to really hurt but enough to shock her and start her crying. I immediately felt ashamed of what I had done and put my arm around her, trying to console her, and myself, for it made me realize that Brenda was also very much a part of the dear and familiar world I was leaving. Tears began to roll down my cheeks.

All this crying came to a stop at the sound of air raid sirens, which started blaring as we arrived at quayside. Father told us to go inside the harbor terminal building, which was made of concrete and might therefore pass for an air raid shelter, at least against shrapnel from nearby bomb hits. Then he drove the car well away from the waiting steamer and the dock, assuming these were the most likely bombing targets. When Father rejoined us, he told us that the steamer's departure would be delayed until after the all clear, so we went to a restaurant inside the terminal for lunch. They were serving five-course meals even though we were still officially in the middle of an air raid.

As we emerged from the building after lunch, a good hour and a half later, we found a crowd outside, looking skyward. A single Heinkel bomber, high in the sky, but not directly over us, was dropping what looked like little white eggs. They were mere specks, but they grew in size as they descended. Then one of these eggs popped apart while it was still high above the ground, and a shower of leaflets scattered across the sky. One by one, about a dozen of these eggs burst open in this fashion. Soon, a snowstorm of leaflets was drifting down over Boulogne. The wind blew them towards the main part of town, away from us, so we were never able to see what the leaflets had to say. Father declared they must be German propaganda.

After circling a few times and dropping more eggs, the Heinkel bomber finally flew away, and the all clear sounded. I kissed Brenda and Mother goodbye and gave Jock a hug and an ear scratching. Then Father and I boarded the steamer, which left the dock without delay because it was running behind schedule. The image of Brenda and Mother standing on the dock with little Jock sitting between them is still clear in my mind's eye. Mother alternated between waving a handkerchief and using it to wipe her eyes.

As the boat steamed out of the harbor, Brenda and Mother became tiny specks, and Father started a concerted effort to cheer me up by taking my hand and walking around the decks, explaining how various things worked. He even obtained permission to take me to the captain's bridge. Later, he took me down to the engine room where the engineer in charge gave us a grand tour of the boilers and machinery. I was fascinated. In those less crowded days, people in such positions took the time to do friendly things, easily and without fear of consequences.

I had never known Father to be so solicitous of my well-being or so interested in talking to me. I suddenly felt privileged and honored. He was doing a great job of keeping my mind off the distant specks on the dock. I asked a lot of questions about the things he was showing me, and he answered them patiently, in a way that I found intriguing and easy to follow. This tour of the steamer was my awakening into the realm of engineering. Until then, I had only been interested in the architecture, the shape and the layout of things, and how the various parts related to their use. I believe it was on this journey that *how and why things worked* first captured my attention in a major way.

Halfway across the Channel, the ship's engines shut down, and we slowed almost to a stop about a hundred yards from a floating sea mine. A sailor in uniform appeared on deck with a rifle and took aim. On the very first shot, the mine exploded, making a deafening noise and sending up a mountain of white foamy water as high as the ship itself. As we steamed forward once more, the sailor with the rifle told the gathered passengers that it was a German mine, dropped in the sea by a plane. "It wasn't supposed to float," he said. "Instead, it's supposed to lie in wait about ten feet below the surface of the water for a passing ship. We're lucky it was floating and visible."

About half an hour later, we slowed again, and a second mine was shot into oblivion. "They must have dropped a bad lot of them," said the sailor this time. "They seldom float up like these two. In the last month, we've had two ships sunk to mines in this stretch of water, and sunk very quickly they did."

Our ship was taking a secret zigzag course through our own elaborate array of mines, which had been placed with the intent of preventing German ships from heading for the open Atlantic by way of the Channel. Father asked the sailor how the captain knew exactly where to zig and where to zag.

The sailor replied that our course was based solely on dead reckoning. Father explained to me that this meant keeping track of speed, direction, and the time traveled on each leg of the course, while making allowances for wind and currents. At that point, the sailor who had been listening attentively to Father, chimed in cheerfully, saying, "That's right, Sir! And if your dead reckoning is wrong, I reckon you're dead!" None of the passengers standing nearby thought he was funny.

Father declared that we would henceforth travel by plane, if at all possible. In the meantime, he instructed me that I wasn't to say a thing to Mother about the mines we had seen. "She would be worried sick if she ever found out about them."

This being a British boat, it was tea time, so we went to the *saloon* (restaurant-bar) and Father ordered a plate of buttered Hovis bread slices, some preserves, and a pot of tea. He explained this would have to be my supper. Our delayed departure, our zigzag course, and stopping for the mines meant that we would not reach Folkestone until after six in the evening, he calculated. There, after going through customs, we would be hustled onto the boat train to London without time for a meal in the station restaurant, as originally planned.

The butter they served turned out to be margarine, which considerably irritated Father. "Agh! First it was those blasted mines, and now this!" he exclaimed in disgust, waving at the plate of "margarined" Hovis bread. "It all means this war is hotting up! In peacetime, margarine is not something they would serve in a first class passenger saloon," he added by way of an explanation. Still sounding unhappy, but trying to put on a positive note for my benefit, he commented that the tea was quite good.

I proposed to Father that he might find the royal slice of bread (without butter but with margarine) quite tasty if the marmalade was *very* thickly spread. This was a bowdlerized reference to *The King's Breakfast*, a poem that Father read to me every time he opened A.A Milne's *When We Were Very Young*. It was his favorite poem in that book. I had never joshed Father before, and he was a bit taken aback, but he quickly recovered and chortled with delight. He seemed to forget his peeve, and we both enjoyed our Hovis thickly spread with marmalade. At least I know I did.

The tea revived us both, for our spirits had been rather dragged down by all this talk of mines and the prospect of the journey extending into darkness as we steamed through mine-strewn waters. For good reason, the ship had been scheduled to make the trip in daylight. It didn't take much imagination to realize that at night, without benefit of searchlights to spot floating German mines, our situation was far more precarious than in daylight.

After tea, Father and I went back on deck where, side by side, we leaned on the ship's rail, watching an incredible sunset. We stood there silently for some time, listening to the churning and frothing of the wake, the swish of the passing sea, and the quiet throb of the ship's engines. On our right, we saw the red ball of the sun end its journey through a patchwork of orange and yellow clouds and descend behind a powdery-blue horizon. To our left, in a deeper blue haze, was the coast of France, and beyond that lay dusky Condette where Mother and Brenda would soon be sitting down to supper. Homesickness crept over me along with the encroaching darkness.

I thought of Mother and Brenda, of Raimond and Françoise, and even of little Jock. One after another, they passed through my mind and I saw them in a remembered moment of pleasure or laughter. All of a sudden I was grievously aware that the carefree, playful existence I had known was almost certainly gone forever, and it seemed brutally unfair that my schooling couldn't continue in France, near my family, and surrounded by a world I was starting to understand and that I loved.

In the presence of Mother, Father had promised that I would come home to France for the Christmas holidays. This promise was all that stood between me and unrestrained despair. I struggled to repress the urge to cry, but couldn't withhold a few silent tears, which I didn't want Father to see. Mother had told me that difficult times like these would be easier to endure if I were brave and strong, and if I didn't cry. That was easy to say, but I didn't seem to have much control over the matter. Father must have sensed the turmoil churning within me. He put his arm around me and said, "Everything will be all right, Sonny, don't you worry."

ABOUT THE AUTHOR

Alan Holmes was born in Paris in 1930, and lived there for ten years. He was educated in France, England, Canada, and at Yale University where he earned his bachelor's and master's in civil engineering. Alan became a US citizen while serving in the army during the Korean War. His multifaceted career includes working as a test engineer for the US army, field engineer for a construction firm, structural engineer at a major architectural firm and, for many years, as a staff scientist at an aerospace company. Alan specialized in the structural analysis of unusual structures and, in the 1950s, performed the structural design and analysis for the Air Force Academy Chapel and for several free-standing spiral staircases found at the Academy. He designed, then built, his own adobe house and a sailboat, and enjoys photography. Alan took up writing when he retired and now lives with his wife in the San Francisco Bay Area.